ANNA WIRTZ DOMAS

Our Sunday Visitor, Inc.
Huntington, Indiana 46750

ISBN: 0-87973-889-8
Library of Congress Catalog Card Number: 78-69994

Cover Design by James E. McIlrath
Detail of Sculpture by Frederick Charles Shrady

Published, printed and bound in the U.S.A. by
Our Sunday Visitor, Inc.
Noll Plaza
Huntington, Indiana 46750

889

Contents

Foreword

Johnstown, Pennsylvania, holds a place in history as the site of one of the most destructive floods in the United States, when some twenty-two hundred persons lost their lives on May 31, 1889. Articles and books on that flood continue to appear through the years. In 1957 Richard O'Connor wrote *Johnstown: The Day the Dam Broke*. In that book he stated how a statue of Mary, decorated for May devotions, had survived the raging waters, to become a source of wonder to those who lived through the tragedy.

Many years later, in the Prints and Photographs Division of the Library of Congress, I was thumbing through thousands of file cards for material I hoped to use as part of an exhibit of religious Americana in my museum. A flick of the finger, and the next card read "Pennsylvania, Johnstown: a group of photographs of the flood." When the file was supplied, there among its eight photos was the statue O'Connor had described. Something happened to me at that moment: Here was O'Connor's research documented "in one picture worth a thousand words." The wheels started turning. If one such picture of Mary in American history existed, why not others? *Mary-U.S.A.* was born at that moment.

The book's several hundred illustrations document dates, places, peoples; these are the variables in a record of five centuries of American history. What is constant, however, is the Marian devotion and association through the years which prompted Americans to action. In considering this record, Mary may become better known, and so more loved, and our history be "illumined" because of her part in it.

All fifty states are represented in material acquired from government agencies, state archives, libraries, museums, historical societies, Chambers of Commerce, churches and individuals. The book begins with the *Santa María* bringing Columbus to the New World; it ends in our Bicentennial Year with the canonization of John Neumann, fourth bishop of Philadelphia and Mary's devoted son, to become the first male American saint. The centuries intervening are considered in seven sections, each with a Marian title appropriate to its content. The section, "Virgin Militant," is independent of the book's chronology for better consolidation of pertinent material.

Persons of all faiths have cooperated in this labor of love; space does not permit listing individual names. The author wishes to acknowledge, however, all those who supplied the illustrations appearing in this book and gave the required permissions for their use. A special debt of gratitude is owed to Irenaeus Herscher, O.F.M., librarian emeritus of St. Bonaventure University, New York. Through his unfailing encouragement and professional assistance he provided the "earthly" motivation for the completion of sixteen years' research. To him, the author's humble thanks.

A.W.D.

Religious Americana Museum
Ringoes, New Jersey

Star of the Sea

DISCOVERY AND EXPLORATION

1492-1602

Virgin of the Seas

This contemporary tapestry, originally housed in the Grande Galería, Madrid, shows the Virgin's mantle protecting Spain's seafarers. Columbus kneels below Mary's left hand. The Santa María is in center foreground. Inscription in Latin at top reads: "With the most ardent Queen of the sea, the vigorous sailors of Spain have endured the dangers of waves and winds." At bottom, "In dangers of the sea, be a protection for us."

Star of the Sea

Before the great era of discovery, sailors knew only navigating by piloting or coasting, that is, sailing within sight of land by dead reckoning and plotting course and position on a chart from the three elements of direction, time and distance. Long voyages over open seas were avoided; where the sailors could not coast they did not go.

When compass and sextant came into use, unknown oceans beckoned, but strong and intrepid sailors, being human, were subject to doubt and uncertainty. For reassurance and comfort they invoked their Star of the Sea, placing their voyages under Mary's protection and invoking her at daybreak and after sunset with the singing of her hymns. Above the creaking of sail could be heard the singing of the ancient hymn *Ave, Maris Stella*:

> *Hail, thou Star of ocean,*
> *Portal of the sky!*
> *Ever-Virgin Mother*
> *Of the Lord most High!*

At fixed hours, when the changing of the watches occurred, when solar and stellar observations were taken, a semireligious ritual was followed to remind sailors that safe voyage depended not on the staunchness of the vessel and their own skill but on the grace of God. Evening prayers consisted of the *Pater Noster, Ave Maria* and *Credo*, and the singing of the *Salve Regina*, the latter hymn a fitting closing to the day.

Explorers coming to the shores of the vast continent of America named landfalls, ports and rivers with Marian titles and feast days. Their gratitude for safe voyage was expressed in many ways: Columbus returned in triumph to Spain, then barefooted and in penitential garb brought his offerings to the Church of Our Lady of Guadalupe; De Soto made provision in his will for a Marian chapel; Cartier vowed a pilgrimage to her shrine; Cortés tumbled heathen idols to the ground, replacing them with images of Mary; Champlain's last will and testament began "I nominate the Virgin Mary my heir."

The explorers' will to conquer was matched by a fervent reliance on Mary's intercession. Since she was the Christ-bearer, to her hands could be entrusted the great mission of sailing the unknown to bring the Cross and Christianity to a new generation of men. The late Samuel Eliot Morison, dean of geographical historians, in his last published work* wrote that "from the decks of ships traversing the two great oceans and exploring the distant verges of the earth, prayers arose like clouds of incense to the Holy Trinity and to Mary, Queen of the Sea."

The European Discovery of America: The Southern Voyages, AD 1492-1616. New York: Oxford University Press, 1974.

Columbus at the Monastery of Santa María de la Rabida

Reproduced by F. Adam after the original of Eduardo Cano, Museo Marítimo, Barcelona, this painting shows Columbus discussing with Franciscan monks his dream of reaching land by sailing west. Of this meeting Lord Acton wrote: "It is the starting point of modern history. The past had ruled the world till then — what began that day was the reign of the future."

To appreciate Mary's association with the discovery of America one must understand the love of her which formed the center and soul of Catholic Spain. Through centuries of Muslim domination, prayers to Our Lady of Guadalupe had been offered at her mountain shrine of Estramadura in Castile. Here Ferdinand and Isabella petitioned for victory against the Muslims in the crucial battle at Granada.

With their prayers finally answered in 1492, they offered trophies of victory and pledged their country to Mary's maternal guidance. Muslim mosques were converted into Marian chapels and she was proclaimed the patroness of the armies. A liberated Spain now became a united Spain, strongly armed and spiritually aroused. The stage was set for one Christopher Columbus, practical dreamer.

6

The year 1485 had found a discouraged Columbus and his young son Diego landing at the Spanish port of Palos. Futile attempts to secure aid from Portugal and Spain in a voyage to the Indies left no choice but to approach France. Walking on the road near Palos they came to the Franciscan Monastery of Santa María de la Rabida and Columbus decided to board Diego with the friars. At the monastery the highly intelligent Antonio de Marchena gave him a letter of introduction to the Duke of Medina Sidonia who in turn provided a contact with a nobleman who offered ships and strongly advised that Columbus again approach Queen Isabella before turning to France.

The queen appointed a special commission to recommend whether to accept or reject the enterprise. For the next six years Columbus battled prejudice, humiliation and indifference in a court engrossed with Muslim occupation problems. A less cou-

A popular sailing ship, on which this model of the Santa María is based, was the caravel. Its hull design, combined with its lateen sail plan, enabled it to sail closer to the wind and faster than any square-rigger. It is modeled after the D'Albertis plans in the Marine Museum, Pegli, Genoa.

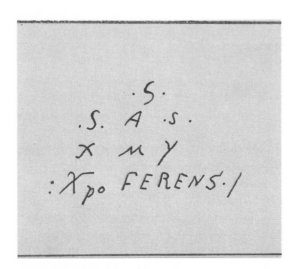

In this signature of Columbus, the initials stand for "Servus Sum Altissimi Salvatoris, Christou Mariae Yiou" (Servant Am I of the Most High Savior, Christ Son of Mary). The last line, "Xpo Ferens," is a Greco-Latin form of "Christopher." Columbus never doubted that his mission was to carry Christianity to lands beyond the sea.

rageous man would have despaired of the voyage but Columbus regarded himself as a child of destiny — "Our Lord revealed to me that it was feasible." He also admitted, quite humanly, that he often "wrestled with God." In late 1490 the commission reported unfavorably.

Columbus's supporters were predominantly priests, especially Franciscans, whose order took more interest in discovery than did any other branch of the Church. On returning to La Rabida to pick up his son Diego, Columbus was persuaded by the prior, Father Juan Perez, to appeal once more to the queen. Now she was receptive, summoning him to court to review the advantages of the voyage. (The year was 1492 and Spain had just taken Granada from the Muslims.) Columbus now raised his former demands for rank, titles and property, and, with the queen agreeing, preparations began for "this great leap over the sea."

On August 2, feast of Our Lady of the Angels, Columbus and his men confessed, received communion in Palos, and placed the voyage under Mary's patronage. The fleet sailed the following day with the singing of the *Salve Regina*; the prayer each day following was "Iesus cum Maria sit nobis in via" (May Jesus with Mary be with us on the way).

Through days of uneventful sailing and the threat of mutiny, Columbus remained constant, telling the crew it was useless to complain "since he had come to go to the Indies, and so had to continue until he found them, with the help of Our Lord." At 2:00 a.m., October 12, on the feast of Our Lady of the Pillar, land was sighted. Going ashore, all rendered thanks, kneeling on the ground, embracing it with tears of joy. Columbus named the island San Salvador (Holy Savior); a second island he named Santa María de Concepción. He offered the entire New World to Mary before officially presenting it to Ferdinand and Isabella.

On his second voyage, 1493-1494, he discovered the island called Taruqueira and named it Our Lady of Guadalupe. Of the first Indians then brought to Spain,

Balboa Claims the Pacific for Spain

four were sent by order of Emperor Carlos V to the Monastery of Our Lady of Guadalupe, "where they may be instructed in the things of our holy Catholic faith and taught to live civilly and decently." Baptized in 1495, they became the first American converts.

The feat of Columbus sparked further concessions by the Church to the kings of Spain. Pope Sixtus IV had already granted extensive concurrent rights over episcopal nominations within their domains and now his successor, Alexander VI, granted the right to name all the missionaries going to the New World, and further conceded all the ecclesiastical tithes in Spain's American possessions to be used for building and support of churches in the colonies.

Further, Julius II in 1508 issued the bull *Universalis Ecclesiae* commanding that no church, monastery, or religious house be built in the colonies without prior royal consent, and that the crown be given the right to nominate all ecclesiastical benefices without exception and in perpetuity.

Spain was about to acquire further world prestige by way of Vasco Núñez de Balboa. He had settled as a planter in Hispaniola (Haiti and the Dominican Republic), went broke and, harassed by creditors, in desperation stowed away on a ship sailing to the Gulf of Darien. A new colony was to be established on the mainland of South America. Sometime after arrival Balboa, a natural leader, suggested that the colony be transferred to Darien and named Santa María de la Antiqua. On being appointed acting governor, Balboa was cautioned that something of a very im-

This statue of Giovanni da Verrazzano in Battery Park, New York, was erected by the Italian Historical Society of America during the Hudson-Fulton celebration of 1909. Verrazzano was the first among Europeans to enter and give a description of the Lower Bay, the Narrows and New York harbor.

GIOVANNI DA VERRAZZANO

portant nature would be expected of him.

Natives had reported that over the mountains from the colony was another sea "where they sayle with shippes as bigge as yours, using both sayles and ores as you doe." On September 1, 1513, Balboa with one hundred ninety soldiers and native guides and porters plunged into the Panamanian jungle with its swamps, snakes, scorpions, polluted water and hostile Indians. On September 24, the feast of Our Lady of Mercy, they reached an elevated plateau after repulsing an attack of nearly a thousand Indians. The following day they gained the summit of the mountain and looked upon the Southern Sea (the Pacific).

Washington Irving has described the dramatic moment when Balboa "took a banner on which were painted the Virgin and Child, and under them the arms of Castile and Leon" and marching into the sea took possession "of these seas and lands and coasts and ports and islands of the south, and all thereunto whatever right or title, ancient or modern, in times past, present, or to come, without any contradiction. . . ."

France joined the impulse to discovery by commissioning an Italian navigator, Giovanni da Verrazzano (or Verrazano, as it is also spelled), to explore the possibilities for settlements in America and to search for a northwest passage to the Orient. Verrazzano, well born and well

The Naming of Annunciata

This manuscript describes how Verrazzano gave the name Annunciata (Annunciation) to a place on North Carolina's Outer Banks on March 25, 1524. The manuscript, which is in the Pierpont Morgan Library, is known as the Cellère Codex for a former owner, Count Giulio Macchi de Cellère. In writing the report to Francis I, the scribes left out entire sentences and Verrazzano made marginal corrections (left, above): "Appellavimus Annunciatam ad die adventus . . ." (We named it Annunciation for the day of arrival . . .). In this report he gave the world the first known description of the Atlantic coast.

Vesconte de Maiollo Map of 1527
Showing Annunciata as La Nunciata

Formerly in the Ambrosian Library, Milan, this map was destroyed by bombing in World War II. An authority has stated that for the information contained in this map and in the map of Girolamo Verrazzano (brother of the navigator), concerning the American coast from North Carolina to Maine, there was no possible source except actual exploration. Arrow indicates La Nunciata (Annunciata) named by Verrazzano in 1524 under the fleur-de-lis of France. The area above Florida is named Mare Indicum (Indian Sea) due to Verrazzano's assumption that the land he named was an isthmus separating the Atlantic from the Pacific! This assumption led to the designation "Sea of Verrazzano" until corrected by later explorations.

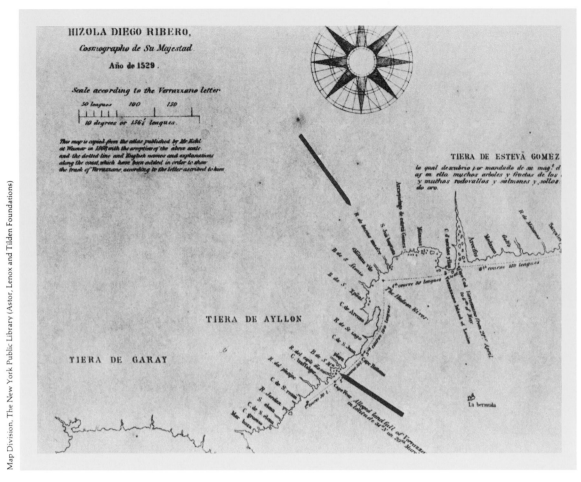

Spanish Explorations Along the Atlantic

This portion of the Diego Ribero map of 1529 shows (lower arrow) Bahía de Santa María (present-day Chesapeake). Upper arrow points to Río de Buena Madre (now the Kennebec River in Maine), which is incorrectly located on the map. Here the Atlantic coast is labeled for the Spaniards, but the dotted line with English titles indicates Verrazzano's route.

educated, was an impressive figure. A contemporary called him "a valiant gentleman." At age thirty-eight he knew more mathematics than most men of his time, and his maritime record was impeccable. His voyage was to be made in *La Dauphine*, a ship of the royal French navy; the necessary funds, however, were supplied by Italian bankers, with Verrazzano contributing a good share.

In January of 1524, Verrazzano said farewell to the Old World. After crossing

the Atlantic he made a landfall near Cape Fear, North Carolina. Cruising north-northeasterly, on March 25 he anchored by the Outer Banks, a few miles north of Hatteras. This spot he named Annunciata because the day was the feast of the Annunciation. He described "an isthmus a mile in width and about 200 miles long, in which, from the ship, we could see *el mare orientale* [the Pacific Ocean, he thought], halfway between West and North." This sea, he wrote, "is the same which flows

12

around the shores of India, China and Cataya [Cathay]." Continuing up the coast he sailed into New York Bay and anchored in the Narrows (now renamed after him and spanned by the Verrazano-Narrows Bridge).

His last anchorage was made off Rhode Island. Sailing northeast past the Maine coast he missed the Bay of Fundy and most of the future Nova Scotia. He decided to return to France, anchoring at Dieppe on July 8. On a voyage made four years later, following the chain of the Lesser Antilles, he anchored off an island, probably Guadaloupe, inhabited by ferocious man-eating Caribs. Unwisely, he rowed shoreward in a ship's boat; then, wading ashore, he was seized by the Indians and murdered.

"To so miserable an end came this valiant gentleman."

Estévan Gomez, a Portuguese pilot in the service of Spain, sought a passage to the East between Florida and Newfoundland. In his ship *La Anunciada* he reached Cape Race, Newfoundland, February 1525. Exploring the Maine coast he gave present-day Whitehead the name Costa de Santa María and the Kennebec River the name Río de Buena Madre (River of the Good Mother).

In 1526 a precedent was set in a northern voyage from a southern colony. Lucas Vásquez de Ayllón, justice of the supreme court of Santo Domingo, fitted out an ambitious armada which explored the Atlantic coast from Florida to Cape Cod. Enter-

Map of Florida

Although the date is uncertain, most historians agree that this map by Hieronymo de Chaves was prepared prior to 1574. Puerto de Santa María (present-day Pensacola) is shown by the arrow.

First Parish Mass

This engraving is from a painting commissioned by Bishop Augustin Verot. It portrays the first parish Mass ever celebrated in what is now the United States. The site is St. Augustine, Florida; the date — September 8, 1565.

ing what is now called Chesapeake Bay, he named it Bahía de Santa María, known also as Bahía de Madre de Dios (Bay of the Mother of God). Without completely supplanting the name Santa María, this terminology was in vogue from 1570 to 1620 in Spanish circles. The name Bahía de Madre de Dios is found on Dutch maps up to the seventeenth century.

Spain would send Ponce de León and a company of about two hundred settlers to explore the Florida coast in 1521, but the expedition was destined to end in failure. Then, in 1522, the ecclesiastical government established the diocese of Santiago de Cuba; this bishopric eventually would have jurisdiction over the first Spanish settlements.

Ayllón's exploration in 1526 was fol-

lowed by the ill-fated expedition of Pánfilo de Narváez near Tampa Bay in 1528. Cabeza de Vaca, one of two survivors, left an intriguing account of an overland trek through the American southwest and northern Mexico, inflaming the minds of treasure seekers with the fabulous riches of the cities of Cíbola.

Hernando de Soto's expedition would occupy three years' time but leave no permanent settlement. Philip II was now thoroughly discouraged, but under the threat of French encroachment he was determined to send still another expedition, this time under Tristan de Luna in 1559. Reporting to His Majesty, De Luna describes the start of the expedition and the subsequent naming of Puerto de Santa María (present-day Pensacola) on the

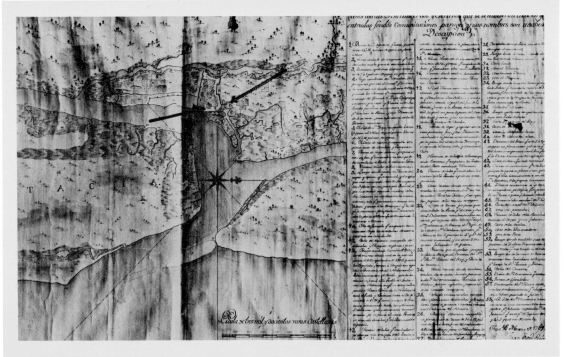

Garrison of St. Augustine, Florida, With Marian Designations

In this plan drawn by John Joseph Elixio de la Puente, Havana, 1769, the legend at right describes, among others, the places marked by the arrows above. Left arrow: "The chapel of Nuestra Señora de la Leche, and lands occupied by the Indians, who subsequently established their town there." Right arrow: "Spot called Nombre de Dios, and is the same where the first Mass was said, September 8, 1565, when the Spaniards went with . . . Pedro Menéndez de Avilés to conquer these provinces, and since then an Indian town has been formed there, with a chapel, in which was placed the statue of Nuestra Señora de la Leche. . . ."

eve of the feast of Mary's Assumption:

"I wrote your Majesty from the city of Tlaxcala that I was going to embark from the port of San Juan de Ulua. I did embark there with five hundred soldiers, one thousand serving people, and two hundred and forty horses, but of the latter there were landed only one hundred and thirty. The fleet being well provided with supplies, I set sail on June 11, and until the day of Our Lady of August [Assumption], when it pleased God that the entire fleet should enter this port of Ochuse, there was nothing done but sail in search of it as we did, both because it is a very good [port] and

because it is in a locality of good land. As we entered on the day I say, and to give it the name of your Majesty, it was named the Bahía Filipina del Puerto de Santa María. . . ."

Though De Luna's venture failed, it prepared the way for the successful expedition of Pedro Menéndez de Avilés, founder of St. Augustine. From that settlement the Catholic faith would spread throughout Florida and Georgia in a great mission chain. (See section entitled "Nuestra Señora.")

Pedro Menéndez de Avilés, admiral of the Spanish fleet of twenty vessels, sailed

15

from Cadiz, Spain, for Florida. Storms scattered the fleet and two thirds of the vessels were lost. Menéndez first sighted the Florida coast on August 28, the feast of St. Augustine. Landing was postponed until September 8, the Nativity of Our Lady, when he led his band on to the beach at a place several miles to the north of what is now known as Cape Canaveral. The event was recorded by Father Francisco López de Mendoza Grajales who had put ashore the previous evening. He wrote:

"I took the cross and went to meet him [Menéndez], singing the *Te Deum Laudamus*. The Admiral, followed by all who accompanied him, marched up to the cross, knelt, and kissed it. A large number of Indians watched these proceedings, and imitated all that they saw done."

In thanksgiving, the Solemn Mass of Our Lady was offered. On the site of this first Mass the Mission of Nombre de Dios (Name of God) was established and here was enshrined the statue of Nuestra Señora de la Leche y Buen Parto (Our Nursing Mother of Happy Delivery), described in the section following.

St. Augustine thus became the first permanent Christian settlement of our country, preceding the English settlement at Jamestown by forty-two years.

Spain's interest westward from the Gulf of Mexico had been fanned by Cabeza de Vaca's tales of golden cities to the north.

Punta de la Limpia Concepción

Arrow on this chart points to Punta de la Limpia Concepción (Point of the Immaculate Conception), the name given by Vizcaino in honor of Mary. Today the headland is known simply as Point Conception.

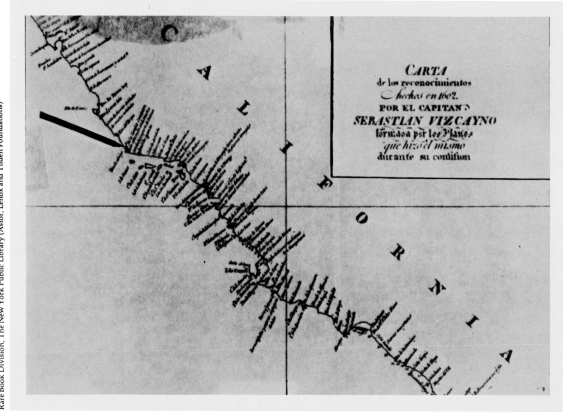

16

Men's imaginations were fired and expeditions moved out in three directions: into New Mexico; across the Rio Grande into Texas; and up into California. On the Pacific coast a rocky point would be named for Mary, predating by eighteen years Plymouth Rock on the Atlantic.

California had been an unexplored land of surf and snowy mountains, sighted by the galleons as they approached the end of their long voyage from Manila to Acapulco, Mexico. Sebastián Vizcaino sailed from Acapulco in 1602, reaching a headland on the Santa Barbara coast, called Cabo de Galera (Cape of the Galley) by Cabrillo be-cause it resembled a seagoing galley. Vizcaino's arrival there on December 8 occasioned naming the headland Punta de la Limpia Concepción (Point of the Immaculate Conception), today known as Point Conception.

Along the coast Vizcaino left other Marian names. In 1603 he discovered Monterey Bay and named it Nuestra Señora de Monte Carmelo (Our Lady of Mount Carmel) for the patroness and protectress of his voyage. Monterey was destined to become the capital of Spanish California and a great center of mission endeavors.

Point Conception, California

Named after Mary, Point Conception is two hundred twenty feet high and marks an abrupt change in the coastline. Because of heavy gales that sweep around the headland, it is called "The Cape Horn of the Pacific." The light station in this picture is a main link in the chain that makes up the Santa Barbara Coast Guard group. The light's candlepower is 1.3 million; its range of illumination is eighteen miles to sea.

U.S. Coast Guard

17

Nuestra Señora

SPANISH BEGINNINGS

1565-1791

Our Lady of the Angels

This oil painting of Nuestra Señora de los Angeles (Our Lady of the Angels) is signed "Año de 1787 Adovosian d. Pasqual Miguel."

Nuestra
Señora

The America that came into being with the discovery of Columbus would forever bear the stamp of Spain. The roots planted in the southern borderlands formed "the calyx upon which blossomed the corolla we call the United States."

These roots were primarily religious; wherever Spain went, the Cross of Christ was displayed for the veneration of all men. Her explorers were committed to sharing the good news of salvation with any distant peoples they might encounter. The Crown insisted the natives be "ennobled" not exploited, and under the mission system to be clothed, their homes improved, and instructed in agriculture and useful crafts. From Florida to California this system proved effective in conversions. Under the missionaries' kind treatment, protected and sustained, the natives were disposed to religious instruction, particularly in learning about the Immaculate

Virgin to whom they were irresistibly drawn.

In achieving the most extensive territorial conquest in history, and in its effective organization, Spain contributed to a Christian civilization from which American prospectors and pioneers would reap the benefits of patience and devotion. Outstanding of her contributions was the founding in 1565 of America's first city, St. Augustine, Florida, a founding which predated that of Plymouth's by more than half a century.

Historians claim Virginia's history began with Jamestown; however, that history began much earlier with the martyrdom of six Spanish Jesuits at the hands of treacherous Indians at the mission of Our Lady of Ajacan. Their deaths became a challenge which was accepted by the Franciscans. In the next century they established forty-four missions along the Florida coast and into Georgia and converted thirty thousand Indians.

The unknown geography, resources and inhabitants of Arizona, Colorado and Utah were first revealed by the explorations of Juan Bautista de Anza, as well as those of Fathers Garcés, Escalante and Domínguez; these explorations provided invaluable guidelines for later frontier expansion. The writings of these men contain continuing acknowledgment of Mary's intercession in their safe traveling.

The Texas and Louisiana forts erected by Spain against the threat of French encroachment were named for Our Lady of Loretto of the Bay and Our Lady of the Pillar of the Adais. No less than the entire state of Texas was the base for the ministry of Venerable Antonio Margil de Jesús. In instructing the natives he followed the Franciscan tradition of special devotion to Mary's Assumption.

The New Mexico missions endowed the state with majestic architecture and interesting historical structures. La Purísima

Concepción at Quarai is one of many listed as national historic landmarks. Missionaries encouraged and enlivened native talent in producing the distinctive art form of *santos*. Many of Mary have been recorded for posterity in the Index of American Design at the National Gallery in Washington. The remarkable progress in converting the natives suffered a serious setback in the Pueblo Rebellion of 1680 when twenty-two Franciscans were martyred. Out of the tragedy would grow the singular devotion to La Conquistadora (Our Lady of the Conquest) whose image in Santa Fe is the oldest Marian statue in the country.

This is the nation's first permanent Marian shrine — Mission Nombre de Dios (Name of God) in St. Augustine, Florida.

Mission Nombre de Dios

While the East was dreaming of independence from Britain, Spain dreamed of new horizons, new beginnings, in the West. Five days before the Declaration of Independence was being read in Philadelphia, Mass was being said by a lake in San Francisco where the sixth mission in Father Junípero Serra's "rosary of missions" would be established. His nine missions would become a decisive deterrent to Russian encroachment of the California coast.

Spanish navigators charted the Pacific from California to Alaska, marking their landfalls, bays, rivers and harbors with the Marian titles of Rosario, Remedios, Angeles, Asunción, Refugio and Concepción. At the tip of Washington is the harbor of Port Angeles, first American port of entry for ships coming in from the Pacific. When first discovered in 1791 it was given the lyrical name Puerto de Nuestra Señora de los Angeles (Port of Our Lady of the Angels). If lesser Marian discoveries do not appear on today's maps, the records at least have survived as documentation.

Fathers Serra and Kino are commemorated in Statuary Hall in the nation's Capitol. They represent California and Arizona, states which proudly recognized the fortitude of these priests. They were but two of hundreds of highly educated men who left cultivated surroundings to secure the moral and material well-being of their Indian brothers.

The Old World devotion to a beloved *Nuestra Señora* did not lessen in transition. Its color, warmth and diversity found eager acceptance in the new land. With Mary as catalyst there came about a happy blending of the separate cultures, prophetic of the emerging America of many peoples.

Forty-two years before Jamestown, and fifty-five years before the Pilgrims landed at Plymouth, Spain's Admiral Pedro Menéndez de Avilés sighted the Florida coast near present-day Cape Canaveral; the date was August 28, 1565. The day being the feast day of St. Augustine, Menéndez gave that name to the settlement made there. This would become the oldest city in the United States, the first Christian mission and parish in this country, and the first permanent shrine to Mary.

The first Mass was celebrated on Mary's birthday, September 8. The site was called Mission Nombre de Dios (Name of God). In 1620 a shrine was established to Nuestra Señora de la Leche y Buen Parto (Our Nursing Mother of Happy Delivery). The original mission and several later structures were destroyed by gunfire during colonial days and later by hurricanes; the present shrine dates from 1915. Within is a replica of Our Lady of La Leche, the ancient title of the statue in Madrid, Spain, Nuestra Señora de la Leche y Buen Parto.

Many believe this document to be our country's oldest existing record. On June 25, 1594, Diego Scobar de Sambrana, "curate and vicar of these provinces of Florida, city and fort of St. Augustine," baptized María Ximenes.

Mission Nombre de Dios

This statue, popularly known as Our Lady of La Leche, can be seen at Mission Nombre de Dios, St. Augustine, Florida. The original statue in the Church of San Luis, Madrid, is called Nuestra Señora de la Leche y Buen Parto (Our Nursing Mother of Happy Delivery).

Mission Nombre de Dios

Thousands of mothers come to the shrine to ask for the blessings of motherhood, beseeching the intercession of Our Lady of La Leche that God will grant them safe and happy delivery and healthy children. The devotion of centuries inspired the establishment of the organization known all

25

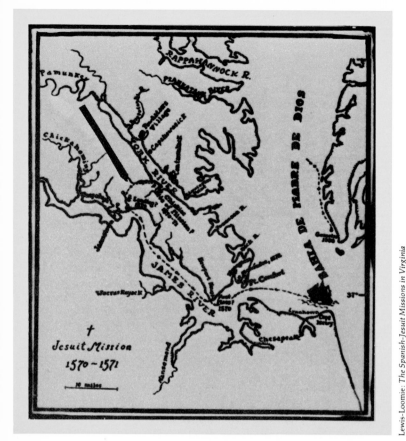

Lewis-Loomie: The Spanish-Jesuit Missions in Virginia

Bahía de Madre de Dios (Bay of the Mother of God) was the name given Chesapeake Bay, Virginia, in this early map. Arrow (upper left) points to the probable location of Mission of the Mother of God of Axacan.

over the world — La Leche League, International. It was begun in Illinois in 1956 by a group of nursing mothers to encourage and instruct mothers in breast-feeding their babies.

What may be the oldest extant record in America is that of a baptism at St. Augustine in 1594. The baby girl was given the name María, her mother being María, and godmother María for good measure. This was the first entry in the parish registers. At one time it was feared these records had been lost forever. The registers had been removed to Cuba in 1763 when Florida was ceded to England, but they had not been returned when the Spaniards came back in 1783. For a hundred years their location was either forgotten or unknown.

Then Bishop Augustin Verot, S.S., went to Cuba and instituted a search, finding the precious volumes and returning them to Florida in 1906 — all but one; that eluded the search until 1930 when it joined its brothers in the cathedral archives. When German submarines were prowling dangerously close to Florida shores in 1942 the cathedral documents were sent to Notre Dame University in Indiana for safekeeping. In 1962 they came home once more.

In founding St. Augustine, Spain made a lasting contribution to the history of America and the Catholic Church. John Dawson Gilmary Shea best expressed it: "The altar was older than the hearth." Today one can find in the city's historic district original residences and several restorations and reconstructions. The present streets, all in the original plan of 1598, are narrow to provide shade and to act as funnels for drafts and breezes. The area has

Killing of Father Segura and Companions, Virginia, 1571

Tanner: Societas Iesu Militans . . . .

26

ST. FRANCIS BARRACKS

A FRANCISCAN FRIARY
1573 - 1763
MILITARY BARRACKS
1763 - 1900
MILITARY DEPARTMENT, STATE OF FLORIDA
SINCE 1907

THESE COQUINA WALLS WERE ONCE PART OF THE CHAPEL AND CONVENT
OF OUR LADY OF THE IMMACULATE CONCEPTION ESTABLISHED BY FRANCISCAN
MISSIONARIES FROM SPAIN WHO CAME TO FLORIDA TO WORK AMONG THE INDIANS.
THATCH ROOFED WOODEN BUILDINGS ON THIS SITE WERE BURNED IN 1599, RE-
BUILT AND AGAIN DESTROYED BY FIRE IN 1702 WHEN ENGLISH CAROLINIAN
FORCES BURNED THE TOWN.

RECONSTRUCTED OF COQUINA, A NATIVE SHELL ROCK, IN 1735-1755, THE
BUILDINGS WERE CONVERTED TO MILITARY USE DURING THE BRITISH OCCUPA-
TION OF FLORIDA, 1763-1784, AND ALSO USED BY THE SPANISH FOR MILITARY
PURPOSES IN 1784-1821, AND BY THE UNITED STATES FROM 1821 UNTIL 1900
WHEN THE GARRISON WAS WITHDRAWN.

THE RESERVATION WAS LEASED TO THE STATE OF FLORIDA IN 1907, FOR
HEADQUARTERS OF THE NATIONAL GUARD. FIRE AGAIN DESTROYED THE INTERIOR
IN 1915, LEAVING ONLY THE COQUINA WALLS STANDING. THE ADMINISTRATIVE
OFFICES WERE MOVED TO ADJACENT BUILDINGS ON THE RESERVATION. IN 1921,
THE PROPERTY WAS DONATED TO THE STATE, AND THE BUILDINGS REMODELLED
FOR USE AS HEADQUARTERS FOR THE MILITARY DEPARTMENT, STATE OF FLORIDA.

MILITARY DEPARTMENT, STATE OF FLORIDA
1964

Military Department, State of Florida

Our Lady of the Immaculate Conception State Marker

*This historical plaque was put up by the State of Florida to commemorate the founding
of the chapel and convent of Our Lady of the Immaculate Conception in St. Augustine.*

been designated a national historic landmark.

From St. Augustine, Florida, Spain extended her domination northward to Port
Royal, South Carolina, establishing little
centers of influence with their missions.
Menéndez sent out ships to explore the
southern Atlantic coast up to St. Mary's
Bay (the Chesapeake). Combining all the
information supplied he was led to believe
that, by ascending for eighty leagues a
river flowing into the bay, it was necessary
only to cross a mountain range to find two
arms of the sea, one leading to the French
at Newfoundland, the other to the Pacific!

To his mind the upper waters of the
Chesapeake, the Potomac and Susquehan-
na, were to be the great carrying place of
eastern trade.

Menéndez appealed to the Jesuits for
missionaries to assist on an expedition and
responding were Father Juan Bautista de
Segura and Father Luis de Quiros. With
six lay brothers and a young boy they left
for Virginia in August 1570. The boy was
later to give an eyewitness account of the
tragedy which befell the party. Sailing up
the Chesapeake they entered the James
River to a spot near what is now Williams-
burg. From here they traveled inland to-

27

John Tate Lanning: *The Spanish Missions of Georgia*

Santa María Mission

This is Willis Physioc's conception of Santa María Mission in what is now St. Marys, Georgia. It was built around 1615-1616.

Historic American Buildings Survey, U. S. Department of the Interior

Well preserved, these ruins at St. Marys, Camden County, Georgia, are the remains of the Franciscans' Santa María Mission.

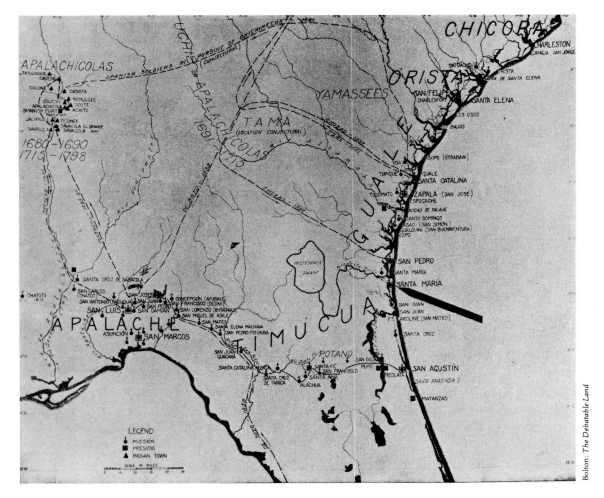

Spanish Missions

Stretching westward from St. Augustine across today's Florida Peninsula and northward along the coast of present-day Georgia as far as Santa Helena, Spain's missions slowly expanded. The arrow on this map points to Santa María Island, now called Amelia Island, Georgia. Santa María Mission (now St. Marys) was erected on the mainland, on the Río Santa María (St. Marys River). The source of this river sparked part of the controversy surrounding the Mason-Dixon Line when the boundary between Pennsylvania and Maryland was being determined.

ward the York River and made camp at a former tribal site, in land unpromising and visited by remnants of area Indians. They "decided to remain there without soldiers or guards other than our Fathers and Brothers, and to trust in God's care and protection and the help of His most Holy Mother...." In this wild country they set up a log house, with its small chapel entrusted to La Madre de Dios de Jacan (the Mother of God of Axacan, Axacan being the name of the Indians of the area).

They endured a winter of great privation, living on nuts and roots; game was scarce and there is no record of any supply of fish. Hoping for relief in the spring they persevered in their ministrations. The Indians showed signs of rebellion and Father Segura prepared his group for death. On February 4 and 9, 1571, treacherous natives killed all but the boy. Father Segura

Shown are the remains of the altar of the first mission dedicated to the Immaculate Conception in what is now New Mexico. Designated a national historic landmark, the mission was built at Hawikuh in 1629.

Frederic Remington's Painting of "Coronado's March"

and his companions indeed had their wish fulfilled "to serve God in earnest." Virginia history thus opened, not with the founding of Jamestown, but with the giving to the world of eight Jesuit martyrs. More than six decades later the Jesuits would be preaching the gospel to the English Catholics of Maryland who had sailed into the Bay of the Mother of God.

Following the martyrdom of the Virginia missionaries the Jesuit Father General, St. Francis Borgia, recalled his remaining priests from the Florida area and assigned them to Mexico. The Franciscans now entered the mission field making St. Augustine the center of activity. Today one can see on St. Francis Street the military barracks which occupies the site of the Convento de Inmaculada Concepción established in 1573. Its chapel was the first in the United States to be dedicated to Mary under this title.

In 1612 the guardian of the Convento, the learned Fray Francisco Pareja, wrote for the Indians inhabiting ten towns in his jurisdiction a *Catecismo en Lengua Cas-*

Reduced to longhand, this carving on Inscription Rock in El Morro National Monument, relating to the Church of La Purísima Concepción in Hawikuh, New Mexico, reads: "They passed on 23d of March of 1632 year to the avenging [the] death of Father Letrado. [Signed] Lujan [a soldier on the expedition]."

Near Grants, New Mexico, these cliffs are known as El Morro National Monument. Early travelers recorded their passing on Inscription Rock (cliff in foreground). Twenty-seven inscriptions concern La Purísima Concepción at Hawikuh.

National Park Service, U.S. Department of the Interior

31

tellana y Timuquano, "Catechism [or Christian Doctrine] in Castilian and Timucuan." Skilled in their language he had no trouble in converting them. They would come to the mission on Saturdays to hear the *Salve Regina* sung and to remain overnight so that they could hear Mass. They faithfully used the catechism and other books written by Father Pareja, including ones on purgatory, hell and heaven, and the rosary. The catechism listed questions (*Pregunta*) and answers (*Respuesta*):

 P. Who is the Holy Virgin Mary?
 R. She is a great Lady, full of all the virtues and graces, the true Mother of God.
 P. Where is this great Lady?
 R. She is in Heaven in body and soul.
 P. And what is that which is in the church?
 R. That represents her image.

Making slow but consistent progress the Franciscans established inland missions westward to the lower reaches of Apalachicola and then on to Pensacola. Northward their coastal missions dotted the Georgia shore (Guale on maps). At the peak of their endeavors (1655) they counted thirty thousand Catholic Indians which they served from forty-four mission centers. One such mission was that of Santa María for the Timucuas located on the Georgia coast near the present town of St. Marys.

Here one can see the best-preserved mission-type ruins in Georgia. The square detached columns, perfectly preserved two-story wall, with thirty-four small windows intact, are silent proof of the skill and zeal of the natives who built the mission in 1615-1616. Used in construction was coquina or tabby, a mixture of crushed oyster shells and cement, poured into molds and tamped down, making a substance that was almost indestructible. The many healthy trees and rich tropical vegetation surrounding the mission are further testimony of the ruins' antiquity.

32

The bishop of Santiago de Cuba, Gabriel Díaz Vara Calderón, visited the Florida missions in August 1674, remaining eight months. In reporting on conditions to Queen Mother Marie Anne of Spain he commented:

"They are very devoted to the Virgin, and on Saturdays they attend the *Rosario* and the *Salve* in the afternoon. . . . They subject themselves to extraordinary penances during Holy Week, and during the

St. Francis Cathedral in Santa Fe, New Mexico, boasts this beautiful statue of La Conquistadora (Our Lady of the Conquest). Carved of Spanish willow, it is the oldest statue of Mary in the country. In March of 1973 it was stolen and a $150,000 ransom demanded. It was recovered by the police, unharmed.

Angelico Chavez, O.F.M.

New Mexico Department of Development

Ruins of La Purísima Concepción, Quarai, New Mexico

Built in 1629, Mission La Purísima Concepción is today a state monument and national historic landmark.

24 hours of Holy Thursday and Friday . . . they attend standing, praying the rosary in complete silence, 24 men and 24 women and the same number of children of both sexes, with hourly changes."

Spain's interest in the southwest had early been aroused by explorers' accounts of the Seven Golden Cities of Cíbola which supposedly lay north of the region now known as New Mexico. Coronado set out in 1540 to find these cities and came to Hawikuh in north central New Mexico. He called it Granada but turned away in disappointment at finding poor pueblos in-

stead of gold. When he returned to New Spain in 1542 three of the expedition's friars remained behind in the hope of converting the Quivira Indians. One of the three, Juan de Padilla, was murdered somewhere in eastern Kansas and became this country's protomartyr.

No permanent colonization of Hawikuh was achieved until Franciscans built La Purísima Concepción in 1629. The church was destroyed fifty years later, but excavations have reconstructed part of its history. Other portions of that history are permanently carved on El Morro National Monument, thirty-five miles to the east in Valencia County. Here on a two-hundred-foot smooth cliff are twenty-seven inscriptions concerning the church and a valiant priest killed by Indians in February of 1630. One message records the expedition sent by the viceroy of Mexico to avenge the death of Father Letrado, first permanent missionary at Hawikuh.

Spain had gradually been forced to move westward from her Florida missions by Indian attacks and English encroachment. In April of 1598, under Don Juan de Oñate, a party of four hundred reached the Río del Norte, New Mexico. A Solemn Mass was offered, followed by Spain's taking possession of the area. The first white settlement of the colony was named Real de San Juan and a church was dedicated on Mary's Nativity.

The colonial capital would be located at Santa Fe and in its mission a skillfully carved image of Mary was enshrined in 1625 and venerated until the Pueblo Rebellion of 1680 when Indians burned the mission, forcing the settlers to evacuate. A brave young woman snatched the statue from its flaming shrine and carried it in her arms for the three-hundred-mile exhausting trek to El Paso, Texas.

Thirteen years later Don Diego de Vargas led the New Mexican exiles back home, first having promised that if peace reigned he would build a chapel in Mary's honor and institute an annual novena. The statue, now bearing the significant title of La Conquistadora, was carried in triumph before her people. De Vargas kept his promise and the devotion thus begun has never lessened over the centuries. Each year on the second Sunday after Corpus Christi the entire town of Santa Fe turns out for an impressive week-long celebration. A specially selected honor guard, "The Caballeros de Vargas," carries the statue on a platform from its shrine in the Cathedral of St. Francis to the Rosario

34

This eighteenth-century bulto of the Virgin and Child, made in New Mexico, consists of an upper part that is solid, with the lower portion being a hollow framework fashioned from sticks.

Chapel three miles distant. In 1960 the statue was given the signal honor of "papal coronation" and received a crown of gold, silver and precious jewels.

In the building of Franciscan missions New Mexico would be endowed with some

Index of American Design, National Gallery of Art, Washington

Retablo of Our Lady of Sorrows

Identified by the tree rings of the wood as having been executed between 1765 and 1812, this retablo, a bas-relief in painted gesso on a wood panel, is comparatively rare. Due to their fragility many retablos were damaged. In the example shown, some pieces are missing.

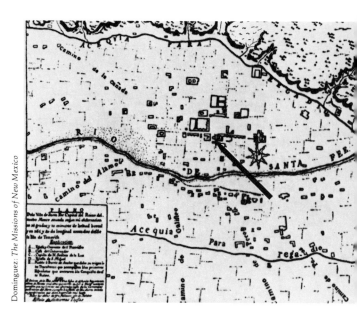

Dominguez: *The Missions of New Mexico*

of its handsomest architecture and most interesting historical structures. La Purísima Concepción at Quarai best exemplifies this tradition. Southeast of Albuquerque lie the Manzano Mountains and near their southern end are the mission ruins, unsurpassed in grandeur of architecture by any that remain of early Franciscan endeavors. A noted historian has stated that "on the Rhine the edifice would be a great superlative, in the wilderness of Manzano it is a miracle."

The walls of church and convent remain standing almost to their original height of forty feet. The pueblo once surrounding them was two and three stories high and enclosed at least three plazas and several ceremonial kivas (chambers). Between 1664 and 1669 an Indian revolt against the Spaniards was plotted here at the mission but was defeated, thus delaying the Pueblo Rebellion until 1680 when most of the missions of New Mexico were destroyed and twenty-two Franciscans were killed.

The missionaries had brought the natives not only a new religion but a new way of life. They had taught new techniques in working in metal, carving and building in stone, and using paint in the European manner. In the resulting style a simplified Spanish element is conspicuous, yet the Indian contribution is also present. In the art of *santo*-making can be found the permanent stamp made on American culture.

Santo was the name given to a representation of a saint, either in the form of a *bulto* or *retablo*. A *bulto* was carved in the round out of cottonwood and covered with gesso and paint; a *retablo* was painted, carved or printed on a flat wood panel. Some *bultos* had removable parts, others

This rendition of Nuestra Señora de la Luz (Our Lady of Light) graces the frontispiece of the constitution of the Confraternity of Our Lady of Light. It was published in Mexico City in 1766.

W. B. Stephens, Mexico City

36

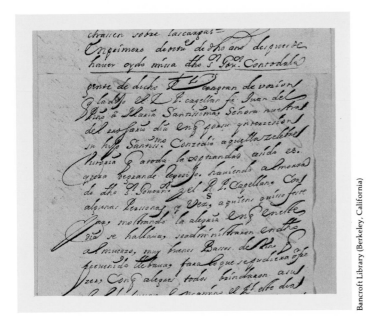

This excerpt from the diary of Governor Antonio de Valverde tells of the first Mass in Colorado celebrated on a Marian feast day. Part of the translation from the diary reads: "On the first day of October of this year [1719], after hearing Mass, the ... governor, with all of the camp and the Reverend Father Chaplain Fray Juan del Pino, prayed with great zeal to the Holy Mary of the Rosary. This was the day on which by her intercession her most holy Son granted that celebrated victory which to all Christendom has been, is, and will be one of great rejoicing. . . ."

Excerpt From Diary Recording First Mass in Colorado

were jointed, taking on the character of puppets. Certain *santos* were carried in procession from the church to private homes for the comfort of the sick and dying. The simplest adobe had its *santo* of Mary under one of many titles: the Most Holy Virgin of Guadalupe, Our Lady of Sorrows, Our Lady of Solitude, and many more. Outstanding examples of these are contained in artists' renderings of the originals in the Index of American Design of the National Gallery of Art in Washington. The index was begun in the late 1930s to record for posterity those craft traditions which are of artistic and historic significance.

By 1700 New Mexico had largely been reconquered following the Pueblo revolt, but the missions never enjoyed their former prosperity. Santa Fe as the center of Franciscan activities in the state was presided over by a military governor appointed by the king. A 1766 plan of the city shows the location of the governor's house and directly below it the military

castrense (chapel) of Our Lady of Light.

Devotion to Mary under this title had begun in Palermo, Sicily, early in the eighteenth century and brought to Mexico by the Jesuits. Our Lady of Light is represented as being crowned by angels while in the act of rescuing a human being from the jaws of Satan. Governor Marin de Valle founded a confraternity of Our Lady of Light principally for citizens of New Mexico, but those of other provinces were not excluded. Members took an oath to defend the doctrine of the Immaculate Conception, to pray for the souls of deceased members, and to have certain Masses said.

The missionaries were not always happy under the military governors who thought the friars should give equal if not more time to soldiers and settlers than to the natives, but when the missions required protection the military department did not fail.

In 1719 Apache settlements to the northeast were being raided by Utes and Comanches. To punish the raiders Gover-

37

Travels of Eusebio Kino

This map shows the extensive travels of Father Eusebio Kino, S.J., in northern Mexico and southern Arizona during the years 1687–1711. The arrow indicates where his first mission, Nuestra Señora de los Dolores, was founded in 1687.

nor Antonio de Valverde, with soldiers and chaplain, left Santa Fe on September 15. They crossed into what is now Colorado in the vicinity of Trinidad and headed towards the Arkansas River. Spies sent out at night found fresh tracks and reported the enemy near. This disturbed Valverde, not because he feared an encounter, but the day happened to be the thirtieth of September, the vigil of the feast of Our Lady of the Rosary, and Valverde wanted to salute the occasion in discharging his guns. But this would alert the enemy! He "mortified himself considerably by omitting the salute."

Early next morning the feast day was observed. Valverde believed in "first things first." Plenty of time later for dispatching the Utes and Comanches!

This feast day marked the victory of the Christian navy over the Turkish fleet at Lepanto on October 7, 1571, a victory which Pope Pius V attributed to the prayers of the faithful, especially the intensified devotion of the confraternities of the Holy Rosary in petitioning Mary's intercession. In gratitude he established the feast of Our Lady of Victory to be celebrated on October 7. His successor, Gregory XIII, altered this title to Our Lady of the Rosary, changing the feast day to the first Sunday in October. When Valverde observed the feast in 1719 the first Sunday fell on October 1. Pope Pius X in 1913 restored the feast to its original date of October 7.

The area which today forms the northern part of Sonora, Mexico, and the southern portion of Arizona, was once called Pimería Alta for the Pima living there. Its Franciscan converts had slowly yielded their faith following the 1680 Pueblo Rebellion but seven years later would come under the persuasive powers of Eusebio Kino, Jesuit apostle extraordinary.

This explorer, historian, astronomer, mapmaker, colonizer, agriculturist and hu-

Arizona's representation in Statuary Hall in Washington, D.C., this bronze sculpture of Father Eusebio Kino, S.J., is the work of Suzanne Silvercruys, Tucson artist. Cross, rosary and astrolabe symbolize the man and his work.

manitarian, traveled some seventy-five hundred miles in more than forty expeditions in all directions. Of the twenty-four missions established, the first he would name Nuestra Señora de los Dolores (Our Lady of Sorrows), to become the center from which his explorations radiated. On one trip along the infamous Devil's Highway to the tip of the Gulf of California in hot, dangerous, waterless land which would become a burial spot for many later pioneers, he records his special devotion to Mary:

39

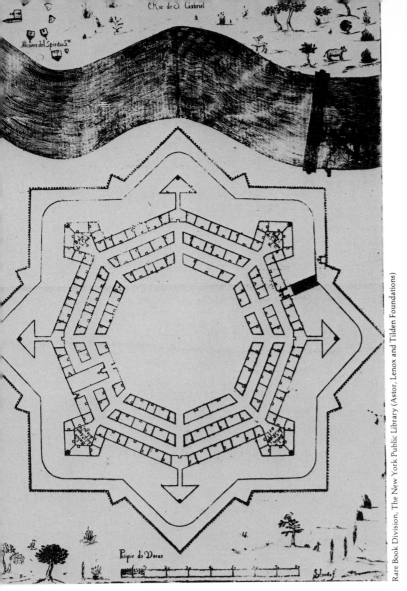

This diagram depicts the layout of Presidio de Nuestra Señora de Loreto en la Bahía (Fort of Our Lady of Loreto of the Bay), eventually shortened to La Bahía Mission. The fort was built near the site of La Salle's abandoned colony at present-day Matagorda Bay, Texas.

"March 9, 1701 . . . On the tenth we set out along the coast toward the northwest, or between north and west, for San Eduardo del Baypia, carrying with us the picture of Our Lady of Loretto. . . . Various parts of the road were made so pleasant and beautiful by virtue of roses and flowers of different colors, that it seemed as if Nature had placed them there for the reception of Our Lady of Loretto. Almost all day we were praying and chanting various prayers

40

and praises of Our Lady in different languages — in Castilian, in Latin, in Italian and also in the California language. . . ."

Father Kino's knowledge of geography produced many maps of the areas traveled; these maps were not to be improved upon for over a century. He discovered that lower California was a peninsula, confirming earlier reports that it was not an island. He introduced stock raising into five or six river valleys and set up ranches at nearly twenty different localities, always placing his endeavors under Mary's protection.

Before his death in 1711 he had baptized over four thousand souls. Memorials to him in equestrian statues best recall this "padre on horseback" and can be found in Phoenix and Hermosillo — the neighboring states of American Arizona and Mexican Sonora. A magnificent memorial in bronze is in the nation's Capitol. As the two hundred fiftieth anniversary of Father Kino's death approached, the Arizona State Legislature voted that a statue of him represent the state in Statuary Hall. It was installed in 1964. In 1976 the Arizona Film Corporation produced a movie, *The Father Kino Story*, in which the talents of fourteen leading male actors shared the honors.

Two forts named for Mary practically mark the beginning and end of Spain's early endeavors in the Texas-Louisiana area. In 1682 La Salle reached the mouth of the Mississippi, claiming the entire Mississippi Valley for France and naming the region Louisiana. Returning to Illinois he built Fort St. Louis and two years later, in 1684, he again set out for the mouth of the Mississippi. He never reached it. Mistaking what is now Matagorda Bay in Texas for the Mississippi's mouth, he dropped anchor. He attempted to establish a colony there but was driven off by Indians. (Like its Illinois counterpart, this colony also was named Fort St. Louis.) Meanwhile Spain, alarmed at this threat of French encroachment, sent soldiers to oust La Salle, but all they found was a demolished fort. Near its site they built the Presidio Nuestra Señora de Loreto en la Bahía del Espíritu Santo de la Provincia de Texas, popularly referred to as the Fort of Our Lady of Loretto of the Bay, and later simply called La Bahía Mission.

Spain gradually came to regard the Matagorda coastal fort as ineffectual protection and decided instead to strengthen the Louisiana frontier. She moved her garrison northeast to Natchitoches, Louisiana, between present-day Shreveport and Alexandria.

The fort was called Presidio Nuestra Señora del Pilar de los Adais (in honor of Our Lady of the Pillar of the Adais). The title was both European and American. *Pilar* is Spanish for pillar, referring to a column of jasper on which a miraculous statue of the Virgin stands in Saragossa, Spain. *Adais* was for the Adaes Indians of the area who were cared for by the expedition's Franciscans. Until its abandonment in 1773 the *presidio* (fort) served as the capital of the province of Texas.

Notable among the missionaries was the Venerable Antonio Margil de Jesús,

Library of Congress

Father Antonio Margil de Jesús Preaching to the Indians

Louisiana Society, Daughters of the American Colonists

This Marian marker at Natchitoches, Louisiana, reads: "The Presidio Nuestra Señora del Pilar de los Adais was founded in 1721 by the Spaniards on the crest of this hill as the eastern outpost of the Spanish empire in the West and for fifty years was the capital of the province of Texas until its abandonment in 1773."

41

known as "The Apostle of Texas." For forty-three years he worked in the mission field of New Spain and attributed the success of all his endeavors to Our Lady of Guadalupe. He followed the Franciscan tradition of special devotion to Mary's Assumption and composed a lengthy hymn honoring that title, one verse which advised:

> *Ye princes of the court of God*
> *Pry open wide the gates of gold,*
> *Asunder tear concealing veils,*
> *Let all her coming home behold.*

As early as 1691 Franciscans were serving central and eastern Texas; in that year Father Damien Massanet erected a cross at the Indian village of Yanaguana and rechristened it San Antonio, later establishing here Mission San Antonio de Valero which would become part of American history as the Alamo.

Near the Louisiana boundary the Asinais were served from Mission Nuestra Señora de la Purísima Concepción, erected in 1716 and moved later two miles below San Antonio where a beautiful church would be erected. Its stone was quarried in the area and legend states the mortar used was mixed with the milk of cows and goats, for strength and endurance, milk which pious women and children had deprived themselves of in honoring the Virgin. This church would be occupied by Texans in their war for independence and suffered some damage in the Battle of Conception. (See section entitled "Virgin Militant.")

While America fought for independence, Spanish colonization of California had already established a third of our future Pacific boundary. Though the Jesuits had been expelled from all Spanish dominions by a 1767 decree of King Charles III, Franciscans had come to fill the gap.

Spain had been keeping a watchful eye

The oldest church of the Immaculate Conception in the United States still in use, San Antonio's Mission de Nuestra Señora de la Purísima Concepción was the scene of the Battle of Conception in the Texas war of independence.

on English, French and Dutch ships poking their prows into an area she considered hers by virtue of early exploration. When Vitus Bering, sailing for Russia, discovered the strait connecting the north Pacific with the Arctic Ocean, Russia became interested in following this discovery down the coast. To safeguard her interests, Spain began a system of missions protected by military detachments, entrusting the undertaking to the remarkable Junípero Serra.

So much has been written about the spiritual Serra that one overlooks the larger picture of him as a truly heroic example of a man of the late Renaissance. From the beginning of his mission work in 1767 he found himself in conflict with the

42

civil military authorities. While they provided protective escorts and small groups of soldiers as mission guards, they considered the religious program secondary to the civil and acted accordingly. Serra was

Chosen by California as its representation in the nation's Statuary Hall, this bronze sculpture of Father Junípero Serra (1713-1784) by Ettore Cadorin was unveiled in 1931.

Collection of the Architect of the Capitol

forced into taking the position of claiming authority for himself over all missions and mission activities and, in spite of resultant conflicts, advanced his progress and overcame obstacles that would have crushed a lesser man.

Stretching along the California coast from San Diego to Sonoma, about six hundred miles, he established nine missions, each a day's travel apart. His sixth was at San Francisco, named after St. Francis of Assisi. That name (referring to the original mission and grounds) over the years has yielded to Dolores for a nearby lake named Los Dolores by Juan Bautista de Anza, having come upon it on the feast day of Our Lady of Sorrows, March 29, 1776. Mass was said here by Father Serra on June 29, five days before the Declaration of Independence.

The mission is one hundred fourteen feet long, twenty-two feet wide, with adobe walls four feet thick, constructed with manzanita pegs, its rough-hewn redwood roof timbers lashed together with rawhide. In the devastating 1906 earthquake and fire it was unharmed while its modern neighbors were leveled.

The interior of Mission Dolores has hand-carved altars and statues, as well as the original confessional doors and a revolving tabernacle. Its ceiling remains as originally decorated by the Indians in bright vegetable colors. The great north bell dates to 1797 and is embossed "Ave María Purísima." For Father Serra, Mary's Immaculate Conception was a dominant theme. He taught and upheld the doctrine long before it was defined as an article of faith. His constant refrain was: "Thou art all fair, O Mary, and the original stain is not in thee."

Of the many evidences he recorded of Mary's intercession, one in particular describes an Indian attack on August 15, 1769, at his first mission at San Diego:

"Our Lady, Our Most Pure Superioress

Mission Dolores

San Francisco's famed Mission Dolores was founded in 1776 under the title of St. Francis of Assisi. A nearby lake had been named Los Dolores (in honor of Our Lady of Sorrows) when Anza came upon it on Mary's feast day, March 29. Over the years the name St. Francis has yielded to Dolores.

This memorial commemorates the founding of the world's largest city named after Mary: Los Angeles, California.

... delivered us on the day of her Assumption. ... I had her in one hand and in the other her Divine Son, the Crucified, when the arrows rained in upon us. ... With such defenses, whether one was about to die or not, all was well, although I am such a great sinner."

A week prior to his death on August 28,

1784, he ministered to the Christian Indians at Carmel, leading them in the singing of Father Antonio Margil's hymn *Our Lady Assumed into Heaven.*

Since 1931 Father Serra has been honored by a statue in the nation's Capitol. It stands in Statuary Hall where each state is permitted two statues of distinguished natives judged worthy of national commemoration. California's first choice was the Franciscan justly called "The Father of California." In the summer of 1976 a twenty-two-foot statue of him was dedicated near Hillsborough, California. Doves were released on the occasion to signify that he had come with the cross of peace and not with the sword.

Going north from San Diego to find the good but long-lost port of Monterey, the military detachment protecting Father Juan Crespi camped on the banks of a nearby river. The date was August 2 and in honor of the great Franciscan Marian feast Father Crespi named the river El Río de Nuestra Señora la Reina de los Angeles de Porciúncula (the River of Our Lady Queen of the Angels of Portiuncula). The latter word means "little portion" and refers to the small chapel of St. Mary of the Angels near Assisi which the Benedictines had given to St. Francis.

The area continued to be known by the river's name and eleven years later Felipe de Neve, governor of the Spanish colonial province of Alta California, founded the pueblo of Our Lady Queen of the Angels (Los Angeles). The first settlement comprised but eleven men, eleven women and twenty-two children; by 1800 the town had seventy families and a population of three hundred fifteen. Today it is California's leading metropolis in wealth, manufacturing, commerce, aviation and ocean shipping, as well as being the world's largest Marian city.

The city contains many impressive memorials, but none is of greater significance

45

Ceremony of Las Posadas ("The Lodgings") in Los Angeles

than the simple cross which stands on Olvera Street amid the brightly decorated stalls and shops of its Mexican community. The area attracts thousands of visitors year round, but especially from December 16-24 when there is reenacted the centuries-old ceremony of *Las Posadas* (The Lodgings), telling the story of Mary and Joseph's journey to Bethlehem in search of a birthplace for Jesus. A platform, containing an artistic tableau lighted by candles, is carried by men dressed in native costume; other attendants playing stringed instruments accompany the colorful procession. On the Saturday before Ash Wednesday Olvera Street is the scene of the ceremony of the Blessing of the Animals, a custom originating with St. Francis of Assisi.

By 1773 San Diego and Monterey had been established by Gaspar de Portolá and Father Serra to lay the foundation of New California; but overland communication with the Mexican mainland was needed, as well as a stronger colony to hold the land. To meet these needs a party of twenty-two soldiers under Juan Bautista de Anza left Tubac, Arizona, on January 8, 1774.

46

Anza's diary relates: "Morning Mass was sung . . . to invoke the divine aid of this expedition, and I named as its protectors the Blessed Trinity and the Mystery of the Immaculate Conception of most Holy Mary. . . ." Anza was accompanied by Father Francisco Garcés who carried a Marian banner with which he was to become famous among the Southwest Indians.

The banner was a large piece of linen cloth with the Virgin and Child painted in colors on one side and a person burning in hell on the other. Father Garcés' diary records his ministrations to the Indians encountered on their route:

"I distributed among them tobacco and glass beads, showed them the image of Holy Mary and the figure of the lost soul and gave them to understand the things of God. All with great joy manifested how much Holy Mary suited them, shouting that all was very good; but the sight of the damned caused them such horror that they wished not to see it."

On leaving Arizona the party went down the Altar Valley of Mexico to Caborca, over the almost waterless Camino del Diablo (Road of the Devil) to Sonoita and then to Yuma, then down the Colorado River thirty-five miles to Santa Olaya.

This map shows the route Anza and Father Francisco Garcés traveled in 1774 to establish an overland route between Mexico and California. Dotted line shows variation in the second expedition of 1775-1776.

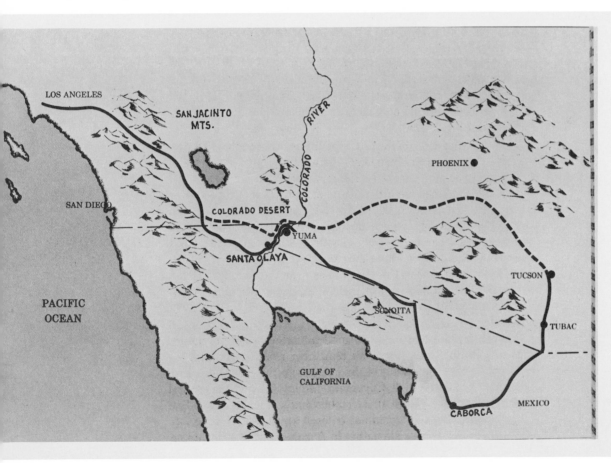

Pourade: *The Explorers*

Anza and Father Garcés Exploring California-Mexico Route
Father Garcés carries his banner depicting Mary and the Child Jesus on
one side, with the other side portraying a soul suffering damnation in hell.

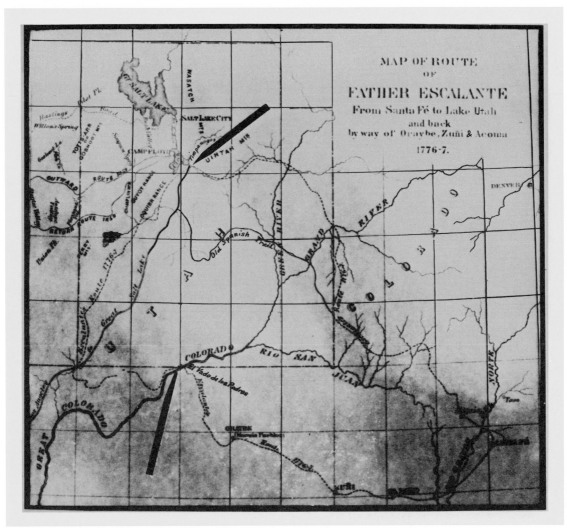

Map Showing Father Escalante's Journey

This map from a U.S. Army report, dated 1859, traces the seventeen-hundred-mile trek made by Father Silvestre Vélez de Escalante and his companions in 1776. Upper arrow points to present-day Utah Valley which the missionaries named Our Lady of Mercy of the Timpanogos. Lower arrow indicates the spot at the Utah-Arizona border where the expedition crossed the Colorado; it was called Holy Conception of the Virgin Mary.

Here the party left the river and struck across the terrible Colorado Desert where for ten days they struggled against sand, heat and lack of water to reach Signal Mountain near the California boundary, only to have to turn back against insurmountable odds. Retracing their way to Santa Olaya, Anza prepared a new start.

He now circumvented the sand dunes, crossed the Colorado Desert, swung north to discover San Carlos Pass over the San Jacinto Mountains, and descended their western slope to Mission San Gabriel near Los Angeles. Mission accomplished!

A year later he led a colony of two hundred forty-four persons over the route,

The Naming of Our Lady of Mercy of the Timpanogos

This painting by Paul Salisbury, owned by the Utah State Historical Society, depicts Father Escalante blessing the Utah Valley and naming it for Our Lady of Mercy of the Timpanogos. The high mountains beyond the valley are the most majestic in Utah and are still called Timpanogos.

arriving at present-day San Gabriel, from where he traveled northward to San Francisco Bay. On March 28, 1776, he established here the *presidio* and mission which were the foundation of what is now known as San Francisco. Father Garcés and three companions would establish two missions at the junction of the Colorado and Gila Rivers where in July 1781 the Yuma Indians revolted and massacred the friars and the adult males of the families. (Of the one hundred forty-two Franciscans who had served the California area up to 1848, sixty-seven died at their posts.)

One of the outstanding peaceful journeys of exploration in American history began on July 29, 1776, when two Franciscans, Silvestre Vélez de Escalante and Francisco Atanasio Domínguez, left their headquarters in Santa Fe to seek an overland route to the California mission headquarters in Monterey. In five months' arduous travel they covered almost seventeen hundred miles in Colorado, Utah, Arizona and New Mexico. They failed to accomplish their objective but revealed the geography, resources and inhabitants of a vast inland area. They were the first white

Formerly located on one of the walls of the Colorado River Canyon, this marker reads: "Nov. 7, 1776. Crossing of the Fathers. At this place Fray Silvestre Vélez de Escalante and Fray Francisco Atanasio Domínguez, with a small party, made the first recorded crossing of the Colorado by white men, on their return to Santa Fe after failing to reach Monterey in California, naming the old Indian ford 'Holy Conception of the Virgin Mary.' "

Places named after Mary by Juan Francisco de Bodega in 1775 are designated on this contemporary map of southeast Alaska. Top arrow points to Puerto de los Remedios (named after Our Lady of Help); bottom arrow — Bahía Guadalupe (Bay of Guadalupe, in honor of Spain's patroness).

51

Bay of the Assumption

Bruno de Ezeta's 1775 map of the northwest coast shows the mouth of today's Columbia River as the Bay of the Assumption.

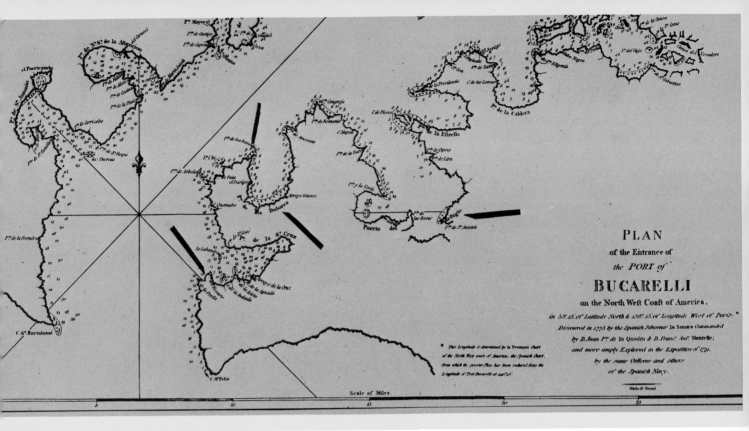

Marian Designations

*Arrows in this 1779 "Plan of the Entrance of the Port of Bucarelli,"
Alaska, show the Marian names of Punta del Rosario, Puerto del
Refugio, Puerto de los Dolores and Puerto de los Remedios.*

men to enter present-day Utah and blazed the route that became the Old Spanish Trail which the Mormons followed seventy years later. (The Mormons have perpetuated their memory by including them in a monument honoring Mormon pioneers, erected in Salt Lake City in 1947.)

The expedition arrived at Utah Valley on September 23, 1776. That day being the vigil of the feast of Our Lady of Ransom (or Mercy), they named the valley Nuestra Señora de la Merced de los Timpanagotzis (Our Lady of Mercy of the Timpanogos). Traveling south, the party crossed the Colorado River at the Utah-Arizona border and named their ford Holy Conception of the Virgin Mary. This spot has now been obliterated by the waters of Glen Canyon Dam, but before the area was flooded the crossing was filmed for the scene of

Christ's baptism in the Jordan in the movie *The Greatest Story Ever Told.*

Though the mission posts had strengthened Spain's hold on lower California, the threat of Russian expansion still required that she explore upper California and the northwest. An expedition was readied in 1775 called the Ezeta-Bodega Expedition in honor of its two captains, Bruno de Ezeta commanding the schooner *Santiago,* and Juan Francisco de Bodega commanding the *Sonora.*

The crews had received a blessing on the voyage at the church in San Blas, Mexico, "and took with them an image of Our Lady, María Santísima [Mary Most Holy]." Bodega in the *Sonora* sailed on March 16 until he reached what is now Alaska. At the entrance to Klokachef Sound, between Kruzof and Chichagof Islands, Bodega made a landing, planted a cross, and took possession in the name of Spain, thus becoming the first Spaniard to set foot on Alaskan soil. He named the port Nuestra Señora de los Remedios (Our Lady of Help); south of this port he named Shelikof Bay the Bay of Guadalupe for Spain's patroness.

Ezeta in the *Santiago* reached Nootka Sound, British Columbia, and then prepared to return to Monterey. On August 17 he and his men "found themselves in latitude forty-six degrees and eleven minutes. At five in the afternoon they discovered a large bay which they called La

Asunción de Nuestra Señora [The Assumption of Our Lady] and they gave names to the two capes which form the entrance. The one on the north they called Cape San Roque and the one on the south Cape Frondoso, on account of the thick growth of trees with which it is covered. While between the two capes, which are about one and a half leagues apart, they observed that the sea penetrates far into the land, making a horizon to the east. . . ."

Thus Ezeta discovered the Columbia River and named it for Mary, seventeen years before Captain Robert Gray entered

Map of Spanish Exploration of the Northwest Coast, 1790-1791

In this map the upper arrow shows Gran Canal de Nuestra Señora del Rosario (present-day Strait of Georgia), while the lower arrow points to Puerto de Nuestra Señora de los Angeles (now Port Angeles, Washington).

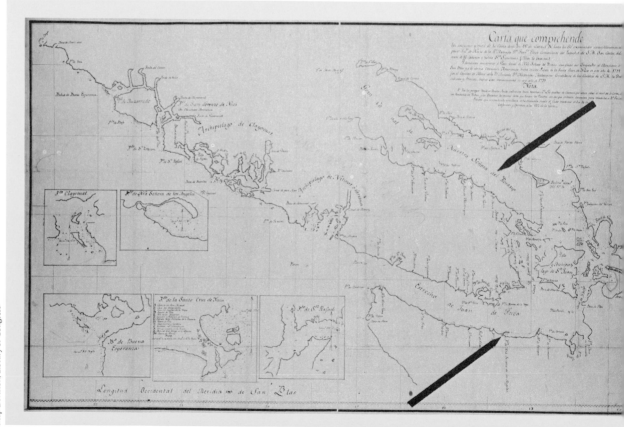

Port Angeles, Washington

This photo shows today's bustling Port Angeles, Washington, originally named Puerto de Nuestra Señora de los Angeles by Spaniards in 1791. At the tip of the claw is a U.S. Coast Guard station; twice weekly its pollution-control flights check for oil spills from foreign and domestic tankers approaching Puget Sound.

it for the first time and naming it for his ship the *Columbia.*

Still another Spanish expedition ventured northward, this time under Bodega and Antonio Maurelle commanding the *La Princesa* and the *La Favorita.* Leaving San Blas, Mexico, on February 11, 1779, the ships became separated by a severe storm on April 19. The captain of the *La Princesa* "made a vow to Our Lady of the Rosary, patroness of the frigate. He promised the foresail as an offering at her shrine, and also that he would carry, barefooted, the mast in procession to the church of San

55

Blas if the Blessed Virgin would deliver us from this and other dangers which we might encounter and should we return safely to harbor. As if to reward us for this promise, Our Lady favored us with her powerful protection. Indeed, it would be difficult to find another example of a voyage of discovery fraught with so many dangers and so happily ended.''

On the third of May they reached Bucarelli Bay on the southern extremity of Prince of Wales Island, Alaska. In gratitude they named their first landfall Punta del Rosario (Point of the Rosary). Exploring deeper into the bay they named several harbors after Mary, among them Puerto de los Dolores and Puerto de los Remedios.

The swan song of Spain's exploration of the Pacific coast would be the Eliza-Malaspina Expedition of 1790-1791. Entering the present Strait of Georgia, British Columbia, and believing it to be the long-sought interoceanic passage, they named it Gran Canal de Nuestra Señora del Rosario (Grand Strait of Our Lady of the Rosary). In sailing they found safe harbor behind a natural seawall in the Strait of Juan de Fuca and named it Puerto de Nuestra Señora de los Angeles (Port of Our Lady of the Angels), today Port Angeles, Washington, whose harbor is the first American port of entry for ships coming into Puget Sound from the Pacific.

Spain's exploration of the Pacific coast had run out. Her control of California would last until 1822 when the province passed under the sovereignty of Mexico. In the interim, "intruders" could hardly be kept out. Not only Russian but English, French and American explorers and traders came in increasing numbers as Spain's hold on the frontiers relaxed. Sailors from the vast reaches of the Pacific, traders eager to exchange goods for furs, hides and tallow, trappers from the Rocky Mountains, all became familiar sights in Monterey, Los Angeles, San Diego, San Jose and San Francisco. Too absorbed in making their own history, they would be unappreciative of the great Marian devotion at the heart of Spain's contributions to the land.

Notre Dame

FRENCH ENDEAVORS

1632-1759

Indian Relic Mold for Mary's Image

Found in 1825 at an Indian campsite in northeastern Pennsylvania's Luzerne County, this mold (circa 1775) is an example of the crucifixes and leaden images of Mary which French traders distributed among the converted Indians. Such images were made by pouring lead into plaster-of-Paris molds. The original of this mold was two inches square. A slightly larger mold shaped the image of the Virgin and Child.

Notre Dame

France's hope for founding an empire in the New World depended on the fur trade and settlements among the natives she hoped to convert. Her first exploration — that by Verrazzano in 1524 — revealed the eastern coast from the Carolinas to Newfoundland; no follow-up to this, however, was possible since France was then at war with Italy.

Ten years later Jacques Cartier's expedition opened the door to Canada; again, further exploration would be delayed by disturbances at home resulting from the Protestant Revolution. Not until 1608, when Samuel de Champlain founded Quebec, would France secure a footing in the St. Lawrence Valley; this footing she would hold for one hundred fifty years.

France's devotion to Mary translated itself into the magnificent cathedrals bearing her name — Chartres, Reims, Amiens and many others — "miracles in stone." These

in turn kept alive a love for the Mother of God which missionaries were eager to share with the New World.

Under Champlain a steady stream of priests came, first Recollects, followed by Capuchins, Sulpicians and Jesuits. The latter's contributions command first place in Franco-American history. The spiritual sons of St. Ignatius Loyola were sent to Indian settlements — the Hurons around Georgian Bay; Algonquins north of the Ottawa; Abenakis in Maine and Acadia; Iroquois south of the St. Lawrence; and Chippewas, Ottawas, Illinois and other tribes of the upper lakes and the Mississippi Valley.

The Jesuits treated the Indians as brothers. They mastered the rich Indian languages and in their published *Relations* preserved a great wealth of ethnographical and geographical knowledge. Their writings reiterate the singular regard which Mary evoked in savage hearts. Whenever martyrdom crowned their efforts it served only to intensify the dedication of this fearless breed of men.

Missionaries with voyageurs and *coureurs de bois* pioneered in opening up large areas of our country and, in the process, perpetuating devotion to Mary. New York has its Lady of Martyrs at Auriesville; Marquette bequeathed to the Mississippi Valley his incomparable devotion to the Immaculate Conception; Michigan's Sault Ste. Marie is host to the thousands who come to see firsthand the marvels of the canal system and Mary's bridge which unites Canada with the United States.

The mighty wheat production of the west owes its beginnings to Frenchmen who pioneered South Dakota, clearing land and planting grain. Alabama has its Notre Dame de la Mobile, Louisiana Our Lady of Prompt Succor, and Tennessee its historic Fort Assumption. The "Golden Triangle" of today's Pittsburgh was once called L'Assomption de la Ste. Vierge à la belle Rivière (the Assumption of the Blessed Virgin at the Beautiful River). For mystery and intrigue no story can match that of the "Lost Virgin" in northern New England.

Without France's support the Revolutionary War might have been lost. When independence was assured, French Catholics eagerly pledged their allegiance to the American cause. Learned priest-refugees of the French Revolution — Flaget, Badin, Dubois, to name but a few — found haven in America at former French communities, or established new areas for diocesan expansion. By their ministrations they enriched the lives of Catholics and Protestants alike. One historian has termed their efforts "a significant stabilizing factor in the maturing process of the states of the Middle West."

In an era of American history marked by difficulties and dangers, France bequeathed from her cultural and spiritual resources a rich Marian heritage. Simple justice requires acknowledgment and full appreciation of the debt owed to *Notre Dame*.

Champlain's discoveries had opened the St. Lawrence River area for settlement and mission activity, and a French vessel sailing down the coast of Maine in 1632 captured a Plymouth Colony trading post on the Penobscot, at what is now Castine. A fort was built and named Pentagöet, and here later the Mission of Our Lady of Holy Hope was begun. The record of that mission's founding came to light in 1863 when a farmer plowing his field turned up a piece of sheet copper. He put it aside, until needing a piece of metal for mending he cut into the plate and then observed its lettering. When the Latin inscription was translated, a bit of Maine history was revealed. That history is perpetuated in a chapel at Castine.

The second Maine mission dedicated to Mary, in 1646, was the outgrowth of an Abenaki petition for a priest to serve them. Since the petition was received at the Jesuit mission at Sillery, Canada, on the vigil of the feast of the Assumption, the priest chosen (Father Gabriel Druillettes) named the mission on the Kennebec, at present-day Norridgewock, for that feast day. It was from here in 1650 that Father Druillettes made his notable visit to the Puritans of eastern Massachusetts to discuss a proposed union between New France and New England against the Iroquois. The union was not realized.

English hunters destroyed the mission's first chapel, but English workmen sent from Boston, according to treaty stipulations, rebuilt it. A much later chapel was erected in 1722 by Father Sebastian Rale, S.J., "dedicated to the Holy Virgin . . . where can be seen her image in relief. . . . There is a holy emulation among the females of the village as to who shall most ornament the Chapel . . . all who have any jewelry or pieces of silk, or calico, or other things of that kind, employ them."

The favorite Marian devotion of the entire tribe was the recitation of the rosary.

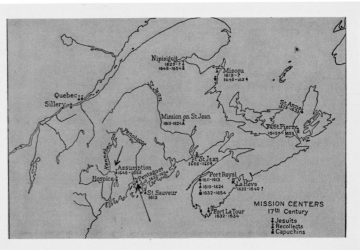

Leger: *Catholic Indian Missions in Maine*

This map of seventeenth-century Maine, New Brunswick and Nova Scotia, shows the mission centers of the Capuchins, Jesuits and Recollects. Two of the missions named in honor of Mary are (lower arrow) Our Lady of Holy Hope (at Fort Pentagöet on the Penobscot), and (upper arrow) Mission of the Assumption (on the Kennebec).

A farmer found this piece of sheet copper in 1863 in Castine, Maine. Translated, the Latin reads: "1648, 8th of June, I, Brother Leo of Paris, Capuchin missionary, laid this foundation in honor of Our Lady of the Holy Hope."

Maine Historical Society

This chapel at Castine, Maine, occupies the site and bears the name of the original mission built in honor of Our Lady of Holy Hope.

Mission of the Assumption, Norridgewock, Maine

the word of God to the savage Mohawks. In July 1636 the newly ordained Isaac Jogues wrote his mother in Orleans, France, of the "excessive joy" he felt on first setting foot in New France "and celebrating my first Mass here on the day of the Visitation . . . indeed a day of the visitation of the goodness of God and our Lady, . . . that I was to be born again to a new life, and a life in God."

This sixty-four-pound bell was found near the Kennebec River eighty-four years after the Mission of the Assumption was raided by the English.

Father Rale met his death at the hands of the English and their Indian allies on August 23, 1724, when the Mission of the Assumption was destroyed in one of many unofficial skirmishes which culminated in the French and Indian War. The Jesuits later rebuilt the mission and continued to evangelize the Abenaki. How this tribe's devotion to Mary persisted through the centuries is attested in the story of the "Lost Virgin" at the end of this section.

The question has been asked: "May not the marvelous growth of the Church in New York State have some connection with the heroism of its first priests?" Those priests were French Jesuits who early in the seventeenth century brought

64

Du Creux: Historiae canadensis seu Novae-Franciae

Martyrdom of Isaac Jogues and His Companions

Today at the Shrine of the North American Martyrs at Auriesville, New York, one may walk the Hill of Torture up which St. Isaac Jogues and St. René Goupil were forced to run the gauntlet in 1642. Goupil perished but Jogues survived, returned to France, and then petitioned to be sent back to the Mohawks. Four years later he was martyred on these same grounds.

In a tree at the shrine can be seen a replica of Our Lady of Foy, a devotion originating with the Jesuits of Belgium. At Foy in 1609 a woodman cutting down an old oak tree found in a pile of black dust an image of Mary estimated to be over two hundred years old. It was placed in a small chapel which gradually outgrew the needs of hundreds of pilgrims. So many cures were reported that a canonical inquiry was instituted which formally approved twenty miracles occurring in ten years' time.

The Jesuits sent replicas of Our Lady of Foy to many countries, one going to the Huron Mission in Quebec. Father Bruyas, superior there, wrote in 1675 of the mission's growth:

"I attribute these conversions to the goodness of the Most Blessed Virgin . . . the church of Agnie [Mohawk] has completely changed its appearance. The older Christians have resumed their former fervor and the number of new ones increases daily. We displayed this precious statue with all possible pomp on the feast of the

Immaculate Conception . . . while litanies were chanted in the Iroquois tongue."

The Mohawk Mission and its Notre Dame de Foy were destroyed by the English in 1684. On the two-hundredth anniversary of the occasion, restoration of the mission site was begun with the erection of a shrine dedicated to Regina Martyrum (Our Lady of Martyrs). A publication entitled *The Pilgrim* was begun "to gather up the memories of the place and to renew its lesson of devotion." The publication is still issued quarterly and the pilgrimages it lists testify to the great honor and reverence paid by thousands to the sacred ground trod by those martyrs, one of whom voiced the spirit of all when he wrote: "We shall be taken; we shall be burned; we shall be massacred. But that is a trifle. One's bed is not always the best place to die in."

The Coliseum Church at Auriesville is a huge amphitheater with a diameter of three hundred fifty-seven feet to provide seventy-two entrances for the seventy-two disciples appointed by Christ. These entrances include eight main portals, each bearing in a niche a statue of one of the eight North American martyrs canonized at Rome in 1930; in that year the building of the church began.

Other Jesuits, undaunted by the martyrdom of their fellow priests, came back into

Loyola Seminary

Martyrs Shrine, Auriesville

Notre Dame de Foy, popularly called the Madonna of the Mohawks, is captured in this artist's rendition. The statue is enshrined in a tree on the grounds at Auriesville, New York.

THE PILGRIM

–OF–

Our Lady of Martyrs

–FOR 1885.–

COMPLETE IN ONE VOLUME.

—COMPRISING—

The History of the Shrine of the Blessed Virgin Mary on the site of the former Mission of the Martyrs, Auriesville, N. Y., with miscellanies on early and recent American Indian Missions.

PUBLISHED AT WEST CHESTER,—N. Y. CATHOLIC PROTECTORY, for Rev. J. LOYZANCE, S. J., St. Joseph's Church, Troy, N. Y.

Coliseum Church, Our Lady of Martyrs Shrine

This view of the Coliseum Church at Auriesville, New York, is from a high rise of ground near Priest's Grove.

northern New York in 1654 when the Iroquois sought peace and trade with the French.

The Iroquois consisted of five tribes — Seneca, Cayuga, Onondaga, Oneida and Mohawk. To the Onondaga Father Joseph Chaumonot came in 1655 and offered the first Mass in New York at Pompey, south of Syracuse. Then Mary was brought into the picture. For her the first settlement of white men in the entire land of the Iroquois was named St. Marie Gannentaha, Gannentaha being the Indian name for the Syracuse area. Here on the shores of Lake Onondaga a fort was built

with its chapel the center and base of missionary operations spreading out to the neighboring Indian tribes.

In addition to the chapel the fort contained officers' quarters, bakehouse and ovens, workshop, smithy and stone forge. Though the French were now well established, the Indians proved unfriendly and the winter of 1657-1658 found the colonists practically besieged. They planned to escape in the spring when the ice in the lake would melt. Meanwhile they secretly built canoes, hiding them under the false floor of the chapel. In the spring they invited the Onondagas to a great feast, and

67

Record of First Mass in New York State (at Pompey), 1655

Beneath this chapel floor the French hid several canoes which they used to make good their escape from hostile Indians at Fort Ste. Marie Gannentaha in what is now Syracuse, New York.

Reconstructed Fort Ste. Marie Gannentaha

made their escape while the Indians slept off the effects of liquid refreshments. (The story forms part of Carl Carmer's book of New York legends, *Dark Trees to the Wind*, in a chapter entitled "The Big Eat-All Dinner.")

Though the settlement proved unsuccessful, the French left their impress on the area in Father Simon LeMoyne's discovery of a spring which proved to be one of the many fountains of salt that became the salt industry of Syracuse and eventually furnished a great part of the money for the Erie Canal.

Moving westward from Syracuse the Jesuits established houses of worship in the westernmost Seneca villages of the Iroquois Confederacy. One such mission was that of La Conception in the vicinity of Rochester Junction. It was a most important location, under the care of Fathers James Fremin, Julien Garnier and Peter Raffeix.

Among its notable visitors were La Salle and Father Louis Hennepin, Recollect. The mission was destroyed by Denonville's army in 1687, after which it was relocated on Spring Brook nearby. Serving here were Fathers Julien Garnier, Vaillant de Gueslis and James D'Heu. When political circumstances compelled the final withdrawal of all French missionaries from this region the ministrations to the Christianized Indians were continued through contacts with Canadian missions where many descendants of the Senecas still persevere in the faith.

When Father Jogues had first come to Quebec he had been sent to work among the Indians south of Lake Huron. Accompanied by Father Charles Raymbaut they reached Michigan and viewed a beautiful waterfall. Legend relates that Father Jogues exclaimed *"Sault"* (falls) and followed this by a fervent *"Sainte Marie!"* — the only name adequate for anything so beautiful. Thus Sault Ste. Marie was named.

Marker Commemorating the Mission of La Conception near Rochester Junction, New York

Joseph J. Domas

Religious Americana Museum

This type of hand-forged iron cross (circa 1680) was given or traded to converted Indians by Jesuit missionaries. This one was excavated in the Syracuse area in the 1960s. Its flat base could be imbedded in a tree branch.

No permanent mission was established here until Fathers James Marquette, Claude Allouez and Claude Dablon came in 1668. Of their first mission, Ste. Marie, the *Relation* states: "We have had a Chapel erected, and have taken care to adorn it, going farther in this than one would dare promise himself in a country so destitute of all things."

Sault Ste. Marie became the center of

69

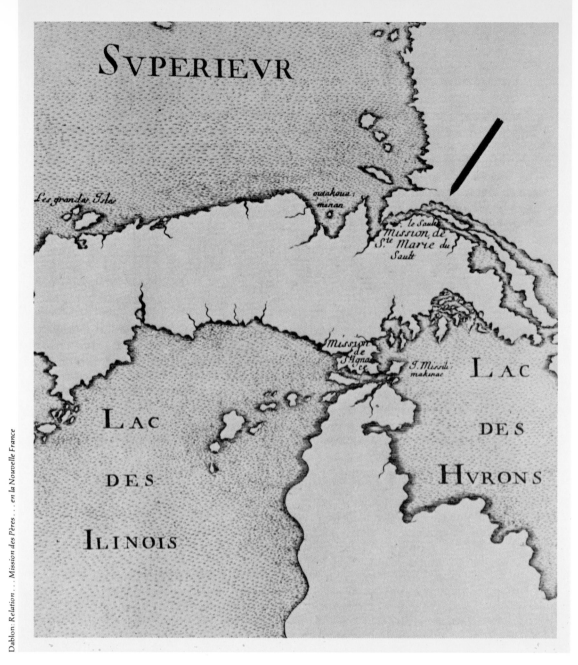

Jesuit Map of Wisconsin, 1672
Arrow points to Mission de Ste. Marie du Sault in what is now Michigan.

the three missions established in the surrounding area, caring for as many as nineteen different Indian tribes. The Sault also became a rendezvous for fur traders who wintered among the tribes, and the area's importance prompted the French to erect a fort to control travel on the river. French claims, however, yielded to England under the terms of the 1763 Treaty of Paris and,

in turn, England yielded her claims to the United States when the American Revolution ended and the 1783 Treaty of Paris ceded to our country all land south of the Great Lakes.

The treaty though did not bring peace. England refused to surrender the region and continued trading with the Upper Peninsula Indians; even after the War of 1812

Carnegie Public Library, Sault Ste. Marie

Catholic Church at Fort Brady

This undated sketch of Fort Brady at Sault Ste. Marie was made prior to 1835. In the background is the Catholic church built sometime after 1822.

the British clung to their holdings. Added to this was the Indians' discontent over infringement of their land claims. Finally in 1817 Lewis Cass, territorial governor of Michigan, boldly carried the American flag into the region and, with reckless courage which almost precipitated a massacre by pro-British Indians, claimed the territory for the United States. He negotiated the Treaty of St. Marys with the Chippewas on June 16, 1820, under which they ceded a four-mile square tract at the Sault on which Fort Brady was erected in 1822. The treaty marked the first real assertion of

American authority in the Lake Superior area.

The Sault has had a colorful history. Trappers and traders settling there found free navigation impossible because the rapids in St. Marys River forced portaging forty-nine miles to reach Lake Superior. When settlement of the Northwest Territory brought increased trade and larger boats it became necessary to unload the boats, haul the cargoes around the rapids in wagons, and reload in other boats. In 1797 the North West Company, a fur-trading organization, constructed a navi-

71

U.S. Army Corps of Engineers

St. Marys Falls Canal, Sault Ste. Marie, Michigan
International Bridge links Sault Ste. Marie, Michigan (left) with Sault
Ste. Marie, Ontario (right). St. Marys Falls are the white water in center.

gation lock thirty-eight feet long on the Canadian side of the river for small boats. This was destroyed by U.S. troops in the War of 1812.

Freight and boats again had to portage until 1855 when the first ship canal was built with congressional aid. This canal had two tandem locks each three hundred fifty feet long. The canal was owned and operated by the State of Michigan with a toll of four cents per ton on boats passing through. Increasing commerce through the canal grew to national importance and, since Michigan did not have the funds to

provide necessary additional facilities, the locks were transferred to the United States Government in 1881, under jurisdiction of the U.S. Army Corps of Engineers who from that time have maintained the locks toll free.

Since the St. Lawrence Seaway opening in 1959, foreign flag vessels are much in evidence, giving the locks all the international flavor of its sister locks at the Panama Canal. The number of passages through the locks averages about seventeen thousand vessels a year. The newest lock, the Poe, can accommodate ships one

Reconstructed Stockade

Holy Rosary Mission (not visible) is beyond the stockade at left. The stockade is on the site of the original post erected by French explorers and fur traders at Grand Portage in Minnesota.

Minnesota Historical Society

thousand feet long and one hundred five feet wide.

French explorers and fur traders, accompanied by missionaries, had established an important post at the eastern tip of Minnesota at Grand Portage, four miles south of the Canadian border. Here the famed nine-mile Grand Portage Trail, connecting Lake Superior to the Pigeon River, provided access to northern waterways. This post, one thousand miles inland, served as depot headquarters and trading settlement and was a lifeline across half a continent.

French Jesuits came as early as 1731 to be followed a century later by the coura-geous Slovenians, Fathers Frederic Baraga and Francis Pierz. The latter dedicated the post's first chapel on July 25, 1838. It was a simple structure of cedar bark and deer-skin made by the Indians themselves for their Lady of the Holy Rosary. Here at the mission Father Pierz opened Minnesota's first Indian school. The chapel was re-placed in 1865 by the present structure made of logs joined by wooden dowels.

The stockaded lake post was recon-structed under the auspices of the Bureau of Indian Affairs, U.S. Department of the Interior. The Grand Portage National Monument, thirty-eight miles northeast of

Holy Rosary Mission, Grand Portage, Minnesota

Grand Marais, was established in 1960 following conferences with the Minnesota Chippewa Tribal Council and the Grand Portage Band of the Chippewa Tribe, through whose reservation the route passes. Holy Rosary Mission continues to serve the Indians of the reservation, many of whose ancestors lie buried in the ground before its doors.

Voyageurs in 1732 sought the Northwest Passage and en route established Fort St. Charles at the top of the Northwest Angle where the little tip of Minnesota holds her own on the Lake of the Woods among her Canadian neighbors. Here Pierre la Vérendrye and a party of fifty men, which included his three sons and the Jesuit chaplain Jean Pierre Aulneau, established what was then the most northwesterly outpost of white men in America. Land was cleared and wheat planted, to

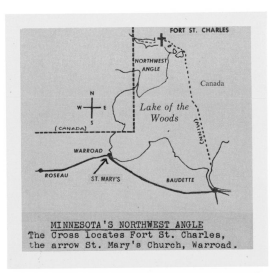

MINNESOTA'S NORTHWEST ANGLE
The Cross locates Fort St. Charles, the arrow St. Mary's Church, Warroad.

This depicts Minnesota's Northwest Angle. The cross locates Fort St. Charles; the arrow points out the site of St. Mary's Church, Warroad, Minnesota.

Jean Baptiste la Vérendrye and Father Aulneau Leaving Fort St. Charles, June 1736

In this drawing by Emile M. Brunet, Pierre la Vérendrye kneels at the shore to bless his son on what will be their last contact.

St. Mary's Church, Warroad, Minnesota — Largest Log Church in the United States

make a pioneer effort in the mighty wheat production of the west. Later from this base two of Vérendrye's sons would explore as far west as Pierre, South Dakota, and still later other Frenchmen would reach the Rocky Mountains.

Flowing into the southwestern end of their Lake of the Woods was a small river made popular as a north and south highway for Indian war parties. "River of bloody ground," the Indians called it; to the French it became *chemin de la guerre*, "the road of war." The English transposed this to Warroad River from which a town was eventually named.

In 1736 Jean Baptiste, oldest son of Vérendrye, in command of nineteen men

Statue of Jean Pierre Aulneau, S.J., St. Mary's Church, Warroad

76

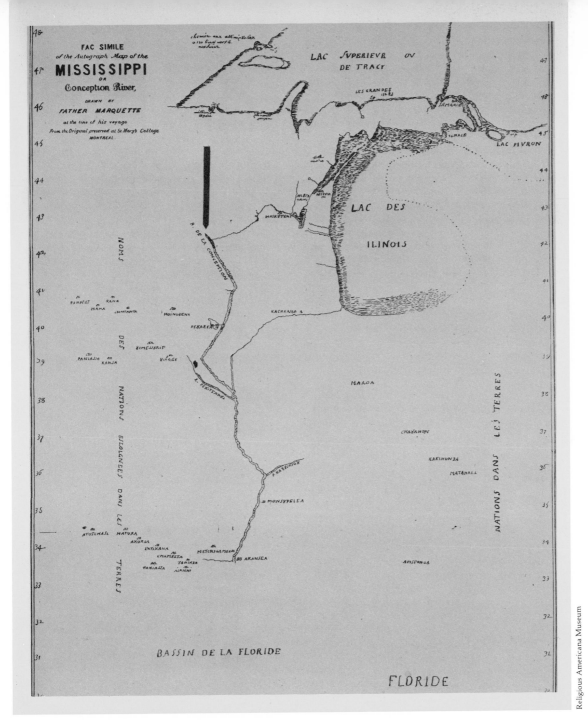

*Father Marquette's Map of 1673
Showing Conception River (the Mississippi)*

and accompanied by Father Aulneau, set out for Mackinac Island, Wisconsin, to bring back much needed supplies. They went in spite of rumors that the Sioux had come down the Warroad River to attack bands of Creeks and Chippewas. The expedition camped overnight on an island where they were attacked by the Sioux and all beheaded. To commemorate the heroism of these men, a Father Aulneau memorial was planned in St. Mary's Church at Warroad.

St. Mary's is often called a "rustic cathedral." Its use of native materials (logs,

This marble statue of Father Jacques Marquette (1637-1675) is Wisconsin's representation in Statuary Hall, Washington, D.C.

Collection of the Architect of the Capitol

cedar shakes, stone) portrays the spirit of the explorers and pioneers meeting the challenge of the elements and the country itself. The logs are from the last stand of virgin timber in the state, where they had to be cut and slabbed, and then hauled one hundred fifty miles to Warroad. The seventy thousand shakes on the roof were

Earliest extant record from the Mission of the Immaculate Conception, this record, dated July 19, 1720, is of the baptism of a girl slave, five or six years of age, who was named Marie Jeanne. It is signed by the pastor, Nicholas Ignatius de Beaubois. The Immaculate Conception Mission at Kaskaskia, Illinois, was named by Father Marquette in 1674 in fulfillment of his promise to the Virgin Mary.

Magazine of American History, VI, 1881

Hamilton: *Mobile of the Five Flags*

In this artist's concept of Mobile, Alabama, in 1711, the procession in the background is approaching the Church of Notre Dame de la Mobile, founded in 1704.

Historic Mobile Preservation Society

split by hand from native cedar, shaved, treated and dipped. Interior furnishings were all made on the grounds, the stained-glass windows cut to fit from the razed St. Mary's Church of Red Lake Falls. All the work was done by parishioners without pay.

The top of the church tower is a replica of the cross and mound of stones erected by the Jesuits in 1905 on Massacre Island where Father Aulneau and his companions met violent death. The statue of the priest

Street signs at a corner of Bienville Square in Mobile, Alabama, attest to the city's French-Spanish origins.

79

This sketch is of the first convent of the Ursuline Sisters in the French quarter of New Orleans. It was replaced by an imposing structure in 1753. Its service to the Church as well as to the State of Louisiana warranted its recent restoration.

at the base of the tower is deliberately out of natural proportions, portraying by outspread, oversized hands the spirit of oblation and self-sacrifice which prompted his missionary endeavors for Christ.

The persistent Indian reports of a river flowing to the great ocean impelled Governor Frontenac to commission Louis Joliet and Father Marquette to find it. Marquette recorded that the orders arrived on "the day of the Immaculate Conception of the Blessed Virgin, whom I had always invoked since I have been in this Ottawa country, to obtain of God the grace to be able to visit the nations on the river Missisipi [sic]. . . . I put our voyage under the protection of the Blessed Virgin Immaculate, promising her, that if she did us the grace to discover the great river, I would give it the name Conception; and that I would also give that name to the first mission which I should establish among these new nations. . . ."

80

Marquette and Joliet's group left their headquarters at St. Ignace, Michigan, canoed to Green Bay, Wisconsin, then up the Fox River to portage to the Wisconsin, and then to travel southwest. Marquette in a separate canoe was rushed along in the turbulent waters which finally joined the broad floodwaters of the Mississippi. The date was June 17, 1673, and Marquette wrote: "We entered the Missisipi [sic] with a joy I am unable to express." Faithful to his promise, he named the river Conception.

In following the river down to the Arkansas (Akansea on map, p. 77) the explorers became convinced that to continue farther would bring them to the Gulf of Mexico and that would mean trespassing on Spanish territory! They turned upstream and returned to Lake Michigan by the Illinois and Chicago Rivers.

Another trip would be made down the

This is the historic Chapel of Our Lady of Consolation. The statue of Our Lady of Prompt Succor was first enshrined in 1810 in the Chapel of Our Lady of Consolation which adjoined the Ursuline convent in New Orleans' French quarter.

Mississippi in the year following, this time to the Kaskaskia in Illinois where Marquette was received "as an angel from heaven" by more than fifteen hundred braves. Here he established the Mission of the Immaculate Conception, near present-day Utica, fulfilling his second promise to Mary. The mission was moved several times in the years following and eventually was located at the junction of the Kaskaskia and Mississippi Rivers. Its church and convent became an important part in American history when George Rogers Clark was forcing the British to vacate the Illinois country. (See section entitled "Virgin Militant.") From 1844 on, flooding of the Kaskaskia area destroyed most of the mission site. Fort Kaskaskia State Park now preserves the memory of this pioneer French settlement.

The eminent Catholic historian John Gilmary Shea, in his *Discovery and Exploration of the Mississippi Valley*, wrote that "Marquette's predominant virtue was a most rare and singular devotion to the Blessed Virgin, and especially to the mystery of the Immaculate Conception; it was a pleasure to hear him preach or speak on this subject. . . . From the age of nine he fasted every Saturday; and from his most tender youth began to recite daily the little office of the Conception, and inspired all to adopt this devotion. . . . So tender a devotion to the mother of God deserved some singular grace, and she accordingly granted him the favor he had always asked, to die on a Saturday."

Many honors have come to this missionary-explorer-discoverer; cities in five states bear his name, also a university, and, most significantly, his statue is included in the nation's Capitol. Though he was neither a native nor a citizen of Wisconsin, the right of that state to commemorate him in Statuary Hall was established by a joint resolution of Congress on October 21, 1893. A seven-foot marble sculpture, ex-

Ursuline Archives, New Orleans

New Orleans, according to this record, is the site of the establishment of the first sodality of the Blessed Virgin in what is now the United States. The date was May 28, 1730.

ecuted by Gaetano Trentanove of Italy, was installed in 1896.

In 1969 Marquette University presented the first Père Marquette Discovery Award Medals to the Apollo II astronauts. The medal is given to men whose achievements bear the same distinguishing marks as those of Father Marquette — a questing spirit, a uniqueness in deed and a consuming dedication to the pursuit of new knowledge for the betterment of man.

Marquette's endeavors were followed by La Salle's exploration of the Mississippi to its mouth and the naming of the valley.

81

Tennessee Historical Commission Marker
Commemorating Fort Assumption

Louisiana in honor of the king. La Salle had convinced Louis XIV that the area would be lost to France if it were not occupied. To establish a settlement La Salle sailed directly from France to the Gulf of Mexico but missed the mouth of the Mississippi and landed at Texas.

France made a second attempt to possess the lower Mississippi Valley, this time from the east, when Pierre Lemoyne, sieur d'Iberville, set up a garrison on Dauphin Island at the entrance to Mobile Bay. Later his brother, Jean Baptiste Lemoyne, sieur de Bienville, established a permanent colony on the present site of Mobile, under the name of Fort Louis de la Mobile, and built

a church, Notre Dame de la Mobile (Our Lady of Mobile).

Mobile came under English control in 1763, then under Spanish in 1779 at which time the church's name was changed to Yglesia de la Purísima Concepción (Church of the Immaculate Conception). The street on which the church was located came to be called Conception Street — one of its intersecting streets is Dauphin, recalling Mobile's French and Spanish roots.

The establishment of Mobile convinced the French that only through such settlements could it control the Mississippi. Though the government was too poor to become involved, it encouraged companies to undertake the task. One such company under John Law established New Orleans, a city which more than any other in America still retains its French flavor.

Governor Bienville needed nuns for the King's Hospital and for the education of the colonists' daughters. To supply that need the Jesuits persuaded Ursuline Nuns to come from Rouen, France, in 1727. Under the valiant Mother Mary of St. Augustine Tranchepain the first order of women in America was founded, providing the first boarding school for girls, the first Catholic orphanage, the first day school and the first instruction classes for Indian and Negro girls and women. Still another first was the establishing of the Sodality of the Blessed Virgin. A perfectly preserved colonial record gives the story:

"Act of establishment of the Congregation of the ladies of the city of New Orleans, directed and governed by the Ursuline Religious of this city . . . in honor of the Most Blessed Virgin Mary, with the permission [among others] of Reverend Mother St. Augustin of Tranchepain, first Superior and Foundress of the Ursuline Religious of this city. . . . The ladies are to assemble every Sunday and feast of the Blessed Virgin in an apartment that will give them no access whatever to the cloister. . . ."

The petition to the Holy See for recognition of the sodality was granted on March 4, 1739, by Pope Clement XII. (The sodality has continued without interruption.)

The Ursuline Order was responsible for Mary's acquiring a new and distinctive title — Our Lady of Prompt Succor; its history involved both France and America. In 1803 the New Orleans community was depleted when fifteen nuns of Spanish extraction left, unhappy that the city had passed from Spanish to French rule. Seven nuns remained. One, Mother St. Andrew Madier, wrote to a cousin in France, Mother St. Michel, appealing for her and

Hess Photographing Company

Public Plaque, Pittsburgh, Commemorating Fort Duquesne and Virgin Alley

others to come to New Orleans, Louisiana.

The French Revolution had expelled this cousin and her community from their convent at Pont-Saint-Esprit; Mother St. Michel had gone to Montpellier to open a boarding school for girls. She was eager and willing to go to America, but her spiritual director and her bishop emphasized how vital her presence in France would be. She was told by Bishop Fournier: "The Pope alone can give this authorization . . . the Pope alone!" These words were equivalent to a determined refusal; the Pope was then incommunicado, a virtual prisoner of Napoleon.

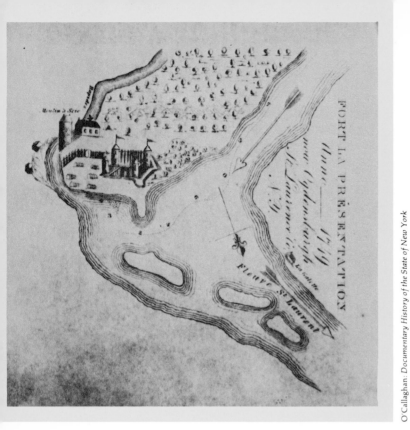

Erected in 1749 on the Oswegatchie and St. Lawrence Rivers in present-day New York, Fort La Présentation was taken over by the British for nearly forty years. In this drawing, the chapel built by Father François Picquet can be seen above the fort.

Undaunted, Mother St. Michel wrote Pope Pius VII on December 15, 1808. With spies everywhere, there was no opportunity for mailing the letter until the following March 19. Meanwhile she had petitioned Mary for "a prompt and favorable reply," promising that if it came she would honor her in New Orleans under the title of Our Lady of Prompt Succor. Miraculously — considering existing conditions — the answer came dated Rome, *April 28*, permission granted.

Fulfilling her promise Mother St. Michel had a statue of Mary carved to accompany her group on the voyage to New Orleans. On their arrival on December 30, 1810, the statue was enshrined in the nuns' choir of the Chapel of Our Lady of Consolation where devotion to Our Lady of Prompt Succor rapidly increased. The im-

84

portance of this devotion in our country's need is told in the story of the Battle of New Orleans in the section entitled "Virgin Militant."

The Ursuline convent, built in 1727, was replaced by a new and imposing structure in 1753. This historic building over the centuries has served as an archbishopric, offices of the diocese, an academy for boys, a meeting place for the Louisiana State Legislature and now is the rectory of St. Mary's Church. As one of the few remaining links with the French capital of Louisiana the convent has been restored, considered an important historic and religious monument in the United States. It is included both in the Historic American Buildings Survey and the register of National Historic Landmarks.

French forts named for Mary were links in the great chain of defense planned by La Salle and Governor Frontenac. The French had a doctrine that the discovery of a river gave them the right to the land drained by its tributaries, and thus claimed the land within the wide arc reaching from the Mississippi to the St. Lawrence. At strategic places along that arc they erected forts to protect their interests.

One such fort grew out of a campaign against the Chickasaw Indians on the bluffs of Wolf River at Memphis, Tennessee. Here in 1739 Jean Baptiste Lemoyne, sieur de Bienville, assembled an army of twelve hundred white soldiers and some Indians, the greatest army that had ever been seen in the interior of America at that time. Since construction of the fort began on August 15 it was named Assumption in honor of the feast day. The French abandoned and destroyed it in 1740 when they made peace with the Chickasaws and Bienville disbanded the Choctaws and his other Indian allies. Though the remains have been obliterated by modern urban construction, a state historical marker indicates the site.

The French had forts along the Ohio to protect their holdings against the Ohio Company made up of Virginia land speculators holding claims from which they expected great profits. Governor Robert Dinwiddie of Virginia sent Washington to look the land over and to tell the French to cease building forts. Washington noted in his journal that a most desirable fort site existed at the triangle of land where the Allegheny and Monongahela Rivers met to form the Ohio. Before the Virginia militia could act on his recommendation, the French built their fort there and named it "Fort Duquesne under the title of the Assumption of the Blessed Virgin." An adjacent burial ground they called L'Assomption de la Ste. Vierge à la belle Rivière. This was the first cemetery in Pittsburgh and the road leading to it was called L'Alleé de la Vierge (Virgin Alley), the first street to be named in all western Pennsylvania.

South of the fort in July 1755 the French defeated the English under General Edward Braddock in the Battle of the Monongahela. Washington escaped injury, but Braddock and the French captain Daniel Hyacinth deBeaujeau were killed. The latter was buried in Mary's cemetery where in succeeding years American soldiers and civilian Pittsburghers were interred, among them Thomas Hutchins, noted geographer, Commodore Joshua Barney, Colonel William Clapham and many Revolutionary veterans important in local history.

Threatened by overwhelming British forces the French destroyed their fort and withdrew from the area. The British built a new fort directly behind Fort Duquesne, naming it Fort Pitt in honor of William Pitt, first earl of Chatham; from this fort the city of Pittsburgh took its name. Today the area's history is preserved in Point State Park and the Fort Pitt Museum. The cemetery and Virgin Alley are gone but the history of the forts is perpetuated by Fort Duquesne Bridge over the Allegheny and Fort Pitt Bridge over the Monongahela. Roadways connecting the two go over the park in modern Pittsburgh's "Golden Triangle." The area is a national historic landmark.

In 1745 a French expedition set out from Quebec to wipe out the English at Fort Edward north of Albany and came to a har-

This is the original cornerstone of Fort La Présentation. Placed by the New York State Education Department in City Hall, Ogdensburg, the stone's Latin inscription reads: "François Picquet laid the foundation of this habitation in the name of Almighty God, 1749."

This seventeenth-century replica of Notre Dame Sous Terre (Our Lady Under Ground) in the Cathedral of Notre Dame at Chartres, France, was the model from which the Abenaki copy presumably was made.

bor on the St. Lawrence at the outlet of the Oswegatchie River. The date was November 21 — feast of the Presentation. The expedition's chaplain, Father François Picquet, observed the harbor's advantages for a mission and trading post. Four years later he erected there Fort La Présentation. A Mohawk war party soon afterward destroyed the fort but Father Picquet began rebuilding immediately. From this fort many Christianized Iroquois were sent south to assist in Braddock's defeat in Pennsylvania.

The priest's courage and stubborn resistance to the English provoked their commander, Sir William Johnson, to call on his Indian allies to "extinguish the fire at Oswegatchie." Father Picquet and his Indians, however, voluntarily abandoned Fort La Présentation and made a new home on a nearby island. He took with him the fort's cornerstone which today may be seen at Ogdensburg, New York.

The British occupied Fort La Présentation from 1760 to 1796 when they evacuated it under the provisions of the Jay Treaty. The town that had grown up about the fort was first called Oswegatchie but later named Ogdensburg for Colonel Samuel Ogden who purchased the land and developed it. The city is today an important transshipping center with far-reaching rail and water connections with the Great Lakes. On the site of Fort La Présentation stands Notre Dame Church, one of the largest in the Diocese of Ogdensburg.

Wampum Belt Sent by Abenaki Indians to Cathedral of Chartres in 1695
This photograph was sent by the bishop of Chartres in 1962 to the Mission of St. Francis de Sales.

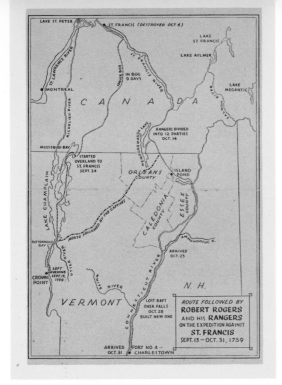

Map Showing Route Taken by Rogers' Rangers to Destroy St. Francis Mission

Shown commemorating the birth of Christ are Abenaki Indians. The site is the Church of St. Francis Odanak, Yamaska, in the Province of Quebec.

Before France yielded her dream of possessing North America she would write one more chapter in the story of Marian devotion. It would involve intrigue, death and hidden treasure, ingredients to captivate the historian and excite the adventurer. More, it would touch the very heart of French history and include the oldest Marian shrine in the world.

In Roman times Chartres was the seat of the Gallic tribe of Canutes and the chief center of Druidic worship. In a grotto on a hill was an altar to "the virgin who should conceive," to whom the local king and his people dedicated themselves. Thus when SS. Polentianus and Savinianus brought the Gospel to Chartres they found, as it were, a shrine to Mary already installed and a people prepared to accept their message. The grotto became the crypt of a church built by Catholics and contained a shrine erected to Notre Dame Sous Terre (Our Lady Under Ground).

Fire in 1020 destroyed the church but left the crypt intact. This was roofed in stone to become the crypt of a basilica,

which later was also destroyed by fire. Then once more the crypt became the starting point for a church, this time the present Cathedral of Notre Dame.

This Abenaki memorial, recalling Rogers' raid, can be seen at Odanak, Yamaska, Quebec Province.

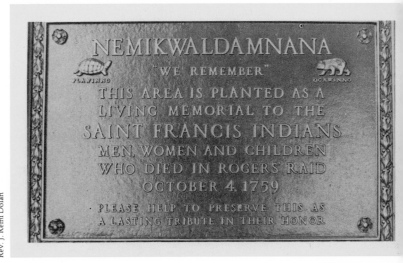

NEMIKWALDAMNANA
"WE REMEMBER"
PLAWISINO   OGAWISNO
THIS AREA IS PLANTED AS A
LIVING MEMORIAL TO THE
SAINT FRANCIS INDIANS
MEN, WOMEN AND CHILDREN
WHO DIED IN ROGERS RAID
OCTOBER 4, 1759
· PLEASE HELP TO PRESERVE THIS AS
A LASTING TRIBUTE IN THEIR HONOR

In the late seventeenth century a replica of the original Notre Dame then being venerated was thus described:

"The Virgin is seated on a chair, holding her Son sitting on her knees, who blesses with His right hand, and in His other holds an orb. His head is bare and His hair quite short. His robe is close-fitting and girdled with a belt; His face, hands and feet, which are bare, are of shining grey-ebony colour. The Virgin is clad in an antique mantle, shaped like a chasuble. Her face is oval, of perfect design and of the same shining black colour. Her crown is plain and only the top is adorned with flowers like small leaves. The chair is one foot in width with four posts, hollowed out at the back and carved. The statue is 29 inches in height."

Now the story's locale shifts to Canada to the Mission of St. Francis de Sales on the east side of the St. Lawrence where Abenaki from Maine had been coming for many years to settle. In 1699 the Jesuit superior, Vincent Bigot, sent to the Cathedral of Chartres a belt of wampum made by the tribe in honor of Mary. Its white letters on a violet background read: "To the Virgin Mother from her most devoted Abenaki." In appreciation cathedral officials sent the Indians a twenty-pound copy of their Madonna Sous Terre which became the Abenaki's most treasured possession, taken from its shrine only on special occasions.

Meanwhile bands of Abenaki had been raiding New England settlements over the years and in retaliation the English and their Indian allies attacked the tribe's Mission of the Assumption at Norridgewock, Maine, burned their church and killed the Jesuit superior, Sebastian Rale. To avenge his death the Abenaki increased their raids into New England, to the point of enraging General Jeffrey Amherst who commissioned Robert Rogers and his Rangers to go to Canada and wipe out the Mission of St. Francis.

Starting out on September 13, 1759,

Rogers and his band of over two hundred men left Crown Point, New York, entered Canada by way of Lake Champlain, and traveling overland came upon the mission in the early morning of October 6. The young braves were away on a hunting trip and the older men and women and children could offer little resistance. All were killed and their houses burned. The convent and valuable manuscripts in the Abenaki language, the output of forty-six years' work, were destroyed. The church was leveled after being stripped of its precious silver statue of Notre Dame Sous Terre, as well as silver-plated copper candlesticks and church ornaments and utensils.

Weighted down by their plunder the Rangers began their return trip, a trip which Rogers later reported to Amherst "was attended by difficulties and distresses." Scores were killed by pursuing Abenaki, others died from starvation and exposure, and those who survived were too exhausted to carry the stolen treasures and buried them along the route, hoping to recover them later, which they never did. Years later a censer was uncovered on an island in the Watopeka River, the statue of a saint near the Magog River, the candlesticks near Lake Memphremagog, but no trace has ever been found of the silver statue of Mary which is supposed to have been buried near Littleton, New Hampshire. Many stories have been written of this "Lost Virgin," even a novel by that name, and many searches made, but the statue has never been recovered.

Today on the site of the destroyed mission is the Church of St. Francis. Devotion to Mary has never lessened through the centuries and was revitalized in 1947 when the pastor visited Portugal and on his return inflamed the parishioners with the account of the apparitions at Fatima. Since that time each evening the Abenaki gather in their church to recite three rosaries in honor of Our Lady of Fatima.

Mother
of
Good Counsel

THE ENGLISH, IRISH AND GERMANS
ON THE ATLANTIC SEABOARD

1634-1790

Coat of Arms of John Carroll,
First Catholic Bishop of the United States

The scroll below the figure of Mary gives the bishop's motto: "Ne Dere-
linquas Nos Domine Deus Noster" (Don't Ever Leave Us, O Lord, Our
God). Thirteen stars for the original colonies encircle Mary and Jesus.

Mother
of
Good Counsel

In his book *The Catholic Church in Colonial Days* John Gilmary Shea credited the Church's progress to a devoted priesthood, a self-sacrificing laity and generous adherence to the faith "amid active persecution, insidious attacks, open violence and constant prejudice, where Catholics were few amid a population trained in unreasoning animosity."

If Maryland Catholics hoped for a continuation of the religious liberty first realized in St. Marys City, that hope was short-lived. Intoleration compelled their removal into surrounding colonies, only to encounter increased prejudice and persecution; even a Catholic name was a rarity. Under such conditions it was natural that the name of Mary would be anathema.

All the more remarkable then is the record of the early churches erected in her honor by the scattered faithful who were being served by heroic English, German and Irish priests. These men kept the faith alive at the risk of their lives and the exhaustion of their energies. Priest and layman alike, strangers in a new land, fearful yet ever hopeful, they clung with childlike trust to their spiritual mother, depending on Mary's counsel for comfort and guidance.

Some respite from prejudice came with William Penn's "holy experiment." Tolerant Quakers defied crowds and Crown to guarantee freedom of conscience to Catholics and their Jesuit pastors. In Philadelphia, St. Mary's Church became the principal and prestigious Catholic church of the city. Jesuits worked westward to establish centers of activity; Marian churches were erected in Lancaster, Conewago and Paradise, the latter name especially appropriate for the Immaculate Heart of Mary Church, first in the nation to be erected under this title. Today on an exterior wall of its rectory one can view a chiseled stone with the initials *C W*, a shears and the date 1761. The stone is from the former home of Caspar Wise, a German tailor. Catholics coming into the area were told that "at the tailor's house Mass will be said."

In the extreme northern tip of Delaware a wealthy Irishman, Cornelius Hollahan, owned property purchased from Penn's daughter, Letitia, and in his home was offered the first Mass in the state. Eventually a log chapel was built at Coffee Run — St. Mary of the Assumption, the first Catholic church in Delaware. From it were served five missions spread through three counties and two states. Numbered among its parishioners were the Du Pont family, their workers, and Irish laborers building the Chesapeake and Delaware Canal.

The entire State of New Jersey was served by one German Jesuit, Ferdinand Farmer, who went about his ministry wearing civilian dress for protection against a civil ruling which stated that "priests are incendiary and disturbers of the public peace and safety, enemies of the true Christian religion, and adjudged to suffer perpetual imprisonment." Undeterred, this remarkable man continued his visitations to scattered Catholics over a one-hundred-mile area, sustaining their faith and encouraging devotion to Mary. When ironworkers in south Jersey built a church they named it St. Mary of the Assumption. At Macopin, in northern New Jersey, Father Farmer told the faithful he would die within the year and pleaded that they meet regularly and say the rosary together, promising them that "the Blessed Virgin will then protect you against apostasy." The group was priestless for twenty-five years, their faith sustained by following Father Farmer's directive.

Catholics in Virginia fared better, having won equality of rights as citizens. When the first permanent church in the state — St. Mary's, Alexandria — was in process of construction, General George Washington expressed his friendliness toward the Catholics by making a donation of money. The Revolution had found Catholics generously responding to the national conflict and by their efforts winning the respect and admiration of all. Anti-Catholic bias was thus diluted at a time crucial to the Church's future when broad foundations were imperative.

It was obvious that the Church in America needed a regularly constituted ecclesiastical organization. After consultation and deliberation Pope Pius VI constituted all of the United States as the Diocese of Baltimore in direct dependence upon the Holy See. The American clergy unanimously elected John Carroll as their bishop and his consecration in England took place on the feast of the Assumption, 1790. To Mary's care he entrusted the great work which lay ahead, confident "that by her intercession the faith, piety and good morals of his flock might flourish and increase."

Founding of Maryland

This is a painting by Emanuel Leutze, famed for "Washington Crossing the Delaware." Mary's banner is by the cross as Father White offers Mass on March 25, 1634. Colonists and Indians exchange gifts. In the harbor the English ships Ark and Dove ride at anchor.

The penal laws in the final years of the reign of Elizabeth I inflicted a meanness of life on Catholics and impelled them to seek a haven abroad. Several furtive attempts failed but George Calvert, first baron of Baltimore (a convert), succeeded in securing a charter for a colony in Maryland. Between two hundred and three hundred persons, with two Jesuits and two lay brothers, sailed from England in late 1633 and landed on an island in Chesapeake Bay which they called St. Clement's. Here the first Mass was offered by Father Andrew White on the feast of the Annunciation, March 25, 1634. Later their capital, St.

Marys City, would be located on St. Marys River.

The Jesuits served both whites and the Indians: Potomac, Patuxent, Anacosts and Piscataway. An Indian king and queen and more than one hundred of their subjects were received into the Church by Father White. He had composed a grammar, dictionary and catechism in the native idiom — the first Englishman to reduce an Indian language to grammatical form, an accomplishment preceding that of John Eliot's among the Massachusetts Algonquins. From the Jesuit headquarters at St. Marys came an unbroken succession of

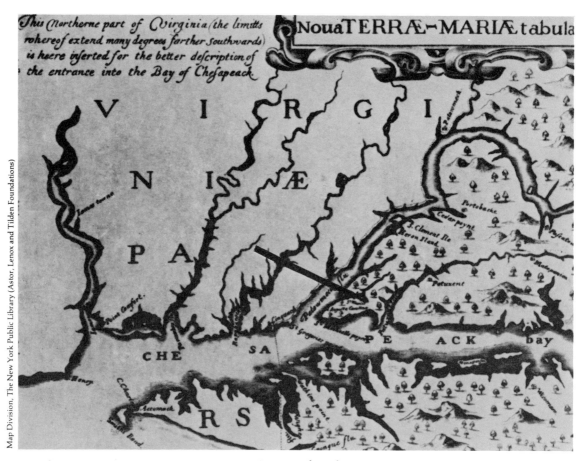

Map of Maryland, 1635

This view is from a point due east. Arrow indicates St. Maries on the St. Marys River.

priests from whose number the first bishop of the United States ultimately was chosen.

St. Marys was Maryland's first capital, Governor Charles Calvert living there in the mid-1600s, his home serving as the meeting place for the earliest sessions of the Maryland General Assembly. With removal of the capital to Annapolis, St. Marys gradually fell into decay. Today the past is being re-created. St. Marys Historic District designation is attracting archaeologists who have already uncovered the foundation of Calvert's manor house. The area is listed in the Historic American

Buildings Survey and the register of National Historic Landmarks. Foundations of approximately sixty buildings are being considered for study, funded under grants from federal and private sources.

A prominent marker calls attention to the role Maryland played as the first colony in America to guarantee religious liberty. At its unveiling in 1960 the late Father John LaFarge, S.J., told the more than one thousand persons present that "seasoned, reasoned dialogue" was needed today on religious issues and on their bearing on contemporary problems. The noted Jesuit was a leader in interracial work, a founder

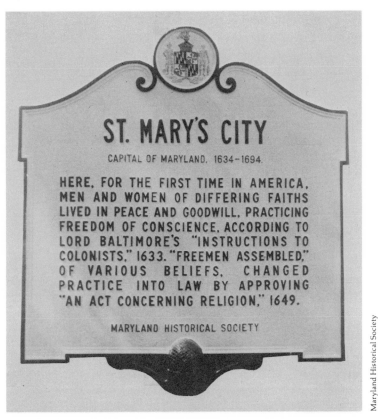

Marker Honoring St. Marys City, First Colony in America Guaranteeing Religious Liberty

and director of the Catholic Interracial Council of New York City and of the National Catholic Rural Life Conference.

The Chesapeake area continued to attract Catholic settlers before 1669, many settling in what is now Dorchester County. On occasions when weather permitted they crossed the bay by boat to attend one of the Jesuit stations at St. Marys or St. Inigoes (Assumption). On these occasions they would bring with them any valuable household goods, *as well as cattle*, to safeguard against destruction by Indians if left behind.

About 1685 a chapel was established at Wye-Town in Talbot County, and in 1704 St. Francis Xavier Mission ("Old Bohemia") was founded at Warwick in Cecil County, ninety miles north of Golden Hill. From these missions Jesuits went south at least twice a year, apart from emergency visits.

In 1769 Richard Tubman gave a piece of property for the building of a chapel for the more than one hundred Catholics in the immediate vicinity of what was then called Golden Hill, now Meekin's Neck. Just when their church was erected is not known, but it was probably before 1790. It was used until 1873 when it was sold to the county as a school building and a new and larger St. Mary Star of the Sea built directly across the road. The building has been deeded back to the Church and is being restored. Descendants of the original settlers still live within a radius of a very few miles.

Under William Penn's "holy experiment" — with its broad grant of freedom of worship and civil rights to all who believed in God — the door was opened to Catholics coming up from Maryland. The tolerant Quakers guaranteed freedom of conscience to Catholics, both lay and clergy. Only eleven persons were in the congregation when Mass was first celebrated on February 22, 1732, in the eighteen by twenty-eight-foot chapel, the beginning of St. Joseph's Church.

"Mission No. 1" of Old St. Joseph's was St. Mary's built in 1763 by Father Robert Harding, an English Jesuit who had served in Maryland from 1732-1749. St. Mary's

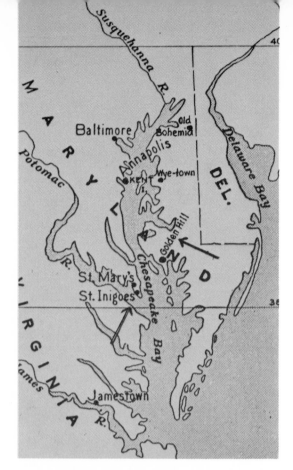

Right arrow points to St. Mary's Church, Golden Hill, while left arrow indicates St. Mary's Church at St. Marys City and Assumption Mission at St. Inigoes.

This simple weathered building, dedicated to St. Mary Star of the Sea, Golden Hill, Maryland, was probably erected before 1790 and used until 1873. It is now being restored.

Okoniewski Studios

would become the principal and prestigious Catholic church of the Philadelphia community, eventually the first cathedral. Of particular interest in its long history is an event reported in *The Pennsylvania Journal and Weekly Advertiser*, Wednesday, July 7, 1779:

"On Sunday last, being the aniversary [*sic*] of the Independence of America . . . at noon the President and Members of Congress, with the President and Chief Magistrates of this State, and a number of other Gentlemen and Ladies went, by invitation from the Honourable the Minister of France, to the Catholic chappel [*sic*], where this great event was celebrated by a well

The Catholic CHURCH OF ST. MARY, Philadelphia.

Old St. Mary's, Philadelphia

This rare lithograph (circa 1830) shows St. Mary's Church as viewed from the Fourth Street side. The fence has been removed and now the entrance is from the Fifth Street side where the first parishioners entered through the graveyard.

adapted discourse, pronounced by the Minister's Chaplain, and TE DEUM solemnly sung by a number of very good voices, accompanied by the organ and other kinds of music."

The French minister was Conrad Alexandre Gérard, first to be named to that office, and his chaplain was Father Seraphin Bandol. The latter's "discourse" was later printed by order of Congress. St. Mary's was the scene of a similar service on November 26, 1781, commemorating the anniversary of the victory at Yorktown.

Among St. Mary's distinguished parishioners were Commodore John Barry, "father of the United States Navy," Mathew Carey, publisher of books and magazines, General Stephen Moylan, cavalry chief under General Washington, and Thomas Fitzsimmons who participated in the Constitutional Convention of 1787.

Jesuits working out of Philadelphia established centers of activity westward — Conewago, Lancaster, Goshenhoppen — ministering to German families and their descendants who formed one of the most flourishing groups of Catholics in colonial America. At Conewago they built the Chapel of St. Mary of the Assumption, also called the Blue Spring Chapel after a spring of water issuing from the limestone rocks beneath it.

99

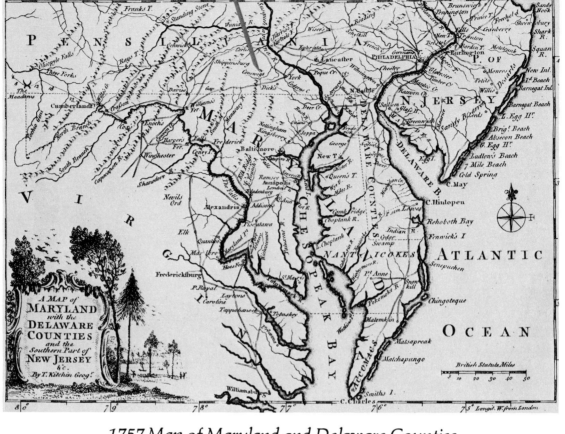

1757 Map of Maryland and Delaware Counties

Arrow points to Conewago, Pennsylvania, where St. Mary of the Assumption Chapel was erected. Dotted line marks the area under dispute in the Mason-Dixon Line controversy.

This chapel is mentioned in a faded record which locates it in Heidelsheim township, *Maryland*. This is not a geographical error! Conewago during the seventeenth and eighteenth centuries lay in the area claimed by both Pennsylvania and Maryland. The latter's charter had stated that its northern boundary was "that Part of the Bay of Delaware on the North, which lieth under the Fortieth Degree of North Latitude where New England is terminated." Penn's party reminded the Calverts of the border being *under* the fortieth parallel, but how far under became the point at issue. If Maryland were to win the

argument then she could claim Philadelphia!

The two states argued for over eighty years and the dispute was finally settled when two English astronomer-surveyors — Charles Mason and Jeremiah Dixon — established the historic Mason-Dixon Line in 1767. Catholics had a special interest in that decision, for in Pennsylvania they were under no penal legislation such as enacted against them in Maryland.

The intrepid Father William Wappeler had been losing no time in establishing churches. A year following the erection of the log chapel at Conewago he was busy in

This excerpt from a faded record in the Jesuit Archives, Maryland Province, details the naming of "the Church of the Assumption" at Conewago where Father Wappeler constructed a combination log dwelling and chapel.

This painting of the Assumption on the ceiling of the historic Conewago Basilica of the Sacred Heart memorializes Mary's log chapel which preceded the present church.

Lancaster building another log chapel, this one the "mission of St. John Nepomucene."

The log chapel was destroyed by incendiaries but replaced in 1762. It was built in keeping with the custom of many centuries that during the Holy Sacrifice of the Mass the priest and congregation faced towards the East, the place and origin of Christianity, and the scene of Christ's birth, death and resurrection. A steeple and belfry were added about 1800. The church was of solid construction and built by parishioners alone. The men gathered stones from nearby farms and the women mixed the mortar. It was so well constructed that it withstood the elements for one hundred nineteen years. In its last years it served as a schoolhouse, when the third structure — Assumption of the Blessed Virgin Mary — was built in 1854.

With the increase of German Catholic settlers in Pennsylvania, Mass would often be said at various unpublicized points along the missionary trail. These were known as "chapel" or "Mass" houses. One belonged to a German tailor, Caspar Wise, who lived in Paradise. To guide Catholics looking for "the tailor's house where Mass will be said," he placed on the front of his home a chiseled stone showing his initials and a scissors, the symbol of his trade, and the date 1761. The stone today holds an honored place in an exterior wall of the rectory of the Immaculate Heart of Mary Church at Paradise. This church, built in 1845, was the first in the country dedicated to Mary under this title. It contains two unusual features — the pulpit which the priest ascends by a hidden stair, and the choir areas above the sanctuary.

In seeking fresh lands Catholics began coming into Delaware from Maryland and were soon being ministered to by English and German Jesuits out of Pennsylvania and northern Maryland missions. In the extreme northern tip of Delaware, Mass

Old St. Mary's Church, Lancaster, Pennsylvania, Erected in 1762

was first offered at the home of a wealthy Irish landowner named Cornelius Hollahan, on property purchased from Penn's daughter, Letitia.

Here in 1772 a German Jesuit, Father Matthew Sittensperger (commonly called Father Manners), purchased a two-hundred-acre farm in Mill Creek Hundred, west of Wilmington, along a stream called Coffee Run. After the Jesuit custom, the land was held in the name of the superior, Father John Lewis. When the Society of Jesus was suspended the following year,

This plaque can be seen in the Church of the Assumption of the Blessed Virgin Mary, Lancaster, Pennsylvania. It commemorates the log chapel built by Father Wappeler in 1742.

102

First Church in America Under the Title of
Immaculate Heart of Mary (Paradise, Pennsylvania)

"Mass House" Marker, Paradise, Pennsylvania

the American Jesuits thereupon became secular clergymen and the Coffee Run land was not developed. Father Lewis upon his death willed the property to another Jesuit, Robert Molyneux, and he in turn devised it to Father Francis Neale of Georgetown.

The history of Coffee Run now jumps to 1790 when an Augustinian, John Rosseter, built a log chapel there which he named St. Mary of the Assumption. It was the first Catholic church in the entire State of Delaware. In 1805, following arrangements with Bishop Carroll and the Jesuits, the property came under the charge of the seculars. St. Mary's history is thus a record of two eras in the annals of Catholicism in

103

SAINT MARY'S CHURCH
SITE OF FIRST CATHOLIC CHURCH IN DELAWARE, USUALLY CALLED "COFFEE RUN" CHURCH. LAND PURCHASED 1772 BY REV MATTHIAS MANNERS. FIRST CHURCH ERECTED SHORTLY THEREAFTER. LAST CHURCH ERECTED BY REV. PATRICK KENNY, REMAINED STANDING UNTIL 1908. SERVICE DISCONTINUED IN 1884 UPON ERECTION O CHURCHES AT HOCKESSIN AND ASHLAND

HISTORIC MARKERS COMMISSION 1933

State Marker on the Site of Delaware's First Catholc Church, St. Mary's

this country — the colonial, with its English and German Jesuit mission-farms, and the national with its parish churches.

Assigned to St. Mary's in 1805 was Father Patrick Kenny who served there until his death. Besides St. Mary's he cared for five missions spread through three counties and two states. His parishioners included members of the Du Pont family, their workers, and Irish laborers building the Chesapeake and Delaware Canal. His diary leaves an unforgettable picture of the physical obstacles he and his faithful four-wheeled wagon, "Dearborn," overcame in serving God and man:

"November 9th — Started about 10 A.M. for Hagley Brandywine [where Du Pont powdermen lived]. Arrived over rocks, through woods, amidst stumps, down precipices, up perpendicular (almost) steeps and bumping of loose stones against my wheels at every step, across Squirrel Run until I got out at Edward Doherty's house. Administered him. From thence through abominable rocky, loose stoney roads through Hagley tanyard, down Brandywine Creek to Hugh Bogan's mother. Administered her. From thence to Peter Quigley's on a bank as high as the third story of the big cotton factory, gave private baptism to his infant child. From

104

Artist's Conception of Original Log Cabin Church of St. Mary of the Assumption, Coffee Run, Delaware

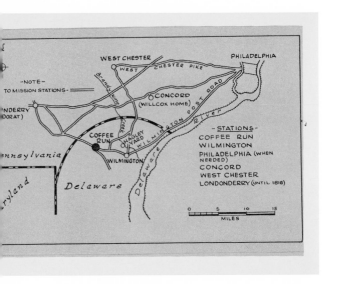

Map Showing Coffee Run (St. Mary's) and Father Kenny's Mission Area

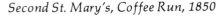

Second St. Mary's, Coffee Run, 1850

Archives of the Catholic Historical Society

thence to Wilmington where I sent my horse and Dearborn to Mrs. McGee's."

The log chapel of 1790 was replaced in 1850 by a church which served until 1884 when churches at Hockessin and Ashland were erected. When the church was razed in 1908 its cross was preserved, to be placed eventually on a field chapel which the Knights of Columbus erected on the site. Each year on the Fourth of July the Fourth Degree Knights of Columbus sponsor a Memorial Mass here for Father Kenny and the honored dead of two centuries. Fifty carved headstones and twelve uncut stone markers are in the Coffee Run Cemetery, now designated as a national historic landmark.

The entire State of New Jersey was served by a German Jesuit, Ferdinand Farmer; he worked out from St. Joseph's Church in Philadelphia, traveling in all kinds of weather, on foot or horseback, against nature's obstacles of rivers, hills and mountains. Added to the hardships of colonial travel was the knowledge that civil authorities had declared priests to be "incendiary and disturbers of the public peace and safety, enemies of the true Christian religion, and adjudged to suffer perpetual imprisonment." Small wonder that Father Farmer wore civilian dress for protection.

Two of his widely separated stops were Batsto in the southern swamps and Macopin in the northern mountains. As the crow flies these places are one hundred miles apart. Batsto had become a settlement in 1760 when three German brothers named Woos found bog iron there and encouraged ironworkers from Germany to join them. The brothers had built a spacious log home which came to be called Shane's Castle (Shane being a corruption of the German *schöen*, "beautiful"). Father Farmer through the years said Mass in secret at Shane's Castle and imparted to all his great love of Mary. Many years later that love was reflected in the naming of the area's first church St. Mary of the Assumption.

The church was built by parishioners themselves on land donated by an Episcopalian mine owner, Jesse Richards, whose own daughter cared for the altar. Services

Father Ferdinand Farmer, Missionary Extraordinary

This is St. Mary of the Assumption, Batsto area, New Jersey. It was also called St. Mary of the Pines, for the forest of Jersey scrub pines where it was located.

Flynn: *The Catholic Church in New Jersey*

Reciting the Rosary at Dominic Marion's Home, Macopin, New Jersey

were held for thirty years until failing fortunes in the ironworks and nearby industries reduced attendance. The unused church was destroyed in a forest fire in 1899. Only the cemetery remains, one of its corner posts bearing the date of the church's erection, 1827.

The State of New Jersey has named Batsto a historical area since its mines once provided munitions for the American forces in the Revolution and the War of 1812. Here also was made the steam cylinder for John Fitch's steamboat *Perseverance.*

The northern limit of Father Farmer's ministry was Macopin in the Ramapo Mountains, an ancient Indian landmark. On clear days the settlers could see the shores of Manhattan thirty miles away. In 1754 a large number of German families settled here to work in the iron ore mines

of Ringwood, Long Pond and Charlotteburg, supplying cannonballs, stoves and other equipment for the Continental Army. Here was forged a portion of the chain stretched across the Hudson River at Bear Mountain and at West Point, New York, to prevent the English fleet from ascending the river.

Among the settlers were three Catholic families from the Black Forest region of Germany: the Marions, Sehulsters and Strubles. Deeply religious, they hungered for a priest to attend them but only one could come, the fearless Father Farmer. He visited Macopin beginning in 1765 and regularly in the twenty years after. On the last visit before his death in 1786 he told the eldest Sehulster: "God will call me from this life within the year, and you will meet regularly and say the rosary together. The Blessed Virgin will then protect you against apostasy." After his death few priests came to Macopin, the last in 1793.

For the next twenty-five years the Catholics were without a priest. During all that time they gathered in the house of Domi-

Memorial to Macopin Catholics, St. Joseph's Church, Echo Lake, New Jersey

1765 1935

THIS TABLET IS DEDICATED
TO THE MEMORY OF
THE CATHOLIC PIONEERS
WHO CAME TO
MACOPIN (ECHO LAKE) IN 1765.
HERE STOOD THE
CRADLE OF THE CATHOLIC CHURCH
IN THE
DIOCESE OF NEWARK.
AND IN ALL
NORTHERN NEW JERSEY.

*St. Mary's Church, Alexandria, First
Permanent Catholic Church in Virginia*

This 1858 print is taken from Ballou's Pictorial Drawing-Room Companion, *a popular
middle-nineteenth-century illustrated magazine. The church today is little changed.*

nic Marion to say the rosary. Mrs. Sehul-ster was a regular missionary to the group; she distributed holy water and taught the children their catechism. Finally in 1829 a priest was appointed and a church built.

Today there are hundreds of descendants of these German families living in the parish whose history is a testimonial to the efficacy of the rosary.

Though Virginia in the eighteenth century was no less bigoted than Maryland, Catholics had at least won a clear equality of rights as citizens. Their number, however, was small; only two hundred could be counted in the entire state by 1785, these assisting at Mass in a log building and later at the home of Colonel John Fitzgerald, aide de camp to General Washington and at one time mayor of Alexandria.

At a St. Patrick's Day banquet in 1788, the erection of a Catholic church was being discussed and given an unexpected assist from two Protestant gentlemen — General Washington offered a donation of money

Memorial Tablet, St. Mary's Church, Alexandria, Virginia

Department of Highways, Commonwealth of Virginia

and Colonel Robert T. Hooe a piece of land at South Washington and Church Streets. St. Mary's Church became a reality in 1795 under the Very Rev. Francis Ignatius Neale, S.J., of Georgetown College.

A second church, in Chapel Alley, was acquired from the Methodists fifteen years later, with the sanctuary and major portion of the present church erected by Father Joseph W. Fairclough.

Washington was a communicant of Christ Church (Anglican) in Alexandria and personally free from religious prejudice; his friendliness toward Catholicism became a matter of record. When his troops had been encamped at Cambridge, Massachusetts, he discovered their intent to burn the Pope in effigy in the annual Guy Fawkes Day celebration. This he forbade, remarking: "To be insulting their Religion, is so monstrous, as not to be suffered or excused."

During the Revolution the Continental Congress sought Canada's support and

109

sent a commission to negotiate. The commission consisted of Benjamin Franklin, Samuel Chase and Charles Carroll, the latter an outstanding Catholic colonist. Carroll was persuaded to invite his cousin, Father John Carroll, to accompany the delegation. The commission failed of its purpose, but Father Carroll was drawn out of obscurity to become a patriot in the minds and hearts of many colonists, particularly Benjamin Franklin, with whom he developed a warm friendship which would ultimately be of great service to the Catholic Church.

Once the Revolution ended and the peace treaty with Great Britain signed, it was obvious that Catholics could no longer be governed by Bishop James Talbot of London. The Sacred Congregation for the Propagation of the Faith (Propaganda for short) then considered organizing the American Church under the rule of a French ecclesiastic, at least temporarily. To this proposal the American clergy demurred. Father Carroll headed a commission of priests meeting at Whitemarsh, Maryland, in an area known as Carroll's Burgh, a clerical estate where clergy from the thirteen original colonies convened on a regular basis.

The commission petitioned the Holy See for a regularly constituted ecclesiastical organization, stating it would not be prudent to have a bishop in the United States under existing conditions, for such an appointment would be resented by the citizens as an undue interference in their affairs and an unwarranted show of power by foreigners.

The Sacred Congregation of Propaganda then ordered the apostolic nuncio at Versailles to review conditions of the Church in America and decide the kind of organization to be set up. Accustomed to dealing with the governments of other countries in ecclesiastical appointments, the nuncio approached Benjamin Franklin,

Mercury Studios

In this stained-glass window George Washington and Father John Carroll are depicted conferring in negotiating for Canada's cooperation in the American Revolution.

our minister to France. After consideration, Propaganda decided to appoint a prefect apostolic and when Father Carroll's name was mentioned as a candidate Franklin expressed his great pleasure and approval. With the naming of Father Carroll as prefect apostolic the Catholic Church was officially established in the United States on June 9, 1784.

The office of prefect apostolic did not carry sufficient authority for the adequate settlement of such problems as lay trusteeism and factious priests, and the American clergy then in 1788 petitioned Pope Pius VI for a bishop with the powers of an ordinary, and not merely those of a titular bishop or vicar apostolic. In their petition they asked permission to elect a bishop themselves, "at least for the first time." With permission granted, the clergy convened at Whitemarsh in May of 1789 and unanimously elected John Carroll as their bishop and requested Baltimore as the episcopal city. Pius VI then constituted all of the United States as the diocese of Baltimore in direct dependence upon the Holy See. The immediate improvement and growth of the Catholic Church that followed attested to the wisdom of John Carroll's leadership.

Scattered Catholics living in Rhode Island had suffered little persecution, for religious toleration was at least inscribed on the statute books. Those living in Providence received unexpected publicity in 1789 when Father Claude Florent Bouchard de la Poterie, former chaplain to the French general Jean Baptiste Rochambeau, celebrated Mass on the feast of the Immaculate Conception and the event was given front-page coverage in *The Providence Gazette and Country Journal*, even copied by the Rev. Ezra Stiles in his literary diary. (Stiles, president of Yale College, in forty-five volumes of his diary provided an interesting record of colonial life.)

There is an interesting bit of Church history connected with Father Poterie. He had settled in Boston at the close of the Revolution, sharing the opinion of some of the secular clergy coming from abroad in imagining that independence included in-

This is the Marian shrine at Whitemarsh (Sacred Heart Church, Bowie, Maryland). This area was once known as Carroll's Burgh, a clerical estate, where clergy from the thirteen original colonies regularly convened.

(Vol. XXVI.)   S A T U R D A Y, December 12, 1789.   (No. 1354.)

News Item on Immaculate Conception

On December 12, 1789, the front page of The Providence Gazette and Country Journal *reported:* "Tuesday last, being the Festival of the Immaculate Conception of the blessed Virgin Mary, the Reverend Abbe de la Poterie, French Roman Catholic secular Priest, and Doctor of Divinity, celebrated the holy sacrifice of the Mass in this Town, at the Request of several Catholics of the Roman Communion; and addressed to the Almighty his humble Prayers for the constant and permanent prosperity of the State of Rhode-Island."

dependence of all ecclesiastical control. He issued a "pastoral letter" giving him "very ample powers," purportedly with the consent of John Carroll, then the prefect apostolic. After a thorough investigation Father Carroll suspended him. (This did not obscure the significance of the celebration of Mass described.)

The publicity of the celebration of this Mass, on a Marian feast day no less, indicated a softening in the attitude towards Catholics in the colonies, due in part to the indebtedness felt owing to Catholic France's assistance in the Revolution and to the colonists' knowledge that Catholics too had fought side by side with their Protestant brothers in securing the precious freedom enjoyed by all.

Some French naval chaplains remained in the country and became part of the permanent clergy. Marriages between prominent Frenchmen and American women deepened the Catholic faith in providing roots for new congregations being formed in the growing nation.

With the exception of three states — Maryland, Pennsylvania and New York — there is little mention of the name of Mary in the history of the colonies. This is not surprising in view of the ingrained prejudice which the English had brought from their homeland. Only in the almanacs is Mary referred to, and this not until 1760.

Almanacs, next to the Bible, were the colonies' most popular reading matter, providing calendars, astrological guides, recipe books, children's primers, summaries of the new sciences, selections from the best British authors, jokes, poems, maxims, etc. The calendars never included saints' days, their absence being explained in a 1646 colonial almanac: "We reject them wholly as superstitious, which being built upon rotten foundations, Idoll dayes, and in the day of their visitation shall perish."

This opinion, of course, was that of the New England Puritans whose quarrel was with the Church of England calendar which largely followed the Catholic. The

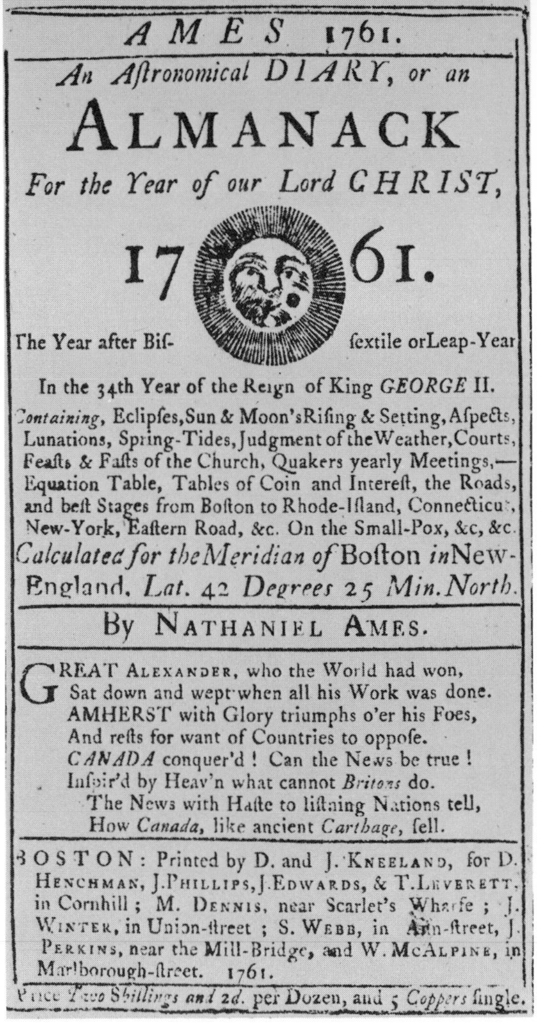

AMES 1761.

An Astronomical DIARY, *or an*

ALMANACK

For the Year of our Lord CHRIST,

17 61.

The Year after Bis- sextile orLeap-Year

In the 34th Year of the Reign of King *GEORGE* II.

Containing, Eclipses, Sun & Moon's Rising & Setting, Aspects, Lunations, Spring-Tides, Judgment of the Weather, Courts, Feasts & Fasts of the Church, Quakers yearly Meetings,— Equation Table, Tables of Coin and Interest, the Roads, and best Stages from Boston to Rhode-Island, Connecticut, New-York, Eastern Road, &c. On the Small-Pox, &c, &c.

Calculated for the Meridian of Boston *in* New-England. *Lat.* 42 *Degrees* 25 *Min. North.*

By NATHANIEL AMES.

GREAT ALEXANDER, who the World had won,
Sat down and wept when all his Work was done.
AMHERST with Glory triumphs o'er his Foes,
And rests for want of Countries to oppose.
CANADA conquer'd! Can the News be true!
Inspir'd by Heav'n what cannot *Britons* do.
The News with Haste to listning Nations tell,
How *Canada*, like ancient *Carthage*, fell.

BOSTON: Printed by D. and J. KNEELAND, for D. HENCHMAN, J. PHILLIPS, J. EDWARDS, & T. LEVERETT, in Cornhill; M. DENNIS, near Scarlet's Wharfe; J. WINTER, in Union-street; S. WEBB, in Ann-street, J. PERKINS, near the Mill-Bridge, and W. MCALPINE, in Marlborough-street. 1761.

Price *Two Shillings and* 2*d.* per Dozen, and 5 *Coppers* single.

Rare Book Division, The New York Public Library (Astor, Lenox and Tilden Foundations)

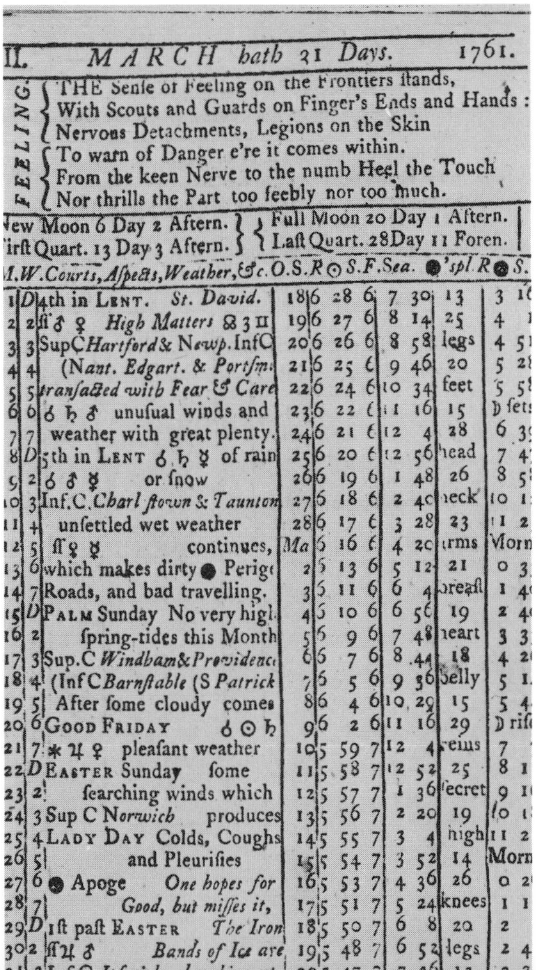

II. *MARCH hath* 31 *Days.* 1761.

FEELING.
THE Sense of Feeling on the Frontiers stands,
With Scouts and Guards on Finger's Ends and Hands:
Nervous Detachments, Legions on the Skin
To warn of Danger e're it comes within.
From the keen Nerve to the numb Heel the Touch
Nor thrills the Part too feebly nor too much.

New Moon 6 Day 2 Aftern. Full Moon 20 Day 1 Aftern.
First Quart. 13 Day 3 Aftern. Last Quart. 28 Day 11 Foren.

M.	W.	Courts, Aspects, Weather, &c.	O. S.	R ☉ S.		F. Sea.	☽'s pl.	R ☽ S.
1	D	4th in LENT. *St. David.*	18	6 28	6	7 30	13	3 1…
2	2	☍♂♀ *High Matters* ☊ 3 ♊	19	6 27	6	8 14	25	4 …
3	3	Sup C *Hartford* & *Newp.* Inf C	20	6 26	6	8 58	legs	4 5…
4	4	(*Nant. Edgart.* & *Portsm.*	21	6 25	6	9 46	20	5 2…
5	5	*transacted with Fear & Care*	22	6 24	6	10 34	feet	5 5…
6	6	☌♄♂ unusual winds and	23	6 22	6	11 16	15	☽ sets
7	7	weather with great plenty.	24	6 21	6	12 4	28	6 3…
8	D	5th in LENT ☌♄☿ of rain	25	6 20	6	12 56	head	7 4…
9	2	☌♂☿ or snow	26	6 19	6	1 48	26	8 5…
10	3	Inf. C. *Charlstown* & *Taunton*	27	6 18	6	2 40	neck	10 1…
11	4	unsettled wet weather	28	6 17	6	3 28	23	11 2…
12	5	☍♀☿ continues,	*Ma*	6 16	6	4 20	arms	Morn
13	6	which makes dirty ● Perige	2	6 13	6	5 12	21	0 3…
14	7	Roads, and bad travelling.	3	6 11	6	6 4	breast	1 4…
15	D	PALM Sunday No very high	4	6 10	6	6 56	19	2 4…
16	2	spring-tides this Month	5	6 9	6	7 48	heart	3 3…
17	3	Sup. C *Windham* & *Providence*	6	6 7	6	8 44	18	4 2…
18	4	(Inf C *Barnstable* (S *Patrick*	7	6 5	6	9 36	belly	5 1…
19	5	After some cloudy comes	8	6 4	6	10 29	15	5 4…
20	6	GOOD FRIDAY ☌☉♄	9	6 2	6	11 16	29	☽ rises
21	7	✱♃♀ pleasant weather	10	5 59	7	12 4	reins	7 …
22	D	EASTER Sunday some	11	5 58	7	12 52	25	8 1…
23	2	searching winds which	12	5 57	7	1 36	secret	9 1…
24	3	Sup C *Norwich* produces	13	5 56	7	2 20	19	10 1…
25	4	LADY DAY Colds, Coughs	14	5 55	7	3 4	high	11 2…
26	5	and Pleurisies	15	5 54	7	3 52	14	Morn
27	6	● Apoge *One hopes for*	16	5 53	7	4 36	26	0 2…
28	7	*Good, but misses it,*	17	5 51	7	5 24	knees	1 1…
29	D	1st past EASTER *The Iron*	18	5 50	7	6 8	20	2 …
30	2	☍♃♂ *Bands of Ice are*	19	5 48	7	6 52	legs	2 4…
31	3	Inf. C. *Ipswich breaking up.*	20	5 47	7	7 36	15	3 2…

1761 Almanac Title Page and Entries for March Showing the 25th as "Lady Day"

Puritans managed to retain their calendar until 1727, when the Anglicans began exerting pressure for the inclusion of theirs. But change was slow in coming. Not until 1760 did Nathaniel Ames, leading New England almanac-maker, include the Anglican calendar, and his competitors quickly followed suit. Of more than ordinary interest is March 25, listed as "Lady Day."

"Lady Day" was originally "Our Lady's Day" in England, marking the beginning of the legal year and the first quarter-day for rents and other payments. Early documents extant in New York and Maryland include the condition for rentals to be received "upon the feast-day of the Annunciation of our blessed Virgin Mary (commonly called Lady Day)."

On the feast of the Assumption Father Carroll was consecrated by Bishop Charles Walmesley, O.S.B., the ceremony taking place in the chapel dedicated to Mary in Lulworth Castle, England. Bishop Carroll chose Mary to grace his coat of arms. The chaplain at Lulworth was Rev. Charles Plowden, close friend of Carroll, and he personally had an account of the consecration published in Ireland.

Bishop Carroll returned to the United States early in December and was installed a few days later in St. Peter's Pro-Cathedral in Baltimore. Washington had come into office a year and a half earlier. In many respects the two men were alike; they shared a common bond in English ancestry, both were close in age — Washington was fifty-seven; Carroll, fifty-four — and while their meetings were few, a mutual respect existed. Both possessed the virtues of prudence and courage demanded for the difficult and uncertain times ahead. Under their leadership America and the Catholic Church steadily advanced.

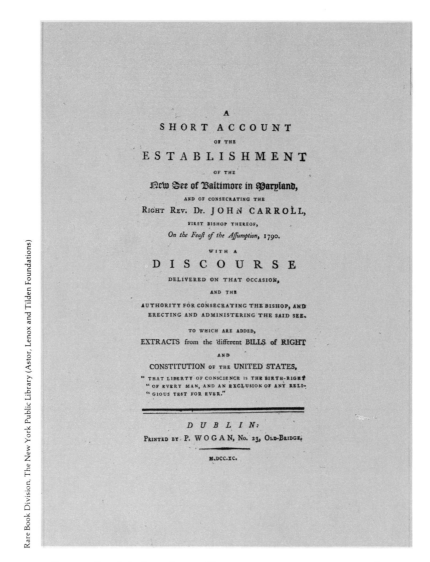

A
SHORT ACCOUNT
OF THE
ESTABLISHMENT
OF THE
New See of Baltimore in Maryland,
AND OF CONSECRATING THE
RIGHT REV. Dr. JOHN CARROLL,
FIRST BISHOP THEREOF,
On the Feaſt of the Aſſumption, 1790.
WITH A
DISCOURSE
DELIVERED ON THAT OCCASION,
AND THE
AUTHORITY FOR CONSECRATING THE BISHOP, AND
ERECTING AND ADMINISTERING THE SAID SEE.
TO WHICH ARE ADDED,
EXTRACTS from the different BILLS of RIGHT
AND
CONSTITUTION OF THE UNITED STATES,
" THAT LIBERTY OF CONSCIENCE IS THE BIRTH-RIGHT
" OF EVERY MAN, AND AN EXCLUSION OF ANY RELI-
" GIOUS TEST FOR EVER."

DUBLIN:
PRINTED BY P. WOGAN, No. 23, OLD-BRIDGE.
M,DCC,XC.

Record of John Carroll's Consecration as Bishop

When John Carroll was consecrated bishop of Maryland on the feast of the Assumption in 1790, a pamphlet recording the event was published in Dublin. In an effort to find additional reference to the occasion, a researcher has examined all existing files of London, Boston and New York papers from August to December 1790, but without result.

Virgin Militant

A NATION AT WAR

1790-1898

Our Lady of Prompt Succor, Patroness of New Orleans and Louisiana

It was before this statue in the Ursuline convent in the French quarter that the people of New Orleans kept vigil in petitioning God for the success of General Andrew Jackson's forces against the British in the Battle of New Orleans on January 8, 1815.

Virgin Militant

In an age when America is deeply involved in world problems, there is a tendency to sacrifice a reverential contact with our country's past and its heroes. It is incumbent on each generation to recapitulate, to evaluate certain events which ultimately determined the present.

The years preceding and following America's establishment as a nation witnessed many bloody conflicts. Their story is here projected in a new dimension. The horrors of war cannot be less horrible; however, an overtone may appear which relieves the picture. That overtone will come from the knowledge that the Virgin Militant was a silent but vital partner in our country's struggles.

When Indians threatened white settlers in the Northwest Territory, Fort St. Mary in Ohio became the lifeline in their protection. The Trenton diocesan Cathedral of St. Mary's now preserves for all time the site of the battle fought there which was the turning point of the Revolution. The War of 1812 witnessed the hardened General Andrew Jackson humbly acknowledging "the signal interposition of heaven" in his victory over the British — the citizens of New Orleans through the preceding night had petitioned God for that victory before the statue of Our Lady of Prompt Succor.

In the Texan fight for independence Mission de la Purísima Concepción became a battleground from which the Mexicans were repelled. In the ultimate conflict of the Mexican War the sloop of war *U.S.S. St. Mary's,* "one of the grandest ships in the Navy," carried the fight into the Gulf of Mexico to terminate hostilities.

The tragic war between North and South found southern Marian churches sheltering the wounded and dying of both armies. Heroic nuns, dedicated to the Mother of God and excelling in devotion to her, gave their lives and resources in caring for casualties. Civil War historians fail to emphasize the important contribution to religious liberty made at Our Lady of Sorrows Cathedral in Natchez, Mississippi, when Bishop William Henry Elder successfully protested the government's interference in the Church's religious practices.

The just and honorable peace Father Peter de Smet effected with the savage Sioux was negotiated under the banner of Mary; to her refuge and help he had entrusted his red brothers. The wounded of land and sea of the Spanish-American War were nursed to health at the Convent of Mary Immaculate in Florida, where the testimonials of a grateful nation are on view today.

These are random incidents of Mary's association in the annals of our country's battles. The victories, however, have been won at great cost. For having been Virgin Militant, Mary embraced the title of Mother of Sorrows — the two are synonymous.

George Rogers Clark Memorial,
Vincennes, Indiana

Not all Catholics served their country by the carrying of arms. One such noncombatant patriot was Father Peter Gibault, pastor of the Church of the Immaculate Conception at Kaskaskia, Illinois. This mission had been founded by Marquette in 1673, in fulfillment of a promise to Mary for her intercession in helping him discover the Mississippi River.

The mission had first been begun near Starved Rock on the Illinois River and then moved several times before finally locating on the Kaskaskia in Illinois. Here the Jesuits built a parochial church in 1753. Ten years later the Treaty of Paris ceded the Illinois area to Great Britain and they established a garrison at Kaskaskia, as well as at the other French posts which had been formed to hem in English colonization.

As the Revolutionary War progressed, Patrick Henry commissioned George Rogers Clark to lead an expedition into the West to seize the English forts, with Kaskaskia the first objective. Leaving Fort Pitt,

Clark and his riflemen sailed down the Ohio to a point forty miles above its mouth. Going overland they marched six days and nights through swamps and forests, at times without food or shelter, reaching Kaskaskia under cover of darkness and capturing it on July 4, 1778. The French inhabitants and their pastor, Father Gibault, rejoiced at Clark's promise of protection and gathered at the Church of the Immaculate Conception to ring out the glad tidings. The church bell is known today as "The Liberty Bell of the West."

Father Gibault allied himself to the American cause and set out with a doctor-companion to Clark's next objective — Vincennes, Indiana — to persuade the French and the Catholic Indians to yield when Clark came. Returning to Kaskaskia Father Gibault blessed the troops, and Clark and his men started out on what became one of the most remarkable feats of the war. The "army" of one hundred twenty-seven men, half of them Frenchmen of Kaskaskia, marched one hundred

120

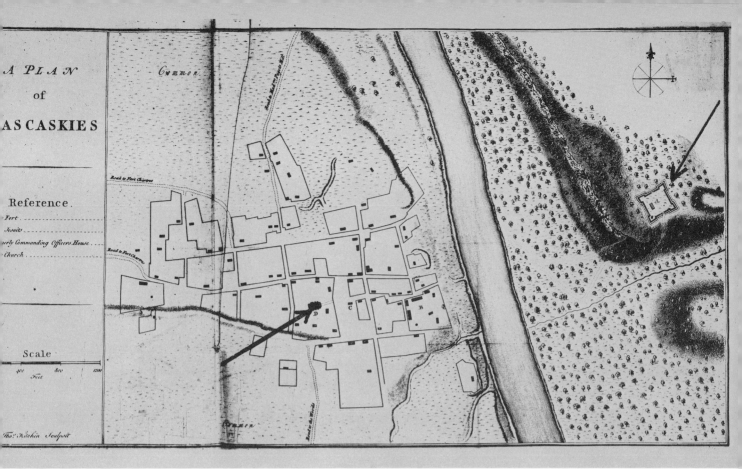

Pittman: *The Present State of the European Settlements on the Mississippi*

British Plan of Kaskaskia, Illinois, 1770

Left arrow points to the location of the Church of the Immaculate Conception while right arrow indicates Fort Kaskaskia.

eighty miles to Vincennes, triumphing over the winter's cold, floods and hunger, to force the surrender of the English garrison on February 24, 1779. Father Gibault's assistance was of great importance. Through his influence Clark was able to take possession of the Illinois country and thus secure it for the United States in the final peace settlement in 1783.

After the capture by Clark, Kaskaskia remained the leading western town and was the capital of Illinois as a territory (1809) and a state (1818). On removal of the seat of government to Vandalia in 1819 Kaskaskia began to decline. The river steadily encroached on the meadow and in 1892 united its course with the Okaw, converting a large part of the old site into an island. After several large floods, the area

crumbled into the river. Much of the area's history is preserved by the state — the bell included.

On the brink of the Revolution the already maligned Catholic population endured further suffering in a deluge of attacks from the colonists who were enraged over England's passage of the Quebec Act guaranteeing freedom of the Catholic Church in Canada. However, when war did come, as true Americans they readily responded in their country's defense.

In December of 1776, after four months of battle losses, a dispirited army on the west bank of the Delaware was preparing an attack on Trenton, New Jersey, where three regiments of Hessians were garrisoned under Colonel Johann Gottlieb Rall. Washington planned the attack for

121

In this old drawing Father Peter Gibault is shown giving George Rogers Clark's men a blessing before their departure in 1779 for Vincennes in present-day Indiana.

The "Liberty Bell of the West" — From the Church of the Immaculate Conception, Kaskaskia

Old Immaculate Conception at Kaskaskia, Later First Capitol of Illinois

early morning of December 26, surmising that Christmas Day would be celebrated with high revelry and the Hessian guard would be relaxed. From the Pennsylvania shore twenty-five hundred men and eighteen field pieces were ferried through the ice-clogged Delaware to a point nine miles above Trenton. The Americans then marched through the night, in sleet and snow on frozen highway, arriving at three in the morning of the twenty-sixth. The surprise attack completely overwhelmed the Hessians. Rall, mortally wounded, was visited by Washington before he died. The victory boosted the morale of soldier and civilian. Historians term the Trenton battle "the turning point of the Revolution."

The site of Rall's headquarters is today occupied by St. Mary's Cathedral, mother church of the Diocese of Trenton, preserving for posterity the famous battleground.

The memory of a Revolutionary patriot is today commemorated at the Trappist Abbey of Our Lady of Mepkin, Moncks Corner, South Carolina. Mepkin Plantation at one time was the residence of Henry Laurens, president of the Continental Congress in succession to Hancock. He sailed in 1779 as minister to Holland for the negotiation of a treaty with that country, but his ship was captured by the British. On suspicion of high treason, Laurens was imprisoned in the Tower of London for fourteen months. At war's end he was exchanged for Cornwallis and then went to Paris where with Adams, Franklin and Jay he signed the preliminary treaty of peace with Great Britain, November 30, 1782. American independence was now recognized and with one stroke of the pen the size of the thirteen colonies was more than doubled in the acquisition of the great territory lying between the Alleghenies and the Mississippi.

Laurens's son John was an aide and often secretary to Washington. In 1781 he was sent to France to obtain money and supplies; bypassing diplomatic precedent he requested and obtained an audience with the king and accomplished his mission. At Yorktown he captured a redoubt and was given the sword of Cornwallis. The year following he was killed in a skirmish south of Charleston.

The origin of "Mepkin," the historic Laurens Plantation, is unknown. It is now the property of the Order of Cistercians of the Strict Observance, on the Cooper River, twenty-two miles north of Charleston. Approaching the Trappist abbey is a state marker detailing the invaluable service which Henry and John Laurens rendered their country.

After the Revolution, settlers streamed into the Northwest Territory to claim land. Those going into the western Ohio country stopped at a trading post on St.

This lithograph is taken from the painting, "Washington Crossing the Delaware," by Thomas Sully (1783-1872).

Shown in this 1776 map of the Battle of Trenton, New Jersey, by Hessian Lieutenant J. Fischer, is the concentrated battleground. Arrow pinpoints the Hessian commander's headquarters, now the site of St. Mary's Cathedral. Roads to the left were used by Washington and his army.

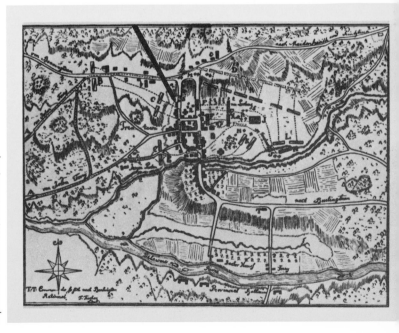

Marys River, named by La Salle in 1680, and the post established in 1769 by French priests. St. Marys River was an important link in the Great Lakes-Ohio River waterway. Indians found by traveling this river, with a portage at the post of only six miles at high water and twenty-six at low, they could go all the way from Lake Erie to the Gulf of Mexico.

Settlers claiming land in the area were soon besieged by Indians who resented intrusion and who retaliated by bloody massacres. To protect the settlers, our new government sent out expeditions, the first in 1790 under General Josiah Harmer who destroyed the Indian villages and supplies but without achieving permanent results. General Arthur St. Clair and two thousand troops then marched against the Miamis under Little Turtle, but the entire army was ambushed and destroyed. These defeats only increased Indian activity.

Now General Anthony Wayne took over. On the west branch of St. Marys River he erected Fort St. Mary's and made it the headquarters and supply depot for his coming campaigns. The fort was to become the most important one of many in this section of the state. Going south, Wayne met the Indians on the Maumee River (near present-day Toledo) and in the Battle of Fallen Timbers completely destroyed them in August 1794.

For future protection, Wayne erected a stockade at the confluence of the St. Marys, St. Joseph and Maumee Rivers in what is now Indiana. (The stockade later became a busy trading post, then a town, and eventually a city in 1840. Today the city of Fort Wayne is the second largest in Indiana.)

In 1795, Wayne and Little Turtle signed the Treaty of Greenville by which the Indians, for about ninety-five hundred dollars in annuities, ceded most of Ohio and a small strip of land along the eastern side of Indiana.

124

St. Mary's Cathedral, Trenton

St. Mary's Cathedral, Trenton — On the Site of the Battle of the Revolution

At St. Marys, Ohio, a treaty was drawn up and signed between spokesmen of the Wyandot, Shawnee and Ottawa tribes, with Lewis Cass and Duncan McArthur signing for the government on September 17, 1818. This treaty opened up large tracts of land for settlement and made possible the organization of a local government at St. Marys for establishing a city.

Georgia and Florida are separated by St. Marys River which traces its history to the Spanish mission era (described in the sec-

Conference on the Treaty of Peace With England

Painted by Benjamin West (1738-1820), this work was never completed because the British commissioners (who were to be on the extreme right) refused to pose. The scene is of the preliminary peace treaty conference in November of 1782. Shown, left to right, are: John Jay, John Adams, Benjamin Franklin, William Temple Franklin and Henry Laurens.

MEPKIN PLANTATION

HOME OF HENRY LAURENS, BORN IN CHARLESTON IN 1724, DIED AT MEPKIN IN 1792, PRESIDENT OF THE FIRST AND SECOND COUNCILS OF SAFETY, 1775-76. PRESIDENT FIRST PROVINCIAL CONGRESS OF S. C, 1775. VICE PRESIDENT OF S. C, 1776. PRESIDENT OF CONTINENTAL CONGRESS 1777-78. ELECTED MINISTER PLENIPOTENTIARY TO HOLLAND 1779, CONFINED 14 MONTHS IN TOWER OF LONDON, EXCHANGED FOR LORD CORNWALLIS, SIGNED IN PARIS, WITH ADAMS, JAY AND FRANKLIN, PRELIMINARIES OF PEACE, 1782.

tion entitled "Nuestra Señora"). On the river's Georgia banks a town grew up in 1788 and was named St. Marys. It became the most southern port of the United States, for Florida was then a Spanish

Mepkin Plantation Marker,
Moncks Corner, South Carolina

125

Our Lady of Mepkin, Trappist Abbey, Moncks Corner

province. Through the port of St. Marys came the commerce of the West Indies, requiring the presence of customs collectors and other federal officials. Here a naval shipyard was established in 1794 and four years later the United States galley *St. Mary's* was launched, the ship becoming part of the country's first permanent navy. The galley was used for coastal defense in the quasi war with France which had resulted from that country's reckless abuse of American shipping in the Caribbean and elsewhere.

No picture of the *St. Mary's* exists, but there is an amusing account in the Georgia Admiralty Records of her involvement in a

"bloodless" incident in 1799, when her commander, Lieutenant Thomas Fowler, confiscated the liquid cargo of a "foreign" yawl.

St. Marys River played an important part in our country's history, attested by a review of Georgia's boundary dispute involving three nations. The state's colonial charter had set the Altamaha River as her southern boundary, but when England secured Florida from Spain she set Georgia's boundary south to St. Marys River, joining the "source" of the river with a straight line westward to the confluence of the Flint and Chattahoochee Rivers. By the Definitive Peace Treaty of 1783 the same

126

boundary was accepted by Spain, who once again owned Florida. Four years later our commissioner, Andrew Ellicott, acting in conjunction with the Spanish commissioner, fixed the two points to be joined by the straight line. He erected a mound near where he *considered* the source of the St. Marys River to be, but he did not run the boundary.

Though various lines were later surveyed or attempted, Georgia by 1830 had definitely come to reject Ellicott's mound as the true head of the St. Marys, claiming a point a dozen miles to the southward and involving almost twenty-five hundred square miles which she wanted! She disputed with the United States from 1819 (when Spain ceded Florida) until 1845 when Florida became a state, and then continued her argument with Florida. Finally a line was agreed upon in 1859.

This painting is believed to have been done by a member of General Anthony Wayne's staff during peace negotiations with Indian tribes in 1795 at Greenville in what is now Ohio. The principal figures at that meeting were Wayne, William Henry Harrison, William Wells, Little Turtle and Turke the Crane.

In this map showing the military posts, forts and battlefields in Ohio during the Indian uprisings and War of 1812, Fort St. Mary's is indicated by the arrow.

A Georgia historian — describing a little known battle of the War of 1812, fought on the St. Marys River — puts it this way: "The British ascended the St. Mary's River for the purpose of burning the mills of Major Clark [near Fort Alert] ... some thirty miles inland. Twenty-three barges, loaded to the utmost limit with troops, started up the river, but while ascending the stream, they were attacked by a party of 28 men, under Capt. William Cone. The heavy growth of palmetto, on either side of the river, shielded Cone's men from the British, so that the latter's guns proved harmless ... the British reported 113 men killed and an equal number wounded. No American loss. . . . In view of the whole-

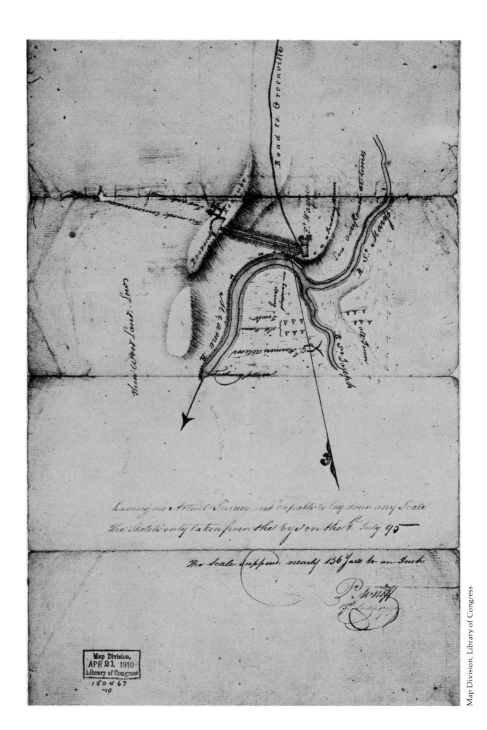

Old Fort Wayne on the St. Marys River, 1795

This map, drawn for General Wayne, was "taken from the eye" of P. Mc-Niff on July 18, 1795. St. Marys River linked Fort Wayne, Indiana, with Fort St. Mary's in Ohio, and was a vital waterway between the two states in the government's efforts to protect the settlers against Indian attacks.

sale slaughter of redcoats wrought by 28 men the feat is almost without parallel in the annals of war."

The war that began in 1812 dragged into 1815. Americans were faring badly in spite of naval victories and the breaking off of power of western Indian tribes. Then American victories at Baltimore and Plattsburg persuaded the British to sign a peace treaty at Ghent, Flanders, on Christmas Eve, 1814.

Unaware of that treaty, General Andrew Jackson prepared to defend New Orleans against eight thousand British under General Edward Pakenham. Jackson's force of five thousand was made up of Mississippi Dragoons, Louisiana Blues, Tennessee Mounted Infantry, U.S. Marines, Choctaw Indians, Santo Domingo Free Men of Color and Jean Lafitte's pirates. Jackson left a sickbed to take command, vowing the British "shall not sleep on our soil."

Jackson's men built a mud rampart on an abandoned millrace running from the Mississippi to an impassable swamp. It was January 7, 1815. All through that night the people of New Orleans were petitioning God for victory before a statue of

Record of 1799 Incident Involving United States Galley St. Mary's

Our Lady of Prompt Succor in the Ursuline convent.

At dawn on the eighth the attack began. The advancing redcoats were blasted from the mud rampart with what looked like "a row of fiery furnaces." In less than two hours two thousand British, including General Pakenham, lay dead or wounded. The American losses were seven dead, six wounded. In New Orleans the people danced in the streets and sang hymns of thanksgiving. One press headline read MOST INCREDIBLE VICTORY.

General Jackson, not known for reli-

St. Marys, Georgia, Historical Marker

Georgia in 1812, When Florida Belonged to Spain

Right arrow indicates Altamaha River, Georgia's southern boundary as set by its colonial charter. Left arrow points to dotted line showing the boundary of the United States in 1812, when England secured Florida from Spain. St. Marys River is shown on the Georgia coast.

St. Marys River, Vicinity of Kingsland, Georgia
*This picture of St. Marys River in Georgia was taken
near the site of a skirmish during the War of 1812.*

gious fervor, admitted that there must have been divine intervention. He addressed a letter to Father Louis Dubourg, S.S., administrator apostolic of the Diocese of Louisiana, requesting that a Mass of thanksgiving be offered in the Cathedral of St. Louis and personally went to the Ursuline convent to thank the nuns for their prayers and their unceasing care of the wounded defenders and captured enemy.

Critics have termed the Battle of New Orleans "needless" in view of the prior signing of the Ghent Treaty. Though Britain and the United States had signed, the treaty had not yet been ratified by the United States Senate, and it contained no provision for an armistice. The treaty specified hostilities were not to end "until this treaty shall be ratified by both parties." Had Jackson been defeated, with Britain's occupation of New Orleans, there is reasonable doubt whether the Senate would have ratified the treaty, and the war might have been prolonged.

Between 1800 and 1820, American traders and military adventurers established commercial relations with Mexico, invited to Texas by the authorities who hoped white occupation would protect their own country from Indian raids and

131

A CORRECT VIEW of the BATTLE ... Near the City of NEW ORLEANS, on the
eighth of January 1815, Under the Command of ... Genl. And ... Jackson, Over 10.000 British Troops, in
... 3 of their most distinguished Generals were killed & ... several wounded and upwards of 3.000 of their choicest
... Soldiers were killed: wounded, ... and made Prisoners. &c

Battle of New Orleans

*This scene of the Battle of New Orleans, which took place on January 8,
1815, shows the mud rampart of the American forces in the background.
The British were picked off with ease from this protective embankment.*

possible aggression by the United States. It soon became evident they had miscalculated when during the period 1820-1830 about twenty thousand Americans, with nearly two thousand slaves, passed into the area. Most were law-abiding, but rougher elements aroused Mexican fears. Further immigration was stopped, restrictive measures passed, and Mexican troops began occupying the province. Relations worsened and attempts by the United States to purchase Texas confirmed Mexican fears of a Yankee plot to seize the territory by force. In turn, Texans rebelled

against restrictions and began their fight for independence.

Before Texan leaders had agreed on military strategy, two of their companies were wiped out, one at the Alamo (the abandoned Mission San Antonio de Valero at San Antonio). Here one hundred eighty-seven Texans, led by William Travis, Davy Crockett and James Bowie, were besieged thirteen days before being killed. From that battle emerged the cry "Remember the Alamo" which rallied Texans in defeating the Mexicans at San Jacinto to conclude their fight for independence.

132

Following the Battle of New Orleans in 1815, General Andrew Jackson wrote this letter to Father Louis Dubourg. Transcribed, it reads in part: "The signal interposition of heaven, in giving success to our arms against the Enemy, ... while it must excite ... emotions of the liveliest gratitude, requires at the same time some manifestation of those feelings. Permit me therefore to entreat that you will cause the service of public thanksgiving to be performed in the Cathedral. ..."

Two previous battles involved Marian missions: La Purísima Concepción and Nuestra Señora del Refugio. Texan soldiers had chosen the former as first in a sort of ring of old missions around San Antonio as camping places for their army. Colonel James Bowie and Captain James Fannin, with ninety-two Texans, occupied the mission in October 1835, waiting for support which never came. Obscured by a curtain of mist, a force of Mexicans were hemming the Texans in on three sides, when a soldier in the mission tower fired a warning signal.

As the fog lifted, enemy infantry fired a heavy volley, then wheeled forward a

It was here, in the historic Cathedral of St. Louis, New Orleans, on January 23, 1815, that a Mass of thanksgiving was said at the request of Andrew Jackson, on his victory over the British.

small brass cannon which soon began its destruction of the mission. Bowie concentrated his sharpshooters in picking off the cannoneers, and under protective fire he and his soldiers weaved their way across the battlefield to reach the cannon. Bowie swung it around and seizing the burning fuse stick from the dead gunner, fired it into the Mexican front line. The enemy stampeded, leaving sixty dead and many wounded. Only one Texan was killed, none wounded. Later, Bowie would die fighting at the Alamo, Fannin before a Mexican firing squad at Goliad.

The Mission of Nuestra Señora del Refugio (Our Lady of Refuge) was the scene of yet another battle. In March 1836, the Mexican army under José Urrea captured the town; the defending soldiers were captured and executed, and the buildings of the town demolished.

The story of that engagement is told in plaques which encircle the twenty-six-foot Amon B. King Monument in Goliad:

"In the early morning of March 14, 1836, twenty-eight Texans under Captain Amon B. King separated from Col. William Ward's command in the Mission Church and late that day in a wood on the west bank of Mission River a half mile below the town fought a desperate battle with part of General Urrea's Mexican Command. Five Texans were killed and five wounded, one of whom joined Colonel Ward in the Church. The others escaped but were captured next day.

"On March 15th, Lieutenant Colonel William Ward with less than one hundred and fifty men successfully defended the Church of the Refugio Mission against four successive attacks by General José Urrea's command and made his escape from the church that night after having lost only three men wounded, two left to care for them, and a few others as couriers or while separated from his command.

"On March 16, 1836, Captain King and fourteen of his men who had been made prisoners by General Urrea's cavalry the day before, were marched to the slope of

Misión de la Purísima Concepción, San Antonio, Texas

This mission, showing part of the damage it sustained in one of the battles for Texas independence in 1836, is a national historical landmark and is listed in the Historic American Buildings Survey.

the hill on the Goliad Road about one mile from the Refugio Church and shot. Their bones were later buried where they fell. . . . James Murphy of Refugio, Colonel Fannin's courier killed nearby on March 14, was buried in their common grave."

During the revolution almost half of the men of Refugio, Irish and Mexican, served in the Texas army and approximately one fourth of the male population died in the Goliad Massacre.

On March 25, 1847, a heavy gun from the *U.S.S. St. Mary's* joined a naval battery (under Commander Matthew C. Perry) bombarding Vera Cruz in the war with Mexico. Shelling was backed up by a fleet of two hundred ships and by nearly fourteen thousand troops under the command of General Winfield Scott. The Americans prepared for their siege by putting men ashore to build gun emplacements, thus adding to the firepower of the naval guns.

Captain Robert E. Lee (destined to make Civil War history) had designed the battery and was by his brother's side during much of the bombarding. He wrote home to his family: "The shells thrown from our battery were constant and regular discharges, so beautiful in their flight and so destructive in their fall. It was awful! My heart bled for the inhabitants . . . it was terrible to think of the women and children."

The *U.S.S. St. Mary's* from her launching in 1844 seemed destined to play an active part in America's history. She was named for St. Marys County, Maryland, and one hundred years later would lend her name to another ship which would see world naval action. (See section entitled "Mother of the Church.")

The record of the *St. Mary's* boasts a variety of missions. In 1857 she visited the Jarvis and New Nantucket Islands in the Pacific when Charles H. Davis, her com-

Our Lady of Refuge Church, Refugio, Texas

This church is on the site of the 1795 mission which became part of Texas history in 1836. The town of Refugio took its name from the mission.

Amon B. King Monument, Commemorating Texas Patriots and Marian Mission Battle Site, 1836

This is a depiction of the U.S. naval battery during the bombardment of Vera Cruz, Mexico, 1847. The U.S.S. St. Mary's gun is second from the left. Third from the right is a gun from the U.S.S. Mississippi under the command of Lieutenant Sydney Smith Lee, brother of Captain Robert E. Lee.

The Sloop of War U.S.S. St. Mary's

mander, took possession of them in the name of the United States. Commander Davis also negotiated terms of capitulation with the filibustering General William Walker who had made hostile expeditions to the Caribbean, Central and South America between the Mexican and Civil Wars. It was the *St. Mary's* which carried Walker and three hundred sixty-four of his followers from Nicaragua to Panama and then to New Orleans. In 1860 the *St. Mary's* landed marines and sailors at Panama to cooperate with the *H.M.S. Clio* in quelling an insurrection there. The governor of Panama turned the city over to this force for their joint occupancy.

When our shipping was at a low ebb in

136

1874, Congress voted to establish nautical schools for states on the seaboard, furnishing ships and equipment to instruct young men in navigation, electricity and steamship marine engineering, so that our merchant marine could be manned and commanded by trained Americans. New York City established its nautical school with the *St. Mary's* and in the capacity of training ship she served her country until 1908.

When the Civil War seemed imminent, one of Lincoln's most pressing problems was what to do about federal forts on Confederate soil, notably the garrison under Major Robert Anderson at Fort Sumter in Charleston harbor, South Carolina. The Confederates had fired on a Union vessel attempting to land supplies, men and arms there, but without Union reprisal.

Now Lincoln faced the dilemma of yielding the fort and acknowledging the power if not the legality of the Confederacy, or of fortifying the garrison, risking bloodshed, and thus appearing the aggressor. He decided to provision Fort Sumter peacefully and notified the South Carolina authorities of his intent.

Now the Confederacy faced a problem:

if provisioned, the fort would stand indefinitely in one of their few good harbors and be a threat to their prestige; if they attacked a peaceful expedition, then *they* would be the aggressor. The southern general Pierre G. T. Beauregard was ordered to request Major Anderson's surrender. Anderson promised to evacuate by April 15 unless relieved or ordered to remain. The Confederates refused to wait and early on the twelfth bombarded Fort Sumter from their position on Fort Johnson. Anderson surrendered the next day. Hostilities had begun.

All during the Union's siege of Charleston the Sisters of Charity of Our Lady of Mercy cared for the sick and wounded of both armies. Shellfire had caused great damage to the asylum they had been maintaining for more than thirty years. When the war ended, the South Carolina Legislature petitioned Congress to remunerate the nuns. A twenty-seven-page booklet offered testimonials of the Sisters' service to North and South "in relieving pain and suffering, dressing and binding up the wounds of the suffering combatants." Congress respected the petition and compensation was made in 1870.

Training Ship "St. Mary's," New York State Nautical School

This painting by Alfred Hutty shows Confederate forces firing on Fort Sumter from Fort Johnson, Charleston, South Carolina, on April 12-13, 1861.

This Marian shrine was built into the earthwork of a Confederate battery during the Civil War. The battery is located on that portion of historic Fort Johnson owned by the Sisters of Charity of Our Lady of Mercy; their motherhouse is located here on Fort Johnson Road.

138

THE PETITION

—OF THE—

MEMBERS OF THE LEGISLATURE

—OF—

SOUTH CAROLINA,

—TO THE—

CONGRESS OF THE U. S. STATES

IN FAVOR OF THE

SISTERS OF OUR LADY OF MERCY,

CHARLESTON, S. C.,

—FOR THE—

REBUILDING OF THEIR ORPHAN ASYLUM,

PARTIALLY DESTROYED DURING THE BOM-
BARDMENT OF THE CITY.

ALSO,

VARIOUS IMPORTANT LETTERS FROM OFFICERS AND SOLDIERS
OF THE UNITED STATES ARMY, TESTIFYING TO THE
HEROIC CHARITY OF THESE GOOD SISTERS, IN
THEIR ATTENDANCE ON THE PRISONERS,
THE WOUNDED, THE SICK, AND THE
DYING, WITHOUT DISTINCTION
OF NORTH OR SOUTH,
OF CREED OR
COLOR.

CHARLESTON, S. C.:
EDWARD PERRY, STATIONER, PRINTER AND BLANK BOOK MANUFACTURER,
155 MEETING STREET.
1870.

Sisters of Charity of Our Lady of Mercy

*Petition to Congress for Compensating the
Sisters of Charity of Our Lady of Mercy*

St. Mary's Church, Troy, New York
This was the first Catholic church to fly the American flag in the Civil War.

A northern church, St. Mary's of Troy, New York, had its share in defending the Union. The bombardment of Fort Sumter occurred on Friday, April 12, and President Lincoln's proclamation calling for seventy-five thousand volunteers was ready on Saturday, the thirteenth. Thinking non-sympathizers might make ill-usage of the Sunday following, it was decided to defer promulgation until Monday, the fifteenth. This information went out to all military personnel, including General

140

John E. Wool, in command of the U.S. Military Department of the East at Troy.

The general's staff included a confidential attaché, a Virginian, who knew that in an arsenal just across the Hudson at Watervliet was a machine for punching bullets out of cold lead, the only machine of its kind in the country. He planned to get this machine on Sunday and ship it out to the Confederates in advance of the proclamation. Southern sympathizers employed in the local nail-making industry were eager to help, but the news of the plot spread to the ears of company officials. They conferred in secret with Father Peter Havermans, pastor of St. Mary's Church, one of Troy's most highly respected citizens and beloved by men of all faiths. He assured the officials that he would intervene.

Father Havermans procured a large American flag and swung it from a window above the clock in the steeple of St. Mary's where at daylight on Sunday it cheered Union hearts. He determined to meet the plotters as they passed the church on their way to the arsenal. As they approached St. Mary's, their leader saw the flag floating and shouted to his men, "The old man is in it." This news completely squelched the plot. The South was out one bullet machine and St. Mary's had the honor of being the first Catholic church

to fly an American flag in the Civil War.

The Confederates had established their capital at Richmond and Congress was tempted into pressuring Union military leaders in first attacking that city. In the campaign the Union army met the Confederates at Manassas Junction, Virginia (Bull Run). Here they were routed on July 21, and this defeat ended early northern complacency. Almost a year later a second attempt to take Richmond failed when General Robert E. Lee repulsed Union forces under George B. McClellan.

Lee placed Stonewall Jackson in command of troops to follow the retreating Union forces and the two armies met, again at Bull Run, on August 29-30, with slaughter on both sides. The battle spread out as far as Chantilly where the Union general Philip Kearney was killed in

Arsenal at Watervliet, New York, 1861
This is now a national historic landmark.

Watervliet Arsenal

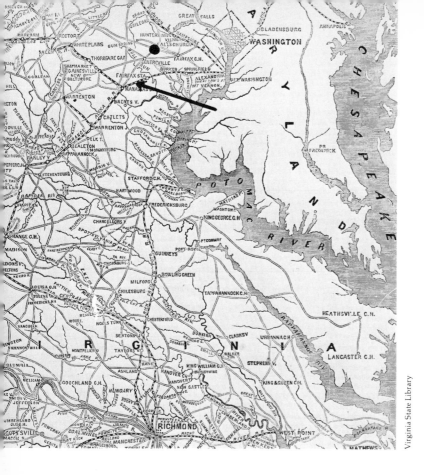

This is a map of Washington and Richmond during the Civil War. The arrow points to Manassas Junction (Bull Run) and Fairfax Station (Church of St. Mary), 1861. Large dot indicates Chantilly battlefield, 1862.

hand-to-hand fighting. General Lee returned his body to the federal lines and before burial it lay in the churchyard of St. Mary's at Fairfax Station, Virginia.

The slaughter at Chantilly would be the compelling force in one woman's efforts to lessen and prevent human suffering. Clara Barton watched as Kearney's leaderless men marched to Alexandria and she helped place the disabled in waiting trains. The warning was already being sounded of approaching Confederate troops. Though

In this representation of the attack on Stonewall Jackson at Chantilly, Virginia, 1862, the wounded and dying are being carried up the thinly wooded slopes of Fairfax Station to St. Mary's Church.

Located at Fairfax Station, Virginia, St. Mary's Church served as a hospital for casualties of the Battle of Chantilly in 1862. Almost a century later it sheltered twenty-five advocates of freedom who fled Hungary during the 1956 revolt.

and around her machinery as a means of protection, a precaution which the Confederacy (lacking iron) frequently took with their small river and coastal ships. The mighty Mississippi would be "home" to the *St. Mary* for her brief life.

The river was a lifeline to the Confederacy and so became the locale of bloody battles. In 1863 Grant, aided by a fleet of gunboats, advanced downriver and took Memphis. Admiral Farragut coming up from the sea had already captured New Orleans, and now only the strongly fortified town of Vicksburg prevented complete federal

physically exhausted from four days and nights' vigil among the dead and dying, she was filled with a determination to be of service in this national emergency. From that day her thoughts and actions were directed to eventually establishing the American branch of the Red Cross.

The history of the *C.S.S. St. Mary* began early in 1862 when she was built at Plaquemine, Louisiana, for service in the Confederate navy. She was just short of ninety feet in length, armed with a 12-pounder gun as well as a 24-pounder, and carried bales of cotton to stack on her deck

This memorial at St. Mary's Church, Fairfax Station, Virginia, also commemorates Clara Barton and her determination to found the American Red Cross.

143

control of the river. Admiral Porter's Union fleet, attacking from the north, tried to reach Vicksburg through a bayou north of the town but was held off at Haynes Bluff by the Confederate fleet. In this fleet of large vessels the *St. Mary* held her own in that battle, one report stating: "The pluck of the little *St. Mary* at the wing and in the center of our line of battle was warmly regarded."

Farther south was Port Hudson where the Confederates had constructed strong defenses. The port was besieged for months, the *St. Mary* assisting in repulsing the enemy. Grant finally took Vicksburg on July 4, 1863, and this, together with the victory at Gettysburg, was the turning point of the war.

Ignoring Vicksburg's surrender the Confederates began fortifying Yazoo City to the north. Grant sent a naval military expedition to capture or destroy the enemy fleet and take the city. Four Union ships and some five thousand troops routed the Confederates who had first destroyed all their ships but one — the *St. Mary*. Taken in tow by the Union, her name was changed to *Alexandria* and she was commissioned at Cairo, Illinois, in December 1863 to go on her way in serving the North as she had served the South.

Among the Civil War papers of south

Confederate States Steamer "St. Mary," on Mississippi, 1862
Between bloody battles of the Civil War one of her crew drew this peaceful scene.

Louisiana Historical Association Collection, Tulane University Library

This is a hand-drawn map of St. Mary and St. Martin Parishes, Louisiana. Arrow points to the engagement at Irish Bend on the Bayou Teche.

central Louisiana is a map covering a portion of the area of the state first founded by Acadians expelled from Nova Scotia by the British in 1755. These devout French Catholics had expressed their religious zeal in place names such as St. Mary, St. James, St. Charles, Assumption. The parish of St. Mary had furnished the Confederacy with a battery called St. Mary Cannoneers, which was captured by Union troops at Fort Jackson, Louisiana. The Confederates fared better at a bend in Bayou Teche known as Irish Bend where on April 14, 1863, five thousand men fought their way out of a federal trap.

A Marian cathedral served as "battleground" when the Church defended, through a courageous bishop, her right to freedom from government interference in religious practices. The commander in charge of Union forces in Natchez, Mississippi, issued a special order threatening any minister who refused to offer prayers for the United States government.

Battle at Irish Bend, St. Mary Parish, Louisiana, 1863

Jones: Christ in the Camp

Most Rev. Richard O. Gerow

Site of Civil War State-Church Controversy

This magnificent edifice is the Cathedral of Our Lady of Sorrows in Natchez, Mississippi.
It served as a "battleground" when the question of Church rights came up following
a government order directing the clergy to pray for the Union during the Civil War.

William Henry Elder, Catholic bishop of Natchez, refused to be intimidated and was taken by Union authority across the Mississippi River to Vidalia, Louisiana, and held in custody of federal troops from July 26 to August 12. He protested first to President Lincoln, then to Secretary of War Edwin M. Stanton, and his release was effected. His diary provides an intimate view

146

of his great anxiety (and determination!) in defense of the Church's rights:

"July 16th. Saturday . . . It had appeared to me from the beginning that I ought not to consent. The more I had studied the matter over in the light of calm reason, the more I was confirmed in the conviction . . . of the duty that I owed to God, & to the Church. — Now, I must confess, when the issue was at hand & the prospect of a guard seizing the Cathedral tomorrow or Monday — turning it into a hospital or barracks, — defacing & desecrating everything beautiful & holy — carrying off the most sacred vessels — driving all the Priests out of the house & leaving the people without Sacraments or religious consolation — I must confess the sight of these awful consequences, depending probably on my single word — it did unnerve me. For a few minutes a severe pain shot across the top of my head — & I feared I was going to have a sharp attack of sickness. — Thanks to God however it passed away.

"July 18th. Monday [meeting with town officials and prominent citizens] . . . I wanted to explain what had been my conduct & the motives for it. — Some Catholics & many more Protestants, were under the impression that my refusal to read the Prayer arises from a preference which I give to the Southern Confederacy. — I wanted them to understand that it was not so — but simply from an unwillingness to acknowledge the right in any secular power to direct our religious worship; — & my own special unwillingness to use my sacred ministry in maintaining either power, or in support of any political views. . . .

"July 26th [removal to Vidalia] . . . Yesterday & to-day many sympathizing friends called — Catholics & Protestants — some who had never been in the house before. — The Sisters & all the Orphans came. Their sobs unmanned me more than anything else. Many were . . . gathered at the Ferry landing to take farewell . . . they all fell on their knees — in the sand & dust, to crave a parting blessing — God forgive me for not doing my duty better by such a people!

"August 12th [returning to Natchez] . . . I went immediately to offer my thanks in Church. — Both bells were rung — . . . what a greeting those good people gave me

Gerow: Civil War Diary of Bishop William Henry Elder

SPECIAL ORDERS NO. 31

Provost Marshal's Office}
Natchez, Miss., June 28, 1864}

Extract - II The Colonel Commanding this District, having been officially notified that the Pastors of many Churches in this city neglect to make any public recognition of allegiance to the Government under which they live, and to which they are indebted for protection; and further, that the regular form of prayer for "The President of the United States and all others in authority," prescribed by the ritual in some Churches, and by established custom in others, has been omitted in the stated services of Churches of all denominations, it is hereby ORDERED that hereafter, the Ministers of such Churches as may have the prescribed form of prayer for the President of the United States, shall read the same at each and every Service in which it is required by the rubrics; and that those of other denominations which have such form, shall on like occasions, pronounce a prayer appropriate to the times and expressive of a proper spirit toward the CHIEF MAGISTRATE OF THE UNITED STATES.

Any Minister failing to comply with these orders will be immediately prohibited from exercising the functions of his office in this city, and render himself liable to be sent beyond the lines of the United States forces, at the discretion of the Colonel Commanding.

The Provost Marshal is charged with the execution of this order.

By Command of B. G. FARRAR
Colonel Commanding
(Signed)
Jas. E. Montgomery, Ass't Adjt. Gen.
(Official) G. D. Reynolds, Major and Provost Marshal
Natchez, June 28 - 4t

This was the controversial Union commander's order which caused the bishop of Natchez, Mississippi, to fight for the rights of the Catholic Church in 1864.

. . . God only knows the happiness of all those hearts. All had been praying . . . making the Novena of the Assumption — hearing Mass every morning . . . there was truly great reason for rejoicing that the cloud had passed & done no harm . . . The true cause is to be sought in the mercy of God, obtained by the intercession of our Holy Mother in answer to all the prayers offered not at Natchez only, but in Vicksburgh, N. Orleans, & no doubt every where that the fact was known."

One of the bloodiest battles of the war took place on the hills outside the city of Nashville, Tennessee. Here from December 15 to 18, 1864, Union forces under

147

Major General George H. Thomas battled and finally routed the Confederates under General John Bell Hood. The dying and wounded were brought into Nashville and every available building of size was turned into a hospital.

On the day following the close of the battle the Nashville *Daily Press* reported that the Cathedral of St. Mary of the Seven Sorrows was "taken possession of by the military authorities." One month later the *Nashville Dispatch* reported the glad tidings of the cathedral's evacuation and the Angelus bell ringing. What was not reported was that the cathedral's interior "appeared to have been the scene of a battle itself and had to be renovated and refitted."

The same bell of St. Mary's which rang in the Civil War can still be heard today. The church is on the register of National Historic Places both for its history and for its architectural excellence. It was designed by the distinguished William Strickland, first American-born and American-educated architect of note. He considered St. Mary's his finest ecclesiastical edifice.

Selma, Alabama, was a Conferederate stronghold, with naval foundry, rolling mill, powder works and armory on the bluffs of the Alabama River. The fortifications had been carefully mapped by a Union officer who noted the scarcity of trained fighters — "One Company of Boys and exempts, 100-County Militia." On April 2, 1865, federal cavalry with drawn sabers engaged Lieutenant General Nathan Forrest's command approaching Selma. The Confederates fought back with rifles and six-shooters in a bloody running fight covering several miles, before retreating. The city was abandoned when the militia fled, and with Forrest's surrender a month later, the war in this area ended.

From 1850 the Catholics of Selma had been served by a priest from Montgomery saying Mass in the homes of the people. The war effort had brought more than two hundred men and their families here, requiring the setting up of a temporary chapel in a city building. After the war ended, the arsenal was dismantled and its

The Battle of Nashville, 1864

Nashville Landmark: The Cupola of St. Mary's of the Seven Sorrows

stones used in building the Church of the Assumption of the Blessed Virgin in 1869.

From the beginning to the end of the war the Sisterhoods of the country made a profound impression upon Catholics and non-Catholics alike by caring for the sick and wounded of both armies. More than eight hundred Sisters heroically offered their services and supplies as they "comforted the dying, nursed the wounded, carried hope to the imprisoned, gave in His Name a drink of water to the thirsty."

Many of these nuns were from communities whose official titles included the name of Mary; all were Marian in the sense their members excelled in devotion to the Virgin. In addition to these were the communities who would have served at the battlefront had they not already been car-

ing for the casualties brought to their very doors.

Sister Angela Heath of the Sisters of Charity, Emmitsburg, Maryland, left a record of conditions under which the nuns worked:

"Left Richmond for Manassas . . . we were five in number & found . . . 500 patients, sick and wounded, of both armies. Mortality was very great, as the sick poor had been very much neglected. The wards were in a most deplorable condition, & strongly resisted all efforts of the broom to which they had long been strangers, & the aid of a shovel was found necessary. [Describing shelters for the wounded] . . . At best they were but poor protection against the inclemency of the season & being scattered, we were often obliged to go through

The stones from the Confederate arsenal were used in the construction of the Church of the Assumption of the Blessed Virgin, Selma.

snow over a foot deep to wait on the sick."

In commemoration of the Sisters' heroic service, the Ladies Auxiliary of the Ancient Order of Hibernians erected a monument on a triangular park at the junction of Rhode Island Avenue and M Street, N.W., Washington, D.C. Former Representative Ambrose Kennedy of Rhode Island had introduced a resolution in Congress autho-

In this diagram of the Confederate fortifications at Selma, Alabama, in 1864, the arrow pinpoints the arsenal.

THEY · COMFORTED · THE · DYING · NURSED · THE · WOUNDED · CARRIED · HOPE · TO
THE · IMPRISONED · GAVE · IN · HIS · NAME · A · DRINK · OF · WATER · TO · THE · THIRSTY

TO THE MEMORY AND IN HONOR OF
THE · VARIOUS · ORDERS · OF · SISTERS
WHO GAVE THEIR SERVICES AS NURSES ON BATTLEFIELDS
AND IN HOSPITALS DURING THE CIVIL WAR

This memorial honoring the "Nuns of the Battlefield" is at the junction of Rhode Island Avenue and M Street, N.W., Washington, D.C.

rizing the erection of the memorial on public ground in the nation's Capitol. When the monument was dedicated on September 20, 1924, Cardinal William O'Connell, archbishop of Boston, commented on the fitness of having such a memorial erected, and predicted that the Catholics of America, in any future emergency "guided by the unfailing light of eternal principles, will again, as ever before, stand valiantly or die gloriously for their nation's just defense of a sacred cause."

As depicted in this drawing, a Sister of Charity of Emmitsburg, Maryland, attends wounded soldiers at the General Hospital in Richmond, Virginia.

The Christian Commission in the Field

This wood engraving, taken from an 1864 edition of Harper's Week-ly, *shows volunteer members of the U.S. Christian Commission.*

Of great humane service was the work of the United States Christian Commission originated by the National Committee of the Young Men's Christian Association "to promote the spiritual good, intellectual improvement and social and physical comfort" of the soldiers. Lincoln remarked: "There is one association whose objects and motives I have never heard in any degree impugned or questioned; and that is the Christian Commission." It commanded the voluntary service, for periods of six weeks or more, of 4,859 men (and Sisters too) and distributed nearly three million dollars' worth of goods, as well as library books, Bibles, hymnbooks and magazines.

The heroic chaplains of North and

South have never quite received adequate recognition. One priest, however, continues to command the interest not only of historians but of poets as well — Father Abram Joseph Ryan of Mobile, Alabama. From youth he was disposed to the military; when the war began it was but natural for him to become involved. On the feast of the Purification, at age twenty-two, he joined the Confederate army. His bravery became a legend; on one occasion he was the only clergyman of any denomination who would enter Gratiot Prison at New Orleans to care for smallpox victims.

His devotion to the Confederacy found expression in poems of high quality. "The Conquered Banner" and "The Sword of

152

This life-size bronze of Father Abram Joseph Ryan is located in Ryan's Park, Mobile, Alabama. The statue's right hand has become shiny from being pressed by thousands of visitors.

while there wrote many Marian tributes. His book *A Crown for Our Queen* was a "month of Mary," thirty-one meditations based on instructions given to his beloved Children of Mary. For him Mary was "the human solo in Creation's Choir." The rosary was his constant source of consolation. He explained in "My Beads":

> For many and many a time, in grief,
> My weary fingers wandered round
> Thy circled chain, and always
> found
> In some Hail Mary sweet relief.

The war had taken thousands of young men away from their homes for the first

Robert E. Lee" won for him the title of "Poet of the Confederacy." He remained an unreconstructed rebel until 1878 when the Gulf States and Tennessee were ravaged by yellow fever. Then the generous response of the North in assisting its victims moved him to heartfelt expression of brotherly love in his poem "Reunion." in 1883 he went on a lecture tour which grossed over a million dollars, all of which he distributed to orphans, charitable institutions and churches impoverished by the war.

From 1870 to 1883 Father Ryan was pastor of St. Mary's Church at Mobile and

Shown here is the title page from A Crown for Our Queen. *This 1882 book by Father Ryan was a "month of Mary," containing thirty-one meditations for his Children of Mary.*

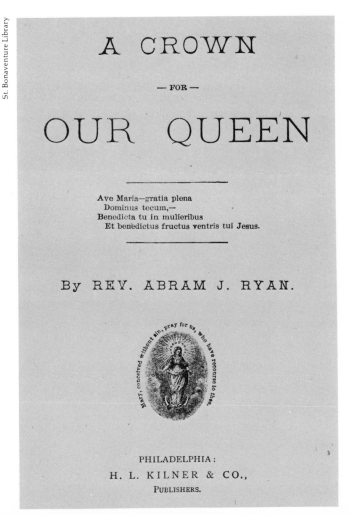

A CROWN

— FOR —

OUR QUEEN

Ave Maria—gratia plena
Dominus tecum,—
Benedicta tu in mulieribus
Et benedictus fructus ventris tui Jesus.

BY REV. ABRAM J. RYAN.

Mary, conceived without sin, pray for us, who have recourse to thee.

PHILADELPHIA:
H. L. KILNER & CO.,
PUBLISHERS.

Father de Smet With His Marian Banner Meets Sitting Bull, 1868

time and many of those who survived were restless and eager for more adventure. Responding to Horace Greeley's "Go west, young man," they found the glamour and excitement they craved. What they had not bargained for was danger.

On the high plains and in the Rocky Mountains alone were over two hundred thousand Indians who resented settlers fencing in lands and slaughtering buffalo. Attacks were many and bloody and the federal government tried to mediate, making promises which were never kept and treaties which were violated. Under such conditions one could not expect the Indians to remain passive.

The Sioux had sworn death to any white man falling within their power but re-

tained in their memory a high regard for the "Black Robes" who had brought the faith to their ancestors. For one such black robe they had a special feeling — Peter de Smet, a Belgian Jesuit. He was "the only white man who never talked to them with a forked tongue."

Father de Smet announced on June 1, 1868, that he was going to confer with the hostile Sioux to induce the chiefs to attend a conference with the government's peace commissioners. His Indian friends warned that such a venture would cost him his scalp, but Father de Smet was not deterred because "before a picture of the Blessed Virgin, Mother and Protector of all nations, six lamps are burning day and night during my absence [from St. Louis] and

154

before these lamps more than a thousand children implore heaven's protection for me."

He set out from Fort Rice in Dakota Territory carrying a banner with the Holy Name of Jesus on one side and a picture of Mary on the other. Sitting Bull and his warriors received him with great joy and prepared a conference at the confluence of the Yellowstone and Powder Rivers in east central Montana where the banner of Mary was prominently displayed.

Father de Smet "expressed the wish that this banner . . . might be for all a pledge of happiness and safety. . . . I recommended the tribe to the protection of Mary, Auxilium et Refugium Indianorum (Help and Refuge of Indians)."

He wrote in his journal: "I was moved to tears by the reception these pagan sons of the desert gave me." The conference re-sulted in complete confidence in De Smet's proposal. Chieftains were selected to accompany him to Fort Rice and from them a bearer was chosen to carry Mary's banner, the honor falling to a warrior covered with scars and distinguished for his exploits.

The party returned to Fort Rice on June 30 and made arrangements with the peace commissioners for a meeting with fifty thousand Indians on July 2, at which time the treaty of peace was signed. The government's commissioners expressed their indebtedness to Father de Smet in a lengthy letter which is now in the National Archives.

Holy Rosary Mission at Pine Ridge, South Dakota, became a part of American history in 1890 when Father John Jutz, S.J., tried unsuccessfully to negotiate between the Sioux and five hundred U.S. Army troops who had come there in antici-

Father de Smet and Sioux in Conference, 1868

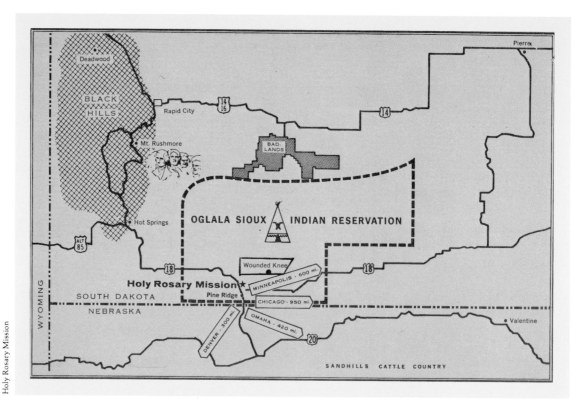

*Map of Southwest South Dakota Showing
Wounded Knee and Holy Rosary Mission*
Site of the battle of December 29, 1890, this area of the state
is famous for its Badlands, Black Hills and Mount Rushmore.

pation of an uprising among the Indians.

Custer's defeat at Little Big Horn had aroused the Sioux war spirit, and this was further intensified by the killing of Sitting Bull as he resisted arrest. Tension mounted when treaty promises were violated and expected rations curtailed. Refugees from Sitting Bull's camp reached Chief Big Foot on the Cheyenne River and, together with the impoverished braves and almost three hundred men and children, a retreat was begun to the Badlands and a return to Pine Ridge. They were intercepted by army troops at Wounded Knee and were promised safe conduct and fair treatment upon surrender of their weapons.

On the morning of December 29, while

156

soldiers were collecting the weapons, an Indian and a soldier struggled over a rifle which fired accidentally. At this first shot the soldiers opened fire, killing one hundred forty-six braves, women and children and wounding many, some of whom died later. Army casualties were twenty-five dead and thirty-nine wounded. The soldiers collected the Indian dead and threw them in a common grave. Priests and Sisters at the mission cared for the wounded and fed the starving survivors. Army historians have continually denied the accusation of "deliberate, intentional shooting of helpless persons."

Wounded Knee was again visited by unrest and death in 1973 when on Febru-

Buffalo Bill and Indian Friends

Shown fourth from right is Buffalo Bill Cody, last of the great scouts. He clasps the hands of two Indian friends. Many braves from Wounded Knee were included in his famous Wild West Shows.

Holy Rosary Mission, Pine Ridge, South Dakota, Established 1888

Chief Red Cloud lies buried on the hill by the school ground with braves who died during World War II at Okinawa, Omaha Beach, Cassino and Normandy.

ary 27 a group led by the American Indian Movement (A.I.M.) occupied the village, taking over the trading post and confronting government marshals and F.B.I. agents who had set up roadblocks around the area. Before the siege ended with an agreement on May 9, two Indians and two federal agents were wounded and two settlers killed.

Tourists previously had been coming for many summers to view the cemetery; their numbers have now increased with the publicity attendant on the A.I.M. siege.

The mission quietly continues its care of descendants of Red Cloud, Big Foot and their companions. With the increase in Indian population, greater than that of any other minority group in the nation, and with heightening Indian pride in their heritage, the reservation now has a broader significance than in the past in preserving the spiritual depth which has sustained the Indian through the years.

A three-year revolt of the Cubans against Spanish misrule had resulted in serious disturbances on the island, and the

The Wreck of the Battleship "Maine"

In this photograph, workers are shown preparing floating derricks designed to raise the ship in Havana Harbor where it sank following an explosion on February 15, 1898.

Cuba and the Wrecked Maine

Temporary Hospital for Casualties

This is the Convent of Mary Immaculate in Key West, Florida, where Sisters cared for soldiers wounded during the Spanish-American War.

American government, believing the lives and property of American citizens to be endangered, ordered the battleship *Maine* to Havana on January 24, 1898. A mysterious explosion the night of February 15 blew up the ship, killing two officers and two hundred sixty of her crew. Though responsibility could not be fixed upon anyone, war with Spain was declared on April 25.

Anticipating that declaration, the Sisters of the Holy Names of Jesus and Mary at Key West, Florida, offered their Convent of Mary Immaculate, as well as two schools and the services of their entire community, to assist in whatever capacity the government desired. In accepting the offer Commander William T. Sampson expressed his personal appreciation for the Sisters' "most generous and patriotic tender."

The convent and two schools for whites and blacks were turned into hospital wards where twenty-three nuns cared for over six hundred wounded and dying of the battles of Santiago and San Juan. Several Sisters, exhausted from their service, succumbed from a malaria attack. A Protestant chaplain termed their service "beautiful in its unselfishness," and Major W.C. Borden

159

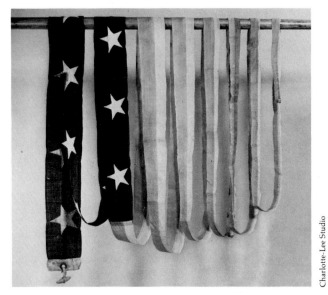

Charlotte-Lee Studio

Found floating in Havana Harbor after the explosion which sent the U.S.S. Maine to the bottom, this pennant was presented to the Convent of Mary Immaculate, Key West, where it is currently kept.

stated, "I am now convinced that the religious communities of your faith are the greatest thing in the world."

The Sisters of the Holy Names of Jesus and Mary had first come to Key West in 1868 and opened a mission in an abandoned army barracks. Their present build-

ing, erected in 1875, is relatively unchanged from the time of its war service, except for the addition of a new wing.

In a museum on the convent grounds are many mementos from the *Maine*, among them the oil-splattered and bloodstained pennant, thirty-nine feet in length and containing thirteen stars, found floating in the harbor after the explosion and recovered by the *U.S.S. Mangrove*, whose captain presented it to the convent.

The war with Spain ended with Admiral George Dewey's victory over the Spanish navy in the Battle of Manila and the subsequent capture of the city on August 13. On Dewey's triumphal return to the States, a flotilla of ships greeted his fleet in the Hudson River. As Dewey's flagship *Olympia* passed the schoolship *St. Mary's* (previously described), "the boys on the St. Mary's won his heart. He called for cheers for them."

Dewey's flagship Olympia *salutes the schoolship* St. Mary's. *This took place on September 29, 1898, when Admiral Dewey returned in triumph from the Battle of Manila.*

Help of Christians

THE FAMILY GROWS

1790-1900

Mary Help of Christians

Carved around 1860 by Matthias Biewer, a parishioner of St. Mary Help of Christians Church, Sullivan, Wisconsin, the Index of American Design terms this "one of the finest examples of native American woodcarving."

Help
of
Christians

To secure unity and uniformity in his diocese, Bishop John Carroll convoked a synod which met in Baltimore in November 1791. After its close he urged the faithful to a fervent devotion to Mary, reminding them that since she had been chosen special patroness of the diocese they were placed under her powerful protection "and it becomes your duty to be careful to deserve its continuance by a zealous imitation of her virtues and reliance on her motherly superintendence."

How well the faithful responded was soon obvious. To Mary they entrusted their first monastery, seminary, cathedral and churches. Though as Catholics they were in the minority on the Atlantic seaboard, their loyalty to Mary unified and strengthened their endeavors. Whenever a settlement was formed, a church would be built to guarantee stabilization, and the church would bear her name. Could any name be *more* Catholic? It is significant that even in unfriendly New England, Marian churches were the first to be erected in Rhode Island, Massachusetts and Vermont, the latter claiming not only its first church in her name but the second and third as well!

Nearing mid-century the Church's membership increased by a million immigrants — different in race, nationality, tradition. Unfamiliar with new customs, life-styles, the polyglot of languages, they were indeed strangers in a strange land. The problem facing the Church was to develop a measure of unity and control in the face of ethnic diversity, a problem somewhat solved by a bond of devotion to the Maternal Mother which slowly but surely emerged.

Many immigrants remained in the cities, but vast numbers moved out to rural areas — to farm or to work on railroads, canals and roads. Now would appear a veritable litany of Marian names, in mountains, rivers, towns — lyrical names found today in twenty-three of our states. Missionaries and diocesan priests, keeping pace with westward-moving populations on lonely plains or busy mining towns, would establish additional locales for Marian "firsts" in churches and schools. Newcomers would find themselves at the doorstep of descendants of early Spanish and French explorers and under the leaven of the One Mother become Americans all.

To time-honored European devotions would be added new expressions of love of Mary, inspired and inculcated in this land of freedom. The bishops, meeting in the Sixth Provincial Council in 1846, responded to the "pious desire then prevalent of paying special honor to Mary," by naming her Patroness of the United States.

American foundations of European religious orders made heroic sacrifices to take root in cities and wilderness; the Marian names of their houses indicate love and dependence on her intercession. How well they constructed these houses is evidenced by the number of churches and institutions included on the roster of the government's Historic American Buildings Survey and the National Register of Historic Places.

The complete story of missionary work among the Indians has been told only in bits and pieces. When the final record is assembled, it will bear the imprint of the endeavors made in the name of Mary, Auxilium et Refugium Indianorum, "Help and Refuge of Indians," as Father de Smet called her.

A country divided by civil war found Mary being invoked as healer and peacemaker. The story of her involvement is found in the section entitled "Virgin Militant." When plague, fire and flood came on the land, the prayers of intercession to Mary produced evidences of consolation which can only be termed "cause for wonder."

As the flow of immigrants increased, so too did the problems facing the Church. The scope of agencies of charity now had to expand in hospitals, orphanages, protective homes and care for the aged and infirm. Many such institutions were founded in the name of Mary who is invoked as Comforter of the Afflicted.

To list the events of the nineteenth century in strict chronology is not a simple matter. The country's simultaneous expansion in widely separated areas requires the historian to dovetail events as best he can. The problem is simplified, however, if one follows the single golden thread unifying the American design: That thread is Mary.

The year 1790 was one of great beginnings: Washington's presidency marked the practical start of constitutional government in this country and the future held much promise for the citizens of the new republic. Seaports, large and small, were the busiest of places with commerce of the area and travelers coming and going.

Four women disembarking at Port Tobacco in southern Maryland occasioned little comment; had they been clothed in religious garb the gossip would have flown fast. They were Discalced Carmelites from Belgium, arriving to establish the nation's first contemplative monastic community for women, devoted to prayer for the salvation of souls. Three were natives of Maryland who had trained at the English convent at Hoogstraet, Antwerp, where the chaplain was also a Marylander, Charles Neale, S.J. He was now accompanying the group to Charles County. Neale was one of five brothers all of whom became priests, descendants of a family which had come to St. Marys City.

Father Neale had exhausted personal resources in obtaining land for the monastery, exchanging his ancestral home, plus a substantial cash bonus, for eight hundred seventy acres of land on the old Georgetown Road, twenty-eight miles from Washington. The nuns' first shelter was an unfinished house, unplastered and unsealed; during the first winter they had to remove the snow from their beds.

Gradually improvements were made, new buildings added. The *Laity's Directory* of 1822, listing the community, described "the happiness enjoyed by these truly respectable ladies, who have excluded themselves from society to enjoy in retirement that peace which the world cannot give, which is a foretaste of the happiness of heaven." Bishop John Carroll earlier had termed the community "a safeguard for the preservation of the diocese."

The nuns sustained themselves by rais-

Founded at Port Tobacco, Maryland, in 1790, the Discalced Carmelite Monastery, the country's first contemplative monastic community for women, is captured in this line drawing.

ing sheep and growing crops of wheat, corn and tobacco. By 1831 deterioration of the buildings, legal difficulties over property titles, and financial losses due to Port Tobacco's demise as a seaport, occasioned the nuns' removal to Baltimore. A century would pass before the monastery's site was

Maryland State Marker Commemorating Monastery's History

rediscovered, the land purchased and restoration begun. A new chapel was added, dedicated to Our Lady of Mount Carmel. A Maryland state marker at the shrine gives the highlights of its history.

The Port Tobacco nuns were members of the Discalced Carmelites founded in 1562 by St. Teresa of Avila and St. John of the Cross. Their community was an offshoot of the Carmelite order named for Mount Carmel in Palestine where over eleven hundred Crusaders lived as hermits. They had built a chapel honoring Mary

Mrs. J. Garesche Ord

This photograph of the Discalced Carmelite Monastery, Port Tobacco, Maryland, shows how it was restored in 1937. A recent chapel dedicated to Our Lady of Mount Carmel (not shown) is located at left.

and became her "firstborn spiritual sons." Saracen victories forced their migration to Europe where in 1247 the Order of the Blessed Virgin Mary of Mount Carmel (as now called) received renewed papal approval. The order's superior general, St. Simon Stock, soon introduced the Brown Scapular of Our Lady as a means of promoting Marian devotion. Sixty-five communities of Discalced Carmelites in thirty-three states trace their foundation, directly or indirectly, to the courageous women of Port Tobacco.

Greatest of the problems facing John Carroll as first bishop of the Catholic Church in the United States was the scarcity of priests to meet the demand, a demand which could not depend on the uncertain supply from Europe. While in England he received, following his consecration, a generous offer from the Society of the Priests of St. Sulpice to found a seminary in America.

The Sulpicians had been one of the leaders in training priests for France and their offer was promptly accepted. In announcing their coming Bishop Carroll wrote:

"I propose fixing them very near to my own home, the Cathedral of Baltimore, that they may be, as it were, the clergy of the church and contribute to the dignity of divine worship. This is a great and auspicious event for our diocese, but it is a melancholy reflection, that we owe so great a blessing to the lamentable catastrophe in France [the Revolution]."

The Sulpicians purchased "One Mile Tavern" in Baltimore and in a second-floor room, fitted up as a chapel dedicated to Mary, the seminary began with Mass on July 20, 1791. The first ordination was that of Stephen T. Badin, future apostle of the Church in Kentucky, followed by that of Prince Gallitzin who would become the glory of Pennsylvania. As the seminary expanded, St. Mary's College was added which in a relatively short time gained such prominence as to be granted the charter of university by the state. At St. Mary's the Third Plenary Council drew up the Baltimore catechism.

St. Mary's was a major seminary with two years of philosophy studies and four years of theology, until the theology section was moved in 1927 to Roland Park, a north Baltimore neighborhood. Before the split, St. Mary's housed more than four hundred students for the priesthood; af-

terward it had about two hundred philosophy (senior college) students a year until its closing in 1969.

Attempts to interest private developers and city agencies in making use of the century-old four-story building brought no response. In 1973 the site was sold to the City of Baltimore and the building demolished to make room for a park. Not included in the sale were the historic Seminary Chapel, St. Elizabeth Seton's house, and the convent building that once housed nuns who had served the seminarians.

The Seminary Chapel is the first Gothic Revival church built in the United States. It was dedicated to Mary under the title Beata Virgo Maria Presentata in Templo (the Presentation of the Blessed Virgin Mary in the Temple). It was built in 1807-1808 by Maximilian Godefroy, captain in the Royal Engineers of Louis XVI, who had come to this country in 1805 and who taught "architecture, drawing and fortification" to the seminarians. Into the chapel's construction went two hundred thousand bricks originally intended for the building of the cathedral but put aside when cathedral sketches grew in number, requiring that stone be used.

Bishop Carroll blessed the chapel and celebrated the first Pontifical Mass on June 16, 1808. The basement became a place of worship for Negro French Catholics who had fled Santo Domingo during the 1791-1803 revolt of Toussaint L'Ouverture. It was also used as a school by St. Elizabeth Seton.

The chapel today lacks the steeple, considered unsafe in 1916 and removed. The structure has acquired the particular aura of age and spirituality that marks it a completely original and unique place of worship. It is maintained by the Sulpicians, used only on special occasions.

The year 1791 witnessed another record in Church history with the opening of an academy at "George Town, Patowmack

River," Maryland, for students of all faiths. The academy developed into the first Catholic college and became headquarters and novitiate for the Jesuits when their order was restored in 1805. At Georgetown originated the establishment of the first college Sodality of the Blessed Virgin and the observance of May devotions in her honor.

The great sodality movement had grown out of Father John Leunis's determination to improve world conditions. Christian Europe in 1563 faced renewed Muslim attacks and the Protestant revolt was in full swing. The Eucharistic Christ and Mary were being exiled from England, the Scandinavia Peninsula, parts of the Netherlands, Germany and France. In that year Father Leunis, teacher at the Jesuit College at Rome, proposed to a group of students that they consecrate themselves to Mary under the twofold purpose of continual advance in apostolic holiness and progressive proficiency in studies, calling their group *sodalitas* (sodality). They were divided into twelve groups, each headed by a sodalist guiding their conduct and studies, all the groups directed by a prefect who answered to a priest-director.

After completing their studies, the original founders initiated sodalities wherever they went. In ten years' time sodalities could be found in twenty-two cities of Italy, France, Spain and Portugal. The movement received canonical status and was enlarged to include divisions for high-school students, collegians and lay persons. On this continent sodalities were established as early as 1647 among the Hurons in Canada.

In 1730 the Ursulines established a sodality for girls and women at New Orleans (see section entitled "Notre Dame") and in that same city one for workingmen was set up six years later. The sodality at Georgetown was the first for collegians; the exact date of founding is uncertain, but it was prior to 1799. In 1830 Father Fenwick, then in charge of the sodality, instituted the custom of May devotions, holding evening services during the entire month of May. Churches and convents outside the college began similar devotions and today they are widespread.

In 1953 the World Federation of Sodalities of Our Lady was established. Today these sodalities are embraced in Christian Life Communities. Composed of groups of men and women, adults and the young, they have joined with other persons involved in living their full Christian vocation and commitment in the world. The governing principles and operating norms of sodalities, revised in the spirit of documents of the Second Vatican Council, were promulgated and approved by Pope Paul VI in 1971. The spiritual exercises of St. Ignatius remain a specific source and characteristic of the spirituality of the movement. Christian Life Communities can be found in forty-two countries; the U.S. Federation is composed of approximately one hundred fifty such communities.

In Bishop Carroll's first pastoral letter he called attention to the advantages of a Catholic education. Naturally responsive was the president of Georgetown, Father Leonard J. Neale. He persuaded "Three Pious Ladies" to found "The Young Ladies Academy at the Convent of the Visitation" at Georgetown. The school was begun in 1799, on the feast of the Nativity of St. John the Baptist, a singularly appropriate day in view of the community's affiliation in 1816 with the Order of the Visitation of France.

Today one can view a quaint "roll call" containing the name of every Sister, living or dead, who belonged to the community from 1799 to 1825, with date of birth (or death if deceased) and kind of work assigned to her. The first name is Alice Teresa Lalor, who with Mrs. Maria Sharpe and Mrs. Maria McDermott, were the found-

This is "One Mile Tavern," Baltimore, Maryland, where the first St. Mary's Seminary was begun in 1791. The tavern was so named for being one mile from the docks of Old Baltimore and a stopping place for Washington-bound coaches.

St. Mary's Seminary and University, School of Theology, Roland Park, Maryland, was built in 1927.

ing ladies referred to. Of much significance is the name of Jerusha Mary Augustine Barber, wife of Dr. Virgil Barber, founder of Catholicism in New Hampshire (described later). The convert daughter of Commodore John Paul Jones (Williamina Stanislaus Jones) is included, as well as the convert daughter of General Winfield Scott of War of 1812 fame.

Georgetown Visitation Convent today is a college preparatory and junior college; among its students are fifth-generation descendants of its first graduates.

Catholic education would further advance in the founding in 1808 of Mount St. Mary's, Emmitsburg, Maryland, in a minor seminary which would develop into a college and full seminary. The "Mount" referred to the Mountain of Mary, the name given to a lower range of the Blue Ridge Mountains by Maryland Catholics coming in 1729 to escape the religious intolerance of St. Marys City.

Father John Dubois, a French Sulpician, came to the area as pastor of Frederick which included the Mount. He built St.

Chapel of St. Mary's Seminary, Baltimore, Erected in 1807-1808
The chapel, listed as a national historic landmark, is cruciform in shape, eighty feet in length and fifty in width. Its appearance today is relatively unchanged, lacking only the steeple which was considered unsafe and subsequently removed in 1916.

Mary's Church in 1805 and in its tower placed a large statue. On the terrace below he began Mount St. Mary's College and Seminary. One day while climbing the lower range he came on a clearing in whose center was a mound shaded by the branches of an ancient oak. Streams of water rushing down the mountainside, and flowing on both sides of this mount, had gradually washed out the earth beneath the tree's great roots, forming a recess or grotto underneath the trunk. At this grotto Father Dubois placed a cross and in that act began the history of today's oldest American Grotto of Lourdes.

Elizabeth Seton and a little band of pioneer Sisters had come to the Mount in 1809 and founded the Sisters of Charity and the first free parochial school in the country. One of the community's spiritual directors and a devoted friend was the Sulpician, Simon Gabriel Bruté, later first bishop of Vincennes, Indiana. Bruté enlarged and improved the grotto, marking

171

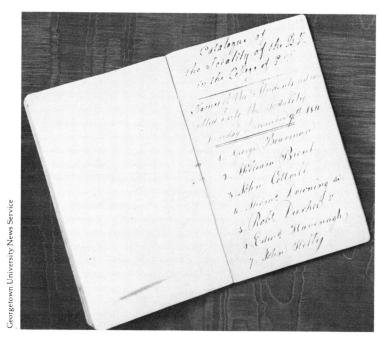

Earliest Extant Document of First College Sodality of the Blessed Virgin

The sodality was founded at Georgetown College prior to 1799.

out paths which would later be made memorable by annual processions. When the oak tree finally rotted away, a stone dam was built to protect the grotto below.

In 1875 a seminarian was reading of Mary's appearance to Bernadette Soubirous at Lourdes, France, and was struck by the similarity of the Mount's grotto to that of Lourdes. He conceived the idea of establishing a similar shrine and, as the idea developed, many improvements were made, a new chapel built, a campanile added. In 1965 the shrine was declared a public oratory. The Maryland State Roads Commission estimates that twenty thousand visitors come monthly between April and November.

The Marian Center at Emmitsburg sends out thousands of scapulars each week. The scapular had been recommended in 1840 by Mary to Sister Justine Bisqueyburu, a Daughter of Charity. Its simple design shows Mary on one side, and on the reverse a pierced flaming heart surrounded by the words "Immaculate Heart of Mary, pray for us now and at the hour of our death."

Bishop Carroll's courage and prudence were effecting steady progress in the affairs of the young Church. Baltimore had been selected as the first diocese, a choice dictated by the American clergy themselves "because this town situate in Maryland, which province the greater part of the priests and faithful inhabit, appeared the most conveniently placed for intercourse with the other States, and because from this province Catholic religion and faith had been propagated into the others."

Acadian French, expelled by the British from Nova Scotia, settled in Baltimore in the winter of 1756-1757 and formed the body of the town's first Catholic congregation. They were served by Jesuits from

This early print shows the Visitation Convent and Young Ladies Academy, Georgetown, Washington, D.C.

nearby Maryland and Pennsylvania missions. Services were held in a two-story brick residence, twenty-five by thirty feet, known as a "mass House," the only kind of church permitted Catholics under Maryland law from the Puritan seizure of the colony until after the Revolution. This simple building came to be called St. Peter's and served as the temporary cathedral and residence of Bishop Carroll after his consecration in England.

In 1805 a more suitable site north of St. Peter's was chosen on which to erect a new cathedral. A non-Catholic, Benjamin Henry Latrobe (designer of the south wing of the nation's Capitol), designed the cathedral free of charge. Since the Roman architecture chosen afforded no position for a belfry, Latrobe employed the Russo-

Roster of Visitation Community in 1825

This memorial, rising one hundred twenty feet, located on the site of St. Mary's "Old Church on the Hill," which was built in 1805, is known as the Pangborn Memorial Campanile.

Built in 1805, St. Mary's Church, Emmitsburg, served the area until 1913. A statue of Mary is visible in the tower.

174

This is Mount St. Mary's College and Seminary, Emmitsburg, Maryland, today. The Pangborn Memorial Campanile is seen in the distance.

Byzantine bell-shaped towers similar to those on the Cathedral of the Assumption in Moscow. The interior duplicated the Chapel of Lulworth Castle, England, where Bishop Carroll had been consecrated. Funds for construction were realized from the receipts of two lotteries and the auctioning of pews, as well as donations from the faithful. Bishop Carroll even asked Napoleon Bonaparte, then first consul of France, for assistance.

The Mother Shrine of Our Lady of Lourdes in the United States, Emmitsburg

Basilica of the Assumption, 1806-1821
—Nation's First Cathedral

Located in Baltimore, Maryland, it ceased being a metropolitan ca-
thedral (though it was granted the dignity of being a perpetual co-
cathedral) when the new Cathedral of Mary Our Queen was dedicat-
ed in 1959. It is listed in the Historic American Buildings Survey.

Beneath the cathedral's altar lie eight of Baltimore's archbishops (including Carroll and Gibbons). In its sanctuary more than thirty bishops and two thousand priests have received their anointing. (In 1937 it was named a basilica.)

At one corner of the basilica grounds is a majestic elm, known as the Rochambeau Elm. The D.A.R. marker at its base commemorates not only the tree's antiquity but the growth of "Baltimore Towne," a Revo-

lutionary battle and its hero, and Mary's Basilica. The Mass it refers to had been ordered by the king of France and sung by Rochambeau's Irish chaplain.

The priesthood of the young Church would have the services of an extraordinary personality in the second priest ordained at St. Mary's Seminary — Demetrius Augustine Gallitzin. Following brief service in Maryland and Conewago, Pennsylvania, he moved westward to the Al-

Joseph F. Siwak

*"Rochambeau Elm" on Grounds of Basilica
of the Assumption, Baltimore*

*D.A.R. Marker Commemorating
the Growth of "Baltimore Towne"
on Grounds of Basilica
of the Assumption*

Joseph F. Siwak

THIS ELM HAS WATCHED THE GROWTH OF "BALTIMORE TOWNE" FOR OVER
100 YEARS, ON FORMER ESTATE OF JOHN EAGER HOWARD, REVOLUTIONARY
AND 1812 OFFICER AND FIFTH GOVERNOR OF MARYLAND. HERE, IN
"HOWARD'S WOODS". COUNT DE ROCHAMBEAU'S TROOPS CAMPED, 1782,
ERECTING AN ALTAR FOR MASS. JAMES, CARDINAL GIBBONS, LIVED HERE,
1877 – 1921, – RESTING, NOW, BENEATH CATHEDRAL ALTAR. (CORNER STONE
LAID, 1806). FAMOUS WORLD VISITORS (CHURCH AND STATE), AND GENERA-
TIONS OF SOLDIERS HAVE PASSED BENEATH THESE PROTECTING
BRANCHES.

GEORGE WASHINGTON BICENTENNIAL MARKER
ERECTED BY WASHINGTON CUSTIS CHAPTER, MD. D.A.R.
1732 – 1932

legheny Mountains where Catholics resided at McGuire's Settlement in Cambria County. He introduced himself simply as Father Smith to conceal his identity as a Russian prince.

Love of Mary prompted naming the colony Loretto in honor of the Holy House of Our Lady of Nazareth enshrined at Loreto, Italy. He encouraged migration by purchasing land and offering it to settlers at low cost, a practice which cost him his fortune and a good part of his mother's as well. He built storehouses for food, medical supplies, tools, farm implements and other basic necessities. He encouraged the building of a tannery, sawmill, gristmill, the raising of cattle, anything which would improve the economy of his people.

Mindful of their need of relaxation from the rigors of pioneer life, he taught the men swordsmanship, and from his trips to the city brought back ribbons and novelties for the women. In 1832 he built a chapel house which also served as his residence and as a home for the many orphans he cared for through the years. Here he lived the last eight years of his life and was buried nearby. On the occasion of the centenary of the town of Loretto in 1899, Charles M. Schwab, founder of Bethlehem Steel Corporation, gave the funds for building St. Michael's Church. At its entrance stands a bronze statue of Gallitzin.

The mounting burdens of the vast territory under Carroll's care compelled him to petition Pius VII for a division of his diocese. Accordingly in 1808 Baltimore was elevated to the rank of Archiepiscopal See and four dioceses created: Boston, New York, Philadelphia and Bardstown (Kentucky). Boston would include all New England and be under the jurisdiction of the saintly John Louis Cheverus, who with Father Francis Montignon had laid a solid foundation for the area's Catholicity.

In Massachusetts, the great Yankee seaport of Salem included Catholic Corsican, Portuguese, Italian, French, Irish and Canadian. These were visited as early as May 1790 by Father John Thayer. He had been a former Congregational minister and chaplain to the governor, and now was the first native New Englander ordained a priest. On one visit he left "catechisms, prayer manuals and other articles" to sustain his people's faith until he could return. Among the "other articles" were twenty-seven rosaries acknowledging his love of Mary which he considered one of the "fruitful blessings" of his newly found faith.

In 1815 a Mr. Newport (English captive of the War of 1812) on his liberation from Dartmouth Prison returned to his home in Salem "and in the fervor of his zeal commenced collecting from house to house, among the little congregation of Catholics, funds for the erection of a small church for their mutual accommodation." Land was purchased by Bishop Cheverus on September 8, 1820, and on it St. Mary's was erected a year later. The parish eventually was called Immaculae Conception, the name it bears today.

The "unfailing and winning courtesy" of Montignon and Cheverus did much to break down New England prejudice and effect conversions so necessary for Church growth. An Episcopalian minister, Daniel Barber of New Hampshire, consulted Cheverus about Catholicism and took home to Claremont several books which became the starting point for study by his son, Virgil, also an Episcopalian minister.

Virgil and his entire family were received into the Church in 1816. For support he opened a private school in which his wife, Jerusha, helped, but his call to the priesthood became so persistent that negotiations were begun for the heroic separation of husband and wife. Mrs. Barber and an older daughter took up residence at the Visitation convent in Georgetown and eventually joined the order. A son, Samuel, was placed in a boarding school at Georgetown and later became a Jesuit. Two younger daughters joined the Ursulines in Quebec. While Virgil Barber was completing preparations for the priesthood, his father, mother, sister (Mrs. Noah Tyler) and a niece came into the Church.

Virgil Barber was ordained a Jesuit in 1822 and took up residence in Claremont at the family homestead where he conducted services for a handful of converts. Through the generosity of Canadian Catholics, funds were secured for building St. Mary's Church in 1824, the second floor of which served as the classroom of Claremont Academy, first Catholic school for boys in New England. Father Barber, assisted by his father, instructed pupils of many denominations who came from a distance of ten to fifteen miles and had to lodge in the Barber homestead adjoining the church. One pupil was his nephew, William Tyler, who became the first bishop of the Diocese of Hartford in 1844.

Catholics in Rhode Island had enjoyed relative freedom from religious intolerance, but their small and widely scattered groups were without a church until St. Mary's was built in Pawtucket in 1829. Benedict J. Fenwick, S.J., then bishop of Boston, visited Providence in 1828 and "waited upon David Wilkinson, Esq. of Pawtucket, and acknowledged his indebtedness for his Christian-like spirit and generous good feeling in presenting the Catholics with a desirable lot whereon to build a church."

On this lot of one hundred twenty-five square feet a simple frame structure was erected the year following and named St. Mary's, first Catholic church in Rhode Island. It served until 1885 when torn down and on the site the present church built in 1887. In 1854 when the dogma of the Immaculate Conception was promulgated, the church's title was changed to the Church of the Immaculate Conception of

178

Rhode Island. Today it is known simply as St. Mary's.

Maine traces its Marian devotion to 1646 with the Mission of the Assumption on the Kennebec and Our Lady of Holy Help on the Penobscot (see section entitled "Notre Dame"). Through the years, that devotion was sustained by the ministrations of missionaries, chiefly Jesuit, of whom one — Sebastian Rale — would give his life in 1724. For half a century the Indian tribes were without regularly appointed clergy until in 1792 Bishop Carroll sent Father Francis Ciquard, to be followed by John Louis Cheverus, later bishop of Boston.

When Jesuits were again sent into the area, the zealous Eugene Vetromile's coming in the 1840s would be an occasion for rejoicing. Vetromile from childhood had the one desire of converting the Indians and for the next quarter century would live among the Abenaki and become a profound student of their language. In 1856 he compiled a perfect gem of a book called *Indian Good Book*, in which the rosary was fully explained for the Penobscot, Passamaquoddy, St. John's, Micmac and other Abenaki tribes. Of their zeal he wrote:

"You cannot find house or wigwam without a picture or image of Our Lady. I have never met an Indian who did not wear a medal, a Rosary, or a Scapular. The first prayer which parents teach their children is the 'Malie Kitalamikol, Hail Mary.'"

Vermont's Catholicity began in 1609 with Champlain's ascendency of the St. Lawrence and entering the lake which now bears his name. On an island in that lake (now Grand Isle) the Sieur de la Motte in 1666 built Fort St. Anne which became an important post in the Colonial Wars when Vermont was the gateway through which contending forces advanced.

East from the island on the mainland the Jesuits built a mission near what is now

Swanton. It became the region's oldest and largest Indian settlement lasting until 1775. Swanton is remembered as the home of General Ethan Allen of Green Mountain Boys fame. His daughter Fanny merited a place in Catholic history by her conversion to Catholicism and profession as a Hospital Sister at Hotel-Dieu, Montreal, thereby becoming New England's first nun.

Swanton's early Marian history traced to the formation of the parish of the Nativity of the Blessed Virgin, formed by Canadians leaving their homeland to avoid involvement in the Papineau Rebellion. The parish eventually came under the care of the Society of St. Edmund, whose subtitle is Oblates of Mary and the Sacred Heart.

Irish laborers and their families settling in Vermont cities in large numbers required priests for their spiritual needs. Those in Burlington were served by a

Pennsylvania Historical and
Museum Commission

This highway marker in Loretto, Pennsylvania, commemorates Prince Gallitzin. The name Loretto derives from the Holy House of Our Lady of Nazareth enshrined at Loreto, Italy, in 1294.

priest from Quebec until Bishop Benedict Fenwick, in charge of the Diocese of Boston which then included all New England,

Prince Gallitzin Chapel House, Loretto, Pennsylvania

Here are his altar (encased in stone), chalice, Mass book, altar cloths, lavabo dish, relic of the True Cross, ancient crucifix carved in wood, confessional chair and other mementos.

Prince Gallitzin Chapel House

Walsh: Origin of the Catholic Church in Salem

First Marian Church in New England — St. Mary's, Salem, Massachusetts, 1821

sent Father James Fitton into the Burlington area. Fitton reported on the friendly reception received, even by Protestants. He was succeeded by Jeremiah O'Callaghan who for fifty-six years discharged his laborious duties "with cheerful fidelity."

O'Callaghan had been given five acres of land on the outskirts of Burlington, a gift from a wealthy Protestant, Colonel Archibald Hyde, later a convert. On this land St. Mary's Church was built in 1832. It had a short life. In 1838 it became the target of a Nativist attack, set on fire by "a small number of men, low shopkeepers, and even . . . some college students." Public meetings of protest and investigations failed to reveal the guilty.

A second St. Mary's was built in 1841 on a more central location. To this church in 1853 came Louis de Goesbriand as first bishop of Burlington. His crosier, with a figure of Mary, testified to his love of her.

180

Entries in his diary on her feast days reveal his faith in her intercession:

"*December 8, 1855:* The effects of these exercises have been unexpectedly profitable to the welfare of the Congregation.

"*March 26, 1856:* Attendance to Church during holy week remarkably good. We continue to feel the effect of the Protection of our Immaculate Mother."

By 1859 the cathedral had become too small for the congregation and a third edifice begun in 1862. Many men of the parish had enlisted in the Union army and the scarcity of laborers delayed completion until 1867. On December 8 of that year it was dedicated to the Immaculate Conception. The statue of Mary on the great tower was the personal gift of De Goesbriand's successor, Bishop John S. Michaud. The statue was saved in the fire which destroyed the cathedral in 1972. Undaunted, the Catholics of Burlington began plans for a new cathedral which was dedicated in 1977.

Connecticut, geographically last of the New England states, was slow in shedding its intolerance of Catholics. The earliest record of services being held is in 1813

St. Mary's Church and Claremont Academy, New Hampshire, built in 1824, is credited with being the first Catholic school for boys in New England.

De Goesbriand: Catholic Memoirs of Vermont and New Hampshire

The Church of the Immaculate Conception of Rhode Island in Pawtucket, Rhode Island, was built in 1887 on the site of the first Catholic church building in the state.

when Bishop Cheverus said Mass for the first time in New Haven at a house on York Street, the residence of a teacher of French at Yale College. A Catholic, writing his friend in 1829, provides an interesting picture of conditions:

"When we heard that a church had been purchased at Hartford [thirty-four miles distant!] and was about to have a priest, we were delighted. This appointment gave us an opportunity of having Mass at New Haven about once in three months, and happy we then were for so great a privilege."

Holy Trinity was the Hartford church referred to and the priest coming to New Haven was Father James McDermot, "a staunch soul if ever there was one," as a New Havener attests. One Christmas Eve, Father McDermot was long overdue to offer Midnight Mass. Several parishioners determined to go and see if they might meet him.

"We did so, and met him on the road, about four miles outside of New Haven.

The sleighing from Hartford had been good part of the way and then failed, till nothing remained but bare ground, and his horse gave out . . . and the good priest, not wishing to disappoint us, determined to walk the rest of the way. . . . He had his valise on his shoulders. The walking being rough and frozen, his shoes were nearly worn out, and when he arrived that night he was scarcely able to preach, though he did so at the end of Mass, after which we secured a conveyance to leave him where he had left his horse, for he had to return to say another Mass at Hartford the same day."

In 1834 Father McDermot built a church in New Haven for his faithful people, two hundred in all. The edifice was described as the most beautiful little Gothic church in all New England; it bore the name of Christ Church. In 1848 it was totally destroyed by fire. A brick building was then purchased from the Congregationalists to become St. Mary's. As the parish grew, plans were made for a new and larger building. Chosen for the site was historic Hillhouse Avenue, named for

The Rosary Explained in Father Vetromile's Indian Good Book, Maine, 1856

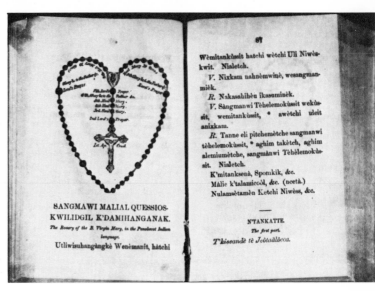

James Hillhouse, treasurer of Yale University in colonial times, active in the Revolution, and Federalist member of Congress. On a wide, beautiful tree-lined avenue the second St. Mary's was built and dedicated in 1874.

At St. Mary's in 1882 occurred the founding of an organization which proved of inestimable service to the Catholic Church. The assistant pastor, Father Michael J. McGivney, in his eagerness to promote the welfare of the men of the parish, organized a fraternal benefit society, the Knights of Columbus. The founding occurred on February 2, feast of the Purification, and its incorporation by the General Assembly of the State of Connecticut took place the following March 29.

Since inception the Knights have been champions of Mary. The organization provided a million dollars for the construction and erection of the Knights Tower (the bell tower or campanile) of the National Shrine of the Immaculate Conception. In 1976 its

Figure of Mary in Crosier of Louis de Goesbriand, Vermont's First Bishop

This is the present Cathedral of the Immaculate Conception, Burlington. It was destroyed by fire in 1972 and rebuilt in 1977.

This replaced the first St. Mary's Cathedral, Burlington, Vermont, erected in 1832 and destroyed by Nativists in 1838.

182

St. Mary's Church, New Haven, Connecticut, 1874
Adjacent to it is the priory of the Dominicans who have administered here since 1886.

membership totaled 1.2 million Catholic men in the United States, Canada, Mexico, the Philippines, Puerto Rico, Guatemala, Panama, Cuba, Guam and the Virgin Islands. It supports educational programs, charitable and beneficent causes, promotes the Catholic faith, and provides care for the sick and needy. Pope Paul told the society's board of directors that "the glory of the Knights of Columbus is not based on humanitarian works alone. Even more ad-

mirable has been your insistence upon the supremacy of God and your fidelity to the Vicar of Christ."

When Bardstown, Kentucky, was created a diocese under the Archiepiscopal See of Baltimore, it had already been the center of Catholic activity west of the Alleghenies. Priests of courage and vision, working out of Bardstown, had been laying the groundwork for a hierarchical organization which would reach west to Iowa in

183

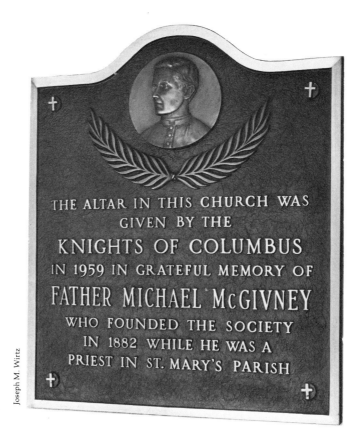

*Plaque in St. Mary's, New Haven, Commemorating
Founding of Knights of Columbus, 1882*

thirty years. Bardstown's second bishop, Stephen T. Badin, was the first priest ordained by Bishop Carroll. Along with Flaget and Bruté he was a product of the French Revolution and it was but natural for him to extend an invitation to religious orders forced out of France by that Revolution to come to America to fill the great need for priests.

A group of Trappists answered the call and settled in Kentucky. Fire destroyed their first monastery in 1809 and forced their removal to Illinois; here they built Notre Dame du Bon Secours (Our Lady of Good Counsel) on an Indian mound. The mound had been erected by aborigines as foundations or understructures for public buildings and temples and as burial grounds. The Trappists planted wheat on one surface of the mound and cultivated a vegetable garden on the step or apron, intending eventually that the topmost surface be the site for a permanent abbey.

At their log cabin monastery they educated the Indians of the area and, in an attempt to secure a school for them, their abbot went to Washington to confer with a senatorial committee to secure title to lands for the school's support. The monks made many improvements, introduced a good breed of cattle, were the first to discover coal in the bluffs east of the mound, and even conducted a watchmaking establishment. During the War of 1812 they helped defend the border against British-led Indian attacks. Crop failures and cholera

Harper's Magazine (May 11, 1860)

This is an 1860 sketch of Monks Mound, East St. Louis, Illinois. The mound, constructed by Indians, was chosen by the Trappist monks as the site for their monastery which they erected in 1809.

This diagrammatic sketch shows how the mound may have originally appeared. Largest earthwork in the world, it is one thousand by seven hundred twenty feet and rises to a height of one hundred feet. The base covers sixteen acres, three times more extensive than the Egyptian pyramid of Cheops.

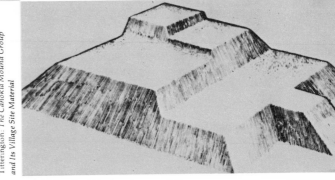

Titterington: The Cahokia Mound Group and Its Village Site Material

forced the monastery's closing and the group eventually returned to France. Their work is not forgotten, however, for the mound bears the name Monks Mound, and is a part of the Cahokia Mounds State Park, East St. Louis.

Another group of Trappists founded in 1848 their first permanent monastery southeast of Bardstown, calling it Our Lady of Gethsemani. West of the Mississippi their first establishment was founded in 1849, Our Lady of New Melleray at Dubuque, Iowa (described later).

Bishop Stephen Badin was blessed by the assistance of Charles Nerinckx, a remarkable Belgian priest who had fled Europe during the French Revolution. On coming to the United States he prepared for mission work by mastering the English language in four months! On a visit to scattered Catholics in Kentucky he found children at Hardin's Creek being taught catechism by Mary Rhodes, a visitor from Maryland. Realizing her great zeal, he persuaded her to enlist the help of several acquaintances in forming a religious order which he named Friends of Mary at the Foot of the Cross, popularly known as Sisters of Loretto. Within the first ten years of its existence eight hundred young ladies were prepared for Holy Communion.

Preparing to go to Europe in 1820, Father Nerinckx drew up his last will and wish for the young community. In this will he indicated his design for the seal of the order, consisting of the letter M surmount-

Museum of Fine Arts, Boston

This rare etching shows the first purely American order of Sisters having no European foundation. Plan of buildings for "Little Loretto," Kentucky, was designed by Father Charles Nerinckx.

The medallion at left gives Father Nerinckx's design of the seal of the Order of the Sisters of Loretto, showing a marked similarity to the medallion at right, the Miraculous Medal described by Mary in her appearance to Catherine Labouré.

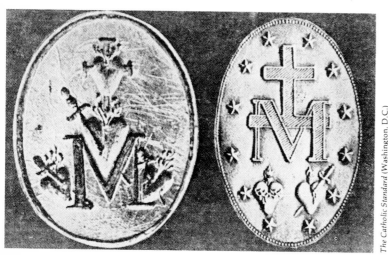

The Catholic Standard (Washington, D.C.)

ed by a cross. On the cross was a sword-pierced heart and beneath it two hearts in a diamond-shaped outline. Father Nerinckx had a metal seal made from the design and it is carefully preserved in the society's general archives in Kentucky. The seal bears a remarkable resemblance to the Miraculous Medal which the Virgin described to Catherine Labouré when she appeared to her in 1830, this being ten years after Father Nerinckx's design.

In the early 1800s the Catholic press in America was represented by numerous journals, short-lived but effective. Some, more political than religious in content, carried such nationalistic names as *Shamrock*, *Erin* and the *Globe and Emerald*. The *Truth Teller* of New York, begun in 1825, continued for thirty years to promote and defend the faith, as did the country's first Catholic newspaper, *United States Catholic Miscellany*, founded by Bishop John England in 1822.

Leading Catholic publisher of the time was Bernard Dornin of Philadelphia, noted for his vigorous writing and editing. It required deep faith, and not a little courage, for him to bring out the first American book entirely devoted to Mary, *The Imitation of the Blessed Virgin*. This was translated from the French of a book composed in 1588 by Francisco Arias, a Spanish Jesuit. Arias had planned the book after the fifteenth-century *Imitation of Christ* by Thomas à Kempis, the book of which George Eliot wrote: "It works miracles ... turning bitter waters into sweetness."

The first American Marian book enjoyed sufficient popularity to warrant a second printing by Fielding Lucas of Baltimore about 1830. Only two copies of this rare book exist today, both in the same building in Washington, D.C. — Georgetown University Library and Woodstock Library.

"Trusteemania" was but one of the Church's growing pains. Under the trustee system congregations were incorporated under the laws of the respective states and management of property and funds placed in the hands of elected lay trustees, many of whom proved to be ambitious meddlers. The Diocese of Philadelphia, which embraced Pennsylvania, Delaware and western New Jersey, experienced such serious trustee trouble as to hasten the death of its first bishop, Michael Egan, O.F.M. Meanwhile trustee rumblings were coming from Charleston, aggravated by serious dissension among the French and Irish clergy.

Into this hornet's nest in 1820 came John England as first bishop of the Diocese of Charleston which included North and South Carolina and Georgia. England was an outstanding example of "the right man in the right place at the right time." He was a genius, under whose tact and versatility peace was effected. He drew up a Charleston Constitution providing for a Convoca-

tion of Clergy and a House of Representatives for the laity, under which "the clergy, and especially the Bishops, are entirely free, and . . . the laity are empowered to cooperate but not to dominate." To establish a sound financial basis, he formed the diocese into a state-approved corporation and for financial assistance founded the country's first Catholic weekly newspaper, *The United States Catholic Miscellany*. At a time when the Church was being assailed by many non-Catholic publications, the *Miscellany* rendered invaluable service.

In covering his vast diocese he often borrowed a courthouse or church from a friendly parson. He preached incessantly and in addition found time to publish in 1833 an *Explanation of the Construction, Furniture and Ornaments of a Church, of the Vestments of the Clergy, and of the Nature and Ceremonies of the Mass*. This fairly substantial volume of one hundred thirty-one pages did much to enlighten its readers and dispel some of the fantastic notions then circulating about Catholicism.

During England's tenure Charleston was ravaged at intervals by fever epidemics which devastated the homes of Irish immigrants, leaving their helpless children as charges of the city. For their care England instituted in 1829 the Order of the Sisters of Charity of Our Lady of Mercy. Their additional objective was the education of Negroes whom England called "his humble Africans." A school for free Negro girls was established in 1835 but had to be discontinued; the white population's fears were being aroused by abolitionist tracts of the North jamming the mails going into southern states.

The welfare of Negroes would continue to involve the Sisters and their resources from their founding until the present day. They conduct and teach in schools in which the enrollment of students is predominantly black. At their motherhouse on James Island (see section entitled "Virgin Militant") they carry out a program of periodically distributing money, food and clothing to indigent Negroes who inhabit the island.

Bishop England manifested his devotion to Mary in the establishment of his first church and a religious order for the "Holy Virgin," as he addressed her in his daily prayers. He petitioned her to "obtain for me from your Son all the graces which my weakness stands in need of."

Thousands of immigrants crossed the Atlantic in the 1820s to swell the Church's membership "in a manner which baffled its friends and exasperated its enemies." Newcomers were looked upon with disfavor; being Catholic they owed obedience to an Italian Pope and to a local bishop who very often was a foreigner.

One such "foreigner" was John Dubois, bishop of New York. He had fled France in the Revolution, arriving in America in 1791. For over a quarter century he would contribute to the Church's growth. He established and directed the seminary and college at Mount St. Mary's, Emmitsburg, and guided Mother Seton and her community of Sisters of Charity.

When consecrated in Baltimore in 1826, the sanctuary of the Cathedral of the Assumption was crowded with priests and ecclesiastics, many of whom owed their education and zeal to his care. When criticism of his nationality arose, he stated: "If we were not long ago American by our oath of allegiance, our habits, our gratitude and affection, thirty-five years spent in America in the toils of the mission and of public education would surely give us the right to exclaim: We too are American! But we are all Catholics. Are not all distinctions of birth and country lost in this common profession?"

One priest in Bishop Dubois's diocese was the Irish-born, Italian-educated Philip J.M. O'Reilly, a Dominican. Dubois deputed him in 1830 "to form missions and build churches on the banks of the Hudson River as far as his zeal would urge him." O'Reilly reported his progress in a letter to the *Truth Teller,* early New York Catholic weekly: "I have now, unassisted and alone, formed five flourishing missions on the Hudson River. The liberality of a Protestant gentleman, whom to name would be to honor, has erected for me a beautiful church in one of them."

The gentleman happened to be an Episcopalian, Gouverneur Kemble of Cold Spring, owner of the West Point Foundry. Cannon was being made here to supply a deficiency of heavy artillery made apparent by the War of 1812. Kemble, sympathetic to the spiritual needs of his predominantly Irish Catholic workers, gave land and a large share of money for the building of a chapel. Catholics were then in the parish of Our Lady of Loretto, meeting in a building used by congregations of other denominations.

As a patron of the arts, Kemble's attention had been attracted to the work of a young Englishman, Thomas Kelah Wharton, who sketched and painted Hudson River landscapes while studying architecture under Martin E. Thompson, leading New York City architect. Kemble engaged Wharton to provide a plan for the chapel and the design ultimately prepared followed the American Greek Revival architecture popular at the time. The chapel was built on a rocky promontory upriver from the United States Military Academy. A landing below the chapel permitted the mooring of boats of cadets and area persons coming for services.

The chapel was the first Catholic church erected outside of Manhattan in the New York Archdiocese, which at that time included all of New York State and a large part of New Jersey. It became a famous landmark on the Hudson, painted by fa-

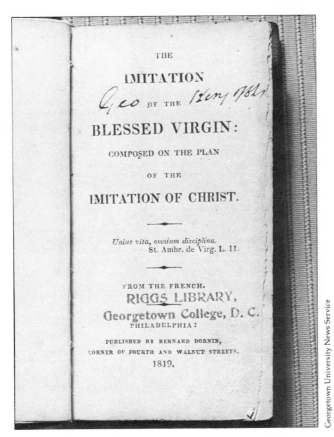

"The Imitation of the Blessed Virgin"
The first American printed book entirely
devoted to Mary, it was published in 1819.

mous artists, praised in books, and its beauty even captured in a rare antique nineteenth-century glass goblet.

When the Civil War came, the chapel was badly damaged due to shock produced in testing guns at the foundry. Kemble's brother-in-law, Robert P. Parrott, rebuilt the chapel, adding two wings and superimposed Victorian steeples. The chapel was used until 1906 when the parish of Our Lady of Loretto moved into the town of Cold Spring. Gradual deterioration reduced the handsome chapel to a mere shell. In the late 1960s a group of interested persons of all faiths formed the Chapel of Our Lady Restoration and engaged a prominent New York architect to restore the building to its original design. This was accomplished and the chapel has been now designated a national historic landmark. As a symbol of faith and mutual love it will be available for wide interfaith usage and for solemn civic and personal religious events.

Irish immigration was aided and abetted by the mania for internal improvements in the country, for which strong-backed Irishmen furnished much of the labor force. Thousands of Irish, with pick and shovel, built the Erie Canal across New

St. Mary's Church — Mother Church
of the Carolinas and Georgia
Located in Charleston, South Carolina, its cornerstone was laid on the feast of the Assumption, 1838.

York. In Ohio they built a reservoir, Lake St. Mary, a link in the Miami-Erie Canal. The section of the canal system extending from Akron to Cleveland was opened in 1827, and Akron traces its history back to the Irish "canallers" who stayed there after their job was completed.

Many of the more adventurous went down the Ohio to the Mississippi and on to New Orleans where lucrative jobs beckoned. Produce of the country was being sent down the river to New Orleans for distribution by coastal boats or overland to widely separated areas. Along the waterfront, between Constance and River Streets, an area was known as the "Irish Channel," for being the "end of the line"

for most of the immigrant keelmen. Here they ruled supreme; hundreds of their craft were tied up so closely side by side, one could walk a mile on their curved decks without going ashore. Two new streets had been cut through a square of land on the waterfront and between them St. Mary's Market was built. This market began the first great development in river traffic and port building which gradually made New Orleans undisputed capital of Mississippi Valley trade.

St. Mary's Market served New Orleans almost a hundred years, providing careers for many successful businessmen and establishing an important shopping section of the city. In later years the market be-

A Sister of Charity of Our Lady of Mercy With Some of Her Little Charges

U. STATES CATHOLIC MISCELLANY.

CHARLESTON, JANUARY 15, 1831.

CORRESPONDENTS.

Letters received from
Richard Byrne, Covington, Ga.—B. Clemont, George-town, D. C.—Rev. F. O'Donohu, N. J.

GEORGIA.

SAVANNAH.—The following gentlemen have been elected to serve together with the *Rev,* JOSEPH STOKES, the pastor, as the Vestry of the Church of St. John the Baptist for the present year.—*viz. John J. Waver,* and *Michael Prendergast,* Church-Wardens; *Paul P. Thomasson,* Treasurer; *Matthew Hopkins,* Secretary; *John Guilmartin, Doctor Chevrier* and *Denis McMahon.*

SISTERS OF MERCY.

It is now more than twelve months since a few unpretend-ing young women have, in this city, placed themselves under the direction of the bishop in a probationary state, with the intention of devoting themselves to the service of God and of their neighbour, under the usual regulations of the church for persons of their sex and condition. They received a short rule of conduct, by the observance of which, they might be able to advance in the practices of piety and industry; and if successful, might aspire to be formed into a more per-manent institute. During the course of the year several applications were made by others for permission to join them; some of the persons who thus petitioned were receiv-ed, and they continued to render themselves useful. On last Sunday the four who first associated were permitted to make vows for one year, which after a retreat of several days spent in prayer and meditation, they emitted on last Sunday morning in presence of the bishop, just before com-munion. The prelate for this purpose, celebrated Mass at a little before eight o'clock, at the lesser altar of the Cathe-dral, which is dedicated under the invocation of the blessed Virgin Mary; and after demanding of each of the candi-dates, in the most solemn manner, whether the act which she was about to perform, was the result of her own free choice, without any influence of any description exercised over her will; and being answered in the affirmative, he permitted the vow to be made; after which, the person mak-ing it received the holy communion, from his hand.

The bishop subsequently addressed to them an instruc-tive and pathetic exhortation respecting the obligation and advantages of the state upon which they had entered.

Several other sections the Union have extensively profited during years by the example, the prayers, and the labours of their religious female institutes, this is the first effort which has been made in this Diocess, and we trust, and pray, that it may receive a blessing from the giver of every good gift. There is no section in which a society of this description is more needed, and we rejoice in the hope which is thus given to us, that we may no longer be deprived of the advantages which result from such establishments.

Sisters of Charity of Our Lady of Mercy

This notice regarding the Sisters of Charity of Our Lady of Mercy appeared in the January 15, 1831, edition of the United States Catholic Miscellany, *the country's first Catholic news-paper.*

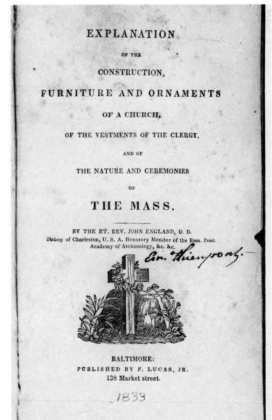

EXPLANATION

OF THE

CONSTRUCTION,

FURNITURE AND ORNAMENTS

OF A CHURCH,

OF THE VESTMENTS OF THE CLERGY,

AND OF

THE NATURE AND CEREMONIES

OF

THE MASS.

BY THE RT. REV. JOHN ENGLAND, D. D.
Bishop of Charleston, U. S. A. Honorary Member of the Rom. Pont.
Academy of Archaeology, &c. &c.

BALTIMORE:
PUBLISHED BY F. LUCAS, JR.
138 Market street.

1833

Religious Americana Museum

This is the title page from a book by Bishop England. The book was published in 1833 to help enlighten the public regarding Catholi-cism.

This page is from the Catholic Amanac of 1835. At this time the Diocese of New York included a large part of New Jersey as well.

came the starting point for the steamboat races which added so much glamour to the Mississippi's history. Today the market's site is a parkway.

Buffalo in 1836 was a boomtown, thanks to the Erie Canal or "Clinton's Big Ditch" as it was called. Ten thousand people had come to this halfway stop to the West. Catholics worshiped at a small structure, Church of the Lamb of God, mother church of all Buffalo. Four unfinished churches awaited a priest — at

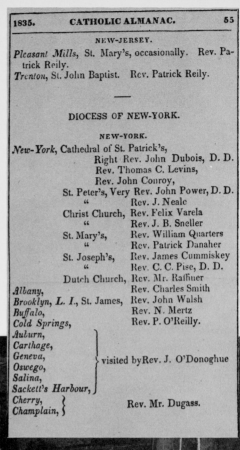

1835.	CATHOLIC ALMANAC.	55

NEW-JERSEY.

Pleasant Mills, St. Mary's, occasionally. Rev. Patrick Reily.

Trenton, St. John Baptist. Rev. Patrick Reily.

DIOCESS OF NEW-YORK.

NEW-YORK.

New-York, Cathedral of St. Patrick's,
Right Rev. John Dubois, D. D.
Rev. Thomas C. Levins,
Rev. John Conroy,
St. Peter's, Very Rev. John Power, D. D.
" Rev. J. Neale
Christ Church, Rev. Felix Varela
" Rev. J. B. Sneller
St. Mary's, Rev. William Quarters
" Rev. Patrick Danaher
St. Joseph's, Rev. James Cummiskey
" Rev. C. C. Pise, D. D.
Dutch Church, Rev. Mr. Raffiner

Albany, Rev. Charles Smith
Brooklyn, L. I., St. James, Rev. John Walsh
Buffalo, Rev. N. Mertz
Cold Springs, Rev. P. O'Reilly.
Auburn,
Carthage,
Geneva, } visited by Rev. J. O'Donoghue
Oswego,
Salina,
Sackett's Harbour,
Cherry, }
Champlain, } Rev. Mr. Dugass.

Metropolitan Museum of Art (Gift of Lyman G. Bloomingdale)

Forging the Shaft

This painting by John Ferguson Weir is of the West Point Foundry in Cold Spring, New York. Here was perfected the Parrott gun and cannon, the latter on Little Round Top saving the Union's left flank at Gettysburg.

192

Rare Antique Engraved Solid
Vaseline Glass Goblet

Chapel on the Hudson is viewed from the north;
below it are the words, "Chapel to Our Lady the
Blessed Virgin Mary at Coldspring New York."

North Bush, Williamsville, Cayuga Creek and Eden. These would be served by the priest who would be canonized St. John Neumann.

Of the four churches, Williamsville was the only one of stone, though floorless and roofless. Under Father Neumann's care it was completed, a parish organized, and the children instructed. Among his parishioners was Joseph Batt and his family, newly arrived from Alsace. (Their experience in the Atlantic crossing has been documented by a great-great-great grandson, Dr. Ronald E. Batt of Williamsville.)

On October 20, 1836, Joseph Batt, his wife, Barbara, eight of their nine children, and a son-in-law left Alsace to embark at Le Havre for America. On November 29, in the North Atlantic, a sudden tropical storm of hurricane proportions tore the sails and masts of the ship, the *Mary Ann.* Weather records at Greenwich, England, recorded the storm's severity damaging every house in England.

All aboard the *Mary Ann* believed she would sink. During the storm's fury Joseph prayed and promised Mary that if he reached America he would build a chapel for her. The ship limped into Cork for repairs. Finally, on February 2, 1837, the

193

ST. MARY'S MARKET.

This is a building in the Rusticated Doric style, deriving its name from being erected for the convenience of the residents of the then suburb St Mary; now the Second Municipality. It fronts (vide map) on New Levee, Tchapitoulas, and North and South Market streets. The edifice is plainly but firmly built, of brick, plastered to imitate granite, with a wooden frame roof and tile covering. It is 486 feet long, by 42 in width; and was constructed at three different periods:

The first section 165 feet long being built by Mitchell & Lemoine A. D. 1822, at a cost of $22,000
The second section of the same length, by J. D Baldwin, 1830, for   13,750
And the third, of about 156 feet long, by the same person, in 1836, for   12,000

    Total cost. $47,750

In A. D. 1834, this market was rented for $13,600
" 1835,   15,050
" 1837,   19,950
" 1838,   24,650

St. Mary's Market is depicted on this page taken from Gibson's Guide and Directory of the State of Louisiana and the Cities of New Orleans and Lafayette.

feast of the Purification, the *Mary Ann* docked at New York Harbor after her voyage of eighty-four days.

The Batt family settled in Williamsville and Joseph told Father Neumann of the trial at sea and his promise to Mary. Father Neumann could sympathize on the dangers of the sea, having made the same voyage a year earlier. He warmly encouraged Joseph's keeping his promise to Mary. He performed the wedding ceremony of Joseph, Jr., and baptized several of the children. Meanwhile, Joseph Batt was making his own bricks, preparatory to fulfilling his promise. Time was needed to

Wharf at New Orleans, Where St. Mary's Market Was Located

make a living for his family, to put aside money from his limited earnings, and then wait for diocesan permission to build. On July 10, 1853, the cornerstone was laid, the chapel blessed and dedicated to "Maria Hilf," Our Lady Help of Christians. It was located south of Williamsville, in the town of Cheektowaga, two miles east of Buffalo.

The Buffalo area had been settled by German-speaking immigrants from Alsace, Baden, Bavaria, Switzerland and Lorraine, who continued their homeland custom of bringing votive offerings to "Maria Hilf." Increasing pilgrimages required the chapel's enlargement in 1871. Joseph Batt, in spite of diminishing eyesight, directed the removal of native limestone (from the now-unused church of Father Neumann's in Williamsville), for constructing a large addition to the front of the chapel. Nearly blind, each day he followed a well-worn path from his home to his beloved chapel. He died the following year and was buried in the cemetery directly behind the chapel.

As Cheektowaga's population in-

This is an 1874 view of the Chapel of Our Lady Help of Christians, Cheektowaga. The rear portion is the original chapel built by Joseph Batt in 1853, fulfilling a promise to Mary. The large front addition was made in 1871 of stone from Father John Neumann's first church in Williamsville, New York.

Present Shrine of Our Lady Help of Christians, Cheektowaga, New York

creased, the establishment of a parish was a necessity; the chapel was then elevated to the stature of parish church. New pilgrimages came, with cures reported and evidenced by braces and crutches on the walls: a "Second Lourdes," the people said. Out-of-door services on May 24 and August 15 became a tradition, people walking from the Buffalo city line two miles away. A second and final stone addition in 1926 provided an outside altar and Mount Calvary Shrine.

A new and larger church was built on the grounds in 1959, its design a pleasing architectural continuity with the former. The original chapel gradually went into disrepair and was closed in 1969. However, 1975 witnessed plans for its reopening and restoration. A Bicentennial project sponsored by the Town of Cheektowaga Youth Bureau, the Bicentennial Commission and the Historical Society, involved many volunteers who enthusiastically painted, plastered, repaired plumbing and restored the one-hundred-year-old pipe organ. They had a deadline to meet — August 15, feast of the Assumption.

In the five-year period 1832-1837, more than fifty thousand Germans came to this country and by 1840 they, along with other Catholic immigrants, were finding life increasingly unpleasant because of Nativists' attacks against their religion and nationality. Hoping for greater freedom in the unexplored wilds, a number of Philadelphia and Baltimore German families banded together to form a German Catholic Brotherhood, and in 1842 purchased land in northwestern Pennsylvania from the Fox Land Company of Massachusetts.

The first settlers left Philadelphia on the first of November and traveled by rail, canal and overland to reach their destination in Elk County. Arriving on the feast of the Immaculate Conception they expressed their gratitude for safe arrival by naming the colony "St. Mary's."

To the herculean task of clearing land, "heaped up like impassable ramparts" of uprooted trees, was added the job of protecting their lives from wolves and bears roaming the area. The Redemptorists, and later the Benedictines, ministered to the colonists and assisted them financially. (Benedictine Sisters coming ten years later would found their first convent in this country.) Primitive living conditions soon drained the settlers' resources, and to attract new colonists pamphlets were printed for distribution in Germany, listing the colony's many attractions and including the fact that the first church built was already too small, "so many of Mary's children already having gathered around their dear Mother" that a new church was being planned.

Present-day St. Marys is a thriving city, proud of its important contribution to

196

St. John Neumann Center

This stained-glass window depicts Father John Neumann as he appeared in 1836-1840 when he was serving nine hundred square miles of territory outside Buffalo, New York. The window, one of twenty-seven showing his life, is in the St. John Neumann Center, Philadelphia.

World War II airpower. During that war Allied bombers were being shot down because carbon brushes in control motors disintegrated at altitudes high enough to protect the bombers from enemy attack. At St. Marys the first high-altitude brush was perfected which permitted the raids over Germany and thus shortened the war.

Wisconsin's rolling fertile lands and vast forests would lure a tide of German immigrants beginning in 1839 and lasting forty years. Those who settled in the

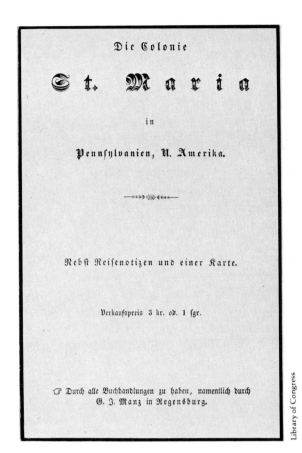

Prospectus Distributed in Germany (Circa 1846) to Attract Settlers to St. Marys, Pennsylvania

southeast found a valley dominated by a huge hill rising two hundred ninety feet from its base. Menominee and Pottawatomie of the area had related how white men passing through the valley placed a cross on the hill's summit. The legend may have inspired two pioneers in 1858 to hew a twenty-foot oak cross, carry it to the hill's summit, and erect it there.

Five years later the hill provided a fitting place for a chapel dedicated to Mary Help of Christians, constructed of sixteen-foot logs which had to be hauled by horse team halfway up the hill and carried the rest of the way on men's shoulders. Now the hill was called Maria Hilfberg, "the hill where Mary is our helper."

Increasing pilgrimages necessitated building a larger structure in 1881. Parishioners fashioned bricks from the area's clay beds to form a base seventy by forty-six feet. Through succeeding years additions have been made, roads added, until the shrine today presents a magnificent appearance, visible for miles. It has an unusually strong attraction to Mexican-Americans who come up from Chicago with Spanish-speaking priests for special Masses. Black people find a like attraction to the Grotto of Our Lady of Lourdes on the grounds. Since 1906 the shrine has been under the care of Discalced Carmelite Fathers.

Minnesota in the 1850s was called "the lily of the west," attracting German immigrants in hordes. Many settled in St. Paul, the name first given by Father Lucien Galtier when he erected a log-cabin chapel there in 1841. The settlers built Assumption Church and School in the heart of the community. Their first simple church of 1858 yielded to a magnificent stone structure designed by the architect to the king of Bavaria. It was dedicated in 1874 and its twin spires are a St. Paul's landmark.

Except for some modernizations, St. Mary's Church, built in 1853 at St. Marys, remains unchanged.

Shown is the Shrine of Our Lady of Holy Hill, Hubertus, Wisconsin. This imposing shrine was erected in 1881 on the second highest hill in Wisconsin.

The Germans were the country's most ardent champions of parochial education; the children of Assumption School had two laymen and two nuns instructing them in a nearby house. A later frame building was destroyed by fire in 1861 and on its ashes was built "a sturdy, noble schoolhouse." This served for seventeen years until a still larger structure was provided, meanwhile being used as a meeting hall. Except for a new roof, the building remains unchanged today. It is Minnesota's oldest grade school building and attracts many visitors to view artifacts of school and church. Present plans call for making a museum here. The school is included in the Historic American Buildings Survey.

The Church in growing with the country recognized the need for stronger bonds of unity and introduced the provincial councils. These brought bishops and their advisors together from all parts of the

198

country to deliberate on current needs. The sixth such council met in 1846 to gratify a pious desire then prevalent of paying special honor to Mary. Twenty-three of the country's twenty-six bishops, with representatives of four religious orders, asked the Holy See for the privilege of inserting in the Office and Mass of December 8 the word *Immaculata* and in the Litany of Loretto the invocation "Queen, conceived without original sin, pray for us." The council declared:

"We take this occasion, brethren, to communicate to you the determination, unanimously adopted by us, to place ourselves and all entrusted to our charge throughout the United States, under the special patronage of the holy Mother of God, whose Immaculate Conception is venerated by the piety of the faithful throughout the Catholic Church. By the aid of her prayers we entertain the confident hope that we will be strengthened to perform the arduous duties of our ministry, and that you will be enabled to practice the sublime virtues, of which her life presents a most perfect example."

The American hierarchy may be proud

Constructed of native limestone in 1864, Assumption School in St. Paul, Minnesota, is the oldest grade school building in the state.

Shea: History of the Catholic Church in the United States

Sixth Provincial Council, Baltimore, 1846, Naming Mary Patroness of the United States

of the fact that this declaration was issued eight years before the dogma of the Immaculate Conception was defined by Pope Pius IX.

The bishops meeting in council may have had varying ideas regarding the erection of new dioceses, but they responded to the needs of Catholics ever moving westward to establish new frontiers. Of five dioceses erected in the 1830s, two — Detroit and Dubuque — would bear the imprint of the remarkable Dominican, Samuel Charles Mazzuchelli, of Milan, Italy. Newly ordained in this country, Mazzuchelli found himself at age twenty-three appointed first resident priest of the vast wilderness of northern Michigan, Wisconsin, Iowa and northern Illinois. Overcoming obstacles, hardships and sufferings, he left a record of conversions which has had few equals. In Wisconsin alone he could say a thousand Menomin-

ees "wore" their rosaries. In baptizing he placed a rosary around the neck of each as a bond between himself and his Indian brother. On three visits to the Winnebagos he instructed and baptized more than three hundred. He attempted, without success, to get government redress for injustices done to them.

Besides his beloved Indians he served pioneer miners, farmers and traders in the Midwest where twenty-four churches of his design and building attest to his tireless and unselfish service. His greatest living monument is the native Dominican Sisterhood, the Congregation of the Most Holy Rosary, which he founded on the feast of the Assumption, 1849. Listed in his personal record is the reception of three of the four Sisters he called the congregation's "cornerstone."

After more than a century Father Mazzuchelli's name is still held in veneration in Wisconsin, Illinois and Iowa. The cause of his beatification, opened in Rome in 1967, is making slow but steady progress.

199

The Dubuque Diocese comprised the entire district between the Mississippi and Missouri Rivers north of the State of Missouri as far as the Canadian border. When its first bishop, Jean Mathias Loras, arrived in 1837, he found the whole diocese had but three churches, built or being built by Father Mazzuchelli. The scarcity of churches was rapidly being remedied by this intrepid priest who moved over the entire area.

In 1841 he was in Iowa City, newly named capital of the Iowa Territory, and built that territory's first capital! Then he erected its first church, St. Mary's. Describing its inception he modestly refers to himself as "our missionary." He wrote:

"By an act of the Iowa Legislature several lots in its Capital City were set aside for church purposes but on condition that

This is Father Mazzuchelli's record of reception of the first members of the Congregation of the Most Holy Rosary, Sinsinawa, Wisconsin, 1847. The bottom entry is for Sister Josephine, admitted in 1848, whose rosary is shown. Attached to it is a medal bearing the date 1898, her golden jubilee.

Father Samuel Mazzuchelli With Menominee Converts Wearing Rosaries, Michigan Territory, 1830s

those Religious bodies who desired to obtain them, should raise thereon a Church building of not less than one thousand dollars in value. In December 1840 our missionary hastened from Burlington to the new Capital and giving over to the proper civil authorities the required security ... secured to the cause of Catholicity one of the finest of the lots reserved for building churches."

St. Mary's served until 1867 when a second church was constructed. Its tower has nineteen bells, one of which merits special attention for having hung in the first church. An interesting story recalls that one day in 1854 a teamster delivered a bell and the resident pastor and Bishop Loras concluded its donor wished to remain

St. Mary of the Assumption, Iowa City, Iowa
This edifice stands on the site of the church built by
Father Mazzuchelli in 1841, it being then the first Catholic
church in the newly named capital of the Iowa Territory.

anonymous. A few days later a man named Hanert, a stranger, informed the bishop that he was the donor. The bell was mounted upon a tower rising twenty-five feet from the ground. Six months after the bell's consecration, the maker of the bell in St. Louis informed the pastor that the bell had been cast for St. Mary's in Sauk City, Wisconsin, and by mistake sent to Iowa City. The Iowans quickly raised the money to keep their bell. Meanwhile Hanert had disappeared.

In Dubuque the ecumenically minded Bishop Loras often lectured to mixed audiences of Protestants and Catholics on the controversial subjects dividing them, one such being the prejudice existing against establishing foundations of religious orders in this country. The bishop concluded one lecture: "Religious orders are a blessing to a country, a source of good example & of usefulness of every sort, both for this world & for the next. Amen."

To prove his point Bishop Loras in 1849

201

offered a gift of four hundred acres of land in Dubuque to Irish Cistercians, newly arrived in America. These men had left their monastery of Mount Melleray in Cork due to overcrowding of facilities, coupled with the great famine. The name Melleray is from the French derivative for "honey." The name was first given to the Cistercian monastery built where a tree stood containing a honeycomb which supplied desperately needed food for two Cistercian Brothers.

Bishop Loras's faith in the Cistercians reaped great rewards for the American Church: Of the initial founders at New Melleray two became bishops, Clement Smyth succeeding Loras in Dubuque, and James Myles O'Gorman becoming vicar apostolic of Nebraska. (The Cistercians of the Strict Observance are commonly called Trappists. Seven of their twelve foundations in this country have Marian titles.)

In answer to the bishops' plea for priests to direct new dioceses and supply educational needs, Father Edward Sorin and six Brothers of the Congregation of the Holy

Our Lady of New Melleray in the Evening Mist

When founded in 1849, the Monastery of Our Lady of New Melleray, Dubuque, Iowa, was the first American Cistercian monastery west of the Mississippi.

Cross settled in Indiana in 1842. They were welcomed by an old log hut, rotting fences, snowclad prairies and frozen Lac St. Marie. Undaunted they began Notre Dame with two students! Father Sorin predicted the college would be "one of the most powerful means of doing good in this country."

In the next year Sisters of the Holy Cross, at Father Sorin's request, came and opened a school. Priests and religious together would make a magnificent effort in caring for the sick and wounded during Civil War years, winning Archbishop John Ireland's praise that "no other order, no di-

Log Chapel on Campus of Notre Dame University
This is located on the site of the first Catholic
sanctuary built by Father Claude Allouez in 1686.

ocese, made for the purpose, sacrificed as did that of Holy Cross."

Sorin's great love of Mary inspired him in 1865 to publish a periodical, *Ave Maria.* He did so against the advice of friends and colleagues who felt its title would provoke cries of "Mariolatry." Sorin, however, felt that the promulgation of the doctrine of the Immaculate Conception had intensified American veneration of Mary and the time was ripe for his publication. The journal was a weekly of sixteen pages of legends, short stories and serials, poetry, theological and devotional articles and essays on the liturgy. On its appearance the *Chicago Tribune* stated that it was "neatly gotten up," and the *Toledo Commercial* noted: "The poetry is of a high order and the articles exhibit a good style and scholarly treatment."

In his introduction to the first issue, Bal-

timore's Archbishop Martin J. Spalding wrote: "A weekly periodical devoted to the Blessed Virgin, successfully established in this cold calculating age of mammonism and in these United States of America, in which perhaps more than anywhere else, the interests of this world are held as paramount and those of eternity are kept in the background, this is truly one of the wonders of the *wonderful* Nineteenth Century."

For over a century the weekly kept pace with changing times in material both original and stimulating. In March 1970, however, subscribers were notified of a change in its title to *A.D. 70;* this failed to prevent the publication's demise six months later due to "financial difficulties." Today a bi-weekly is published, its title being *A.D. Correspondence.*

Father Sorin's prediction about Notre

Dame's potentials is evidenced by its enrollment (1976) of nearly nine thousand students attending Colleges of Arts and Letters, Business Administration, Engineering, Science, the Law School, Graduate School, Medieval Institute and Lobund Laboratory of Microbiology.

Chicago's location on Lake Michigan early attracted adventurers and agents trading with the Pottawatomie and marrying with them. Their descendants would be joined with the military personnel and settlers coming when Fort Dearborn was built as a link in the defense of the North-

This page is from the first edition of Ave Maria, a magazine started in 1865 by Father Sorin at Notre Dame, Indiana.

This statue of Our Lady of Notre Dame University, South Bend, Indiana, replaces one erected in 1865 and destroyed in the fire of 1879. It is sixteen feet high, weighs forty-four hundred pounds, and was designed by Giovanni Meli. It is a replica of the one erected by Pius IX in the Piazza de Spagna, Rome, to commemorate the promulgation of the doctrine of the Immaculate Conception in 1854.

AVE MARIA.

A Catholic Journal: Devoted to the Honor of the Blessed Virgin.

Vol. I.	NOTRE DAME, IND., MAY 1, 1865.	No. 1.

FOR THE AVE MARIA.

BY BISHOP TIMON.

BUFFALO, April 5, 1865.

Very Rev. and Dear Sir:—

I rejoice at your pious thought of the AVE MARIA. It must succeed. In the pardoning judgment upon fallen man, and in the merciful promise to our guilty first parents, cursing the hellish serpent, God said: "I will put enmities between thee and the woman, and between thy seed and her seed. She shall crush thy head, and thou shalt lay in wait for her heel." He thus designated a woman, Mary, the second Eve, to be the dawn of our hope, and her Son to be our Saviour-God. This "oracle of oracles," as the ancients, whether Jews or Gentiles, called it, was in some form treasured up in every nation; and what the prophet Isaiah said: "behold *the* Virgin shall conceive and bear a son," the Emmanuel or God with us, for, as had been promised, "God himself did come to save us," and He sent His fishermen to convert the world to the faith of "His human and divine natures, in the one person of the Eternal Word, *made flesh for us.* And these fishermen, His apostles, had to speak of Mary when they preached Jesus the God-Man. Hence, from the first judgment and sacred promise of redeeming mercy, down to the redemption; at the angel's salutation; at the sacred birth; at His first miracle; even at the foot of the Cross, Mary was present, wonderfully associated with the divine victim. A woman and a man thus became associated in the history of redemption, as a woman and a man was in that of the fall.

And now, when the great rebellion against "the Church of the living God, which is the body of Christ, and the fullness of Him," is crumbling away in multiplied divisions, the sweet and bright "AVE MARIA" of the archangel is the harbinger of many conversions. "*Gaude Maria Virgo, cunctas hæreses sola interemisti, in universo mundo*," it is also the harbinger of that restored unity for which the Saviour-God so touchingly prayed, in the 17th chapter of St. John's Gospel. Hence, I rejoice at your enter-

prise, and request you to put me down as a subscriber, and accept for the good work the enclosed sum, which I would wish that my means would permit me to increase a hundred fold.

With great respect and esteem,

Your most ob'd't humble serv't,

✝ JOHN, BP. OF BUFFALO.

Very Rev. E. SORIN.

AVE MARIA.

The AVE MARIA is, in the true and widest sense of the word, a *Family Newspaper,* in which we intend to speak exclusively of our own family affairs. It is published to meet the wants, and interest the heart of every Catholic, from the grey-haired grandsire who tells his beads at eventide, to the prattling child who kisses his medal as he falls asleep in his downy cradle, with rosy dreams in which the loved images of his mother on earth and his Mother in heaven are sweetly blended.

It is our family chronicle, wherein is emblazoned, in glorious heraldic characters, the glorious deeds of our ancestors. In these chronicles our brave soldier-brothers and fathers will find that the practice of religious duties and devotion to our Blessed Mother are not incompatible with the true military spirit. Here they will meet a brilliant array of noble warriors, commencing with the brave Centurion, who, converted at the foot of the Cross, feared not to proclaim, in the midst of the Roman legions, Mary's Son as his God; and ending with our gallant Garesche and Mulligan. One of whom invoked the Mother of God to pray for him, in that his hour of death, with the same dying breath in which he besought his comrades to lay him down and save the flag he loved so well. And the other one prepared for his last battle by devoutly assisting at Mass and receiving Holy Communion. In the thickest of the fight, when the tide of victory seemed turning against his standard, he was seen to leave the scene of action for a time, and prostrating himself in prayer, he renewed the offering he had already made, at Mass, of his own life, in order that his country might be preserved. Another instant he was in the front rank, bat-

west frontier. To their numbers would be added immigrants coming on the highway provided by the opening of the Erie Canal in 1825. In five short years Chicago was transformed from a typical frontier trading center and military outpost into a bustling community.

Up to 1830 there are but three recorded visits of priests. Then in 1833 a petition for a resident priest was addressed to Bishop Joseph Rosati, C.M., of St. Louis, who was then acting as vicar general in Eastern Illinois on behalf of the bishop of Bardstown. The petition, drawn up in French, guaranteed adequate material support for a priest in this "new and flourishing city." It was signed by thirty-six families, representing better than fifty percent of the population! Included were the names of persons who would become prominent in Chicago's growth: Major William Whistler, commandant of Fort Dearborn; Major Thomas Owen, Indian agent and first president of the Board of Town Trustees (equivalent to mayor); John S. Hogan, first postmaster; Anderson Taylor, builder of the first bridge over the Chicago; Colonel Jean Beaubien, merchant-trader, and Alexander Robinson, Pottawatomie chief.

Bishop Rosati sent the able Father John Mary Irenaeus St. Cyr who found such enthusiastic support — financial and physical — that St. Mary's Church was built within the year. Being the first church building it attracted much attention; a Presbyterian deacon even helped in actual construction. The lumber used was the first sawed lumber imported into Chicago, brought across Lake Michigan from St. Joseph by David Carver in a schooner he had built himself. Father St. Cyr bought the entire shipment of lumber, paying twelve dollars a thousand for it. When the construction bill of four hundred dollars was presented to the chairman of the building committee, he pulled from under his bed a half-bushel basket of new half-dollars and counted out eight hundred.

A church thirty-six by twenty-four by twelve feet in size was built on a canal lot on Lake Street. At its dedication it was still unplastered and without paint on the outside. Indian women cleaned and prepared for dedication services and among the first worshipers were three hundred of the thousand Pottawatomie assembled in Chicago for the sale to the government of their lands in Michigan, Indiana and Illinois.

The church was later moved to Madison Street where it was enlarged and an open belfry added. It served until 1844 when a brick church was built on Wabash Avenue; both structures were destroyed in the great fire of 1871. The following year a third St. Mary's was housed in a complex formerly owned by the Plymouth Congregational Society. Today it is under the care of the Paulist Fathers.

The Church's expansion in area and population triggered envy, fear and hostility among many non-Catholics. The "Irish invasion and the Teutonic tide" were viewed as a threat to their established American way of life, for the immigrants were clustering together in cities, voting in blocs, working for low wages and maintaining their foreign customs. Protest soon came in the active hostility known as Nativism. In 1844 Philadelphia witnessed three days of destruction; the toll was thirteen lives, two churches and personal property, all because local Catholics attempted to have their children excused from compulsory reading of the Protestant Bible in public schools. Similar incidents of harassment, violence and church burnings paved the way for the formation of a secret political party called the Know-Nothings. One of their attacks failed because of the courageous mothers of St. Mary's in Elizabeth, New Jersey.

Elizabeth, as the state's oldest settlement, was slow in shedding its colonial intolerance of Catholics; in 1829 three "papists" had to leave the city for no one would employ them. Four years later, construction of the New Jersey Central Railroad brought the first general influx of Catholics. These faithful souls traveled ten miles to Newark to hear Mass, until in 1844 a resident pastor was assigned them and he encouraged the building of St. Mary of the Assumption.

St. Mary's faced desecration and possible destruction in the 1850s when Know-

Nothing members, armed with clubs and axes, with their leader carrying an open Bible, marched on the church, only to be met by a group of mothers holding their babies. In front was Mary Whelan, known to the mob's leader. To his cry, "Stand aside, Mary, with your child," she replied: "No, Sam, I will not. You cannot enter this door but over the dead body of my child and myself." In the face of such courage the mob wilted and St. Mary's was left unharmed.

Among St. Mary's distinguished parishioners were John Dawson Gilmary Shea and the convert Orestes Augustus Brownson. Brownson has been called "one of the first thinkers and writers, not merely of America, but of the age in which he flourished." Shea's *History of the Catholic Church in the United States* has placed all succeeding historians in his debt. His thirteen Indian grammars and dictionaries have preserved more of the aboriginal languages than any one person working without government aid. To express his deep love of Mary he included "Gilmary" (servant of Mary) in his name.

The hatred, bigotry and prejudice of the 1850s was viewed by one man as "a last desperate lunge of an enemy that had spent its fury to its own destruction." That man was Isaac Thomas Hecker, a convert, whose contributions to the Catholic Church would produce inestimable results.

Son of Methodist German immigrants living in New York, Hecker had been of a deeply socioreligious bent from early childhood. As a boy he worked on a Methodist newspaper, in a type foundry, and with his brothers in their bakery on Rutgers Street. He managed to find time to study the injustices suffered by American workingmen and to deliver speeches of protest on street corners.

In 1841, at age twenty-two, he met Orestes Brownson who exercised tremendous influence on the next three years of his life. Brownson was a lecturer, writer and editor, and introduced Hecker to the Transcendentalist group at Brook Farm in Massachusetts. Here George Ripley was conducting a sociological experiment in which such notables as Nathaniel Hawthorne and Ralph Waldo Emerson participated. Through the educational advantages at Brook Farm, Hecker's inherent asceticism deepened, resulting in his conversion to Catholicism.

In 1845 he entered a Redemptorist novitiate in Belgium and on ordination five years later, with four companions (all American-born converts), began mission work in New York. The group at first devoted their attention to German immigrants, addressing them in that tongue. Gradually they recognized that the Redemptorist congregation would grow more rapidly and appeal more readily to Americans if an English-speaking house were established to attract non-Catholics. Such an apostolate favoring the needs of Protestants suffered from the suspicion of many Catholics who distrusted this type of approach.

Misunderstanding and tension finally prompted Father Hecker and his group to plead their cause before the Redemptorist superior general in Rome. After many months of ordeal, Pope Pius IX dispensed the group from their Redemptorist vows and gave permission for founding a new order, the Missionary Society of St. Paul the Apostle, known today as the Paulists. From its beginning in 1858 it impressed on non-Catholics the idea that the Church was not merely a conglomeration of Europeans but was universal and therefore had the right of existence in a democratic society.

From its inception a magazine, *The Catholic World*, was published with Father Hecker editing and contributing. (The magazine has enjoyed uninterrupted publication to the present day.) Tirelessly he

St. Mary's Church — First Church Building in Chicago
The original building, erected in 1833, was enlarged and the belfry
added when it was moved from Lake Street to Madison Street.

planned, directed, wrote, lectured, traveled. From his earliest years in the priesthood he acknowledged his dependence on his "dearest Mother." In an essay "On the Blessed Virgin Mary" he petitioned the Blessed Mother in this manner: "Through thee I expect all the graces necessary to accomplish the designs of Almighty God in my creation . . . the strength to overcome all enemies and all obstacles to my vocation. . . . Oblige me to love thee more and more."

For him the rosary was a distinctive devotion. On mission engagements he gave inspired explanations of the rosary and by his fervent recitation before congregations acquired the title "Father Mary" which clung to him for years.

In pulpit and press Father Hecker laid the groundwork for the following century's ecumenism. Before leaving Rome he wrote: "I believe that Providence calls me to America to convert a certain class of persons amongst whom I found myself before my own conversion. I believe that I shall be the vile instrument which He will make use of for the conversion of a multitude of those unhappy souls who aspire after truth without having the means to arrive at and possess it."

Today the Paulists are in charge of twenty parishes, as well as eighteen Newman Foundations on college campuses. They conduct information centers in seven major cities to provide accurate information and opportunities for discussion of the faith. The Paulist Press includes pastoral educational services and audio-visual materials.

Converts often attest to the ardent love

207

TAMPERING WITH THE BIBLE.

This Thomas Nast cartoon is taken from an anonymously published book entitled Miss Columbia's Public School; or, Will It Blow Over? *The book's seventy-two illustrations vilify the Pope, the Jesuits and the Irish.*

of Mary accompanying their entry into the Church. One such convert, an Episcopalian minister, made of that love an unparalleled tribute. Before conversion Donald Macleod had established a reputation as novelist, dramatist and historian. His life of Mary Queen of Scots drew high praise from Washington Irving with whom he enjoyed membership in a literary club.

On his conversion Macleod studied for the priesthood and on ordination in 1861

delivered his first sermon on the purity of Mary, refuting a tract then being circulated which denied her virginity. His praise of Mary included "Legends of Holy Mary," "Our Lady of the Litanies," and the historical-spiritual work *Devotion to the Blessed Virgin in North America.* This work of nearly five hundred pages remains the only one of its kind ever written. In it he detailed the growth of devotion from Columbus to the missionaries of the western plains. He carefully defined the true basis of Catholic devotion to Mary and pleaded that she be shown the honor that is her due.

The book first appeared as an appendix to the English translation of Abbé Mathieu

The Know-Nothings Attempt to Destroy St. Mary's, Elizabeth, New Jersey

Father Isaac Hecker,
Founder of the Paulist Fathers, 1858

This is a painting by George P. Healy (1813-1894),
known as the "painter of Presidents," for his series of
Presidents in the Corcoran Gallery, Washington, D.C.

Orsini's *Life of the Blessed Virgin*, but the need for a more convenient form for general reading prompted the publisher to issue it separately in 1886. Father Macleod did not live to see this publication; he was killed by a train while going on a night sick call.

The growth of the Mississippi and Ohio River valleys would attract thousands of pioneers whose independence and self-reliance would be challenged by isolation from the Atlantic seaboard. New Orleans would become the market for their pro-duce and the time and distance involved in transport would be but a preparation, a "westering," for the day when many would make the great leap across the plains to Oregon and California.

Catholic settlements would grow along the rivers, one resulting from a vision which Alexander Creel had while sailing down the Ohio in the late 1840s. The Virgin pointed to a portion of the West Virginia side of the river and told him it would be the site some day of a happy and prosperous city. Creel bought the land but then

209

Father Donald Macleod, Marian Historian

DEVOTION

TO THE

BLESSED VIRGIN MARY

IN

NORTH AMERICA.

BY

THE REV. XAVIER DONALD MACLEOD,

PROFESSOR OF RHETORIC AND BELLES LETTRES IN ST. MARY'S COLLEGE,
CINCINNATI.

WITH A MEMOIR OF THE AUTHOR,

BY

THE MOST REV. JOHN B. PURCELL, D.D.,

ARCHBISHOP OF CINCINNATI.

NEW YORK:

VIRTUE & YORSTON,

12 DEY STREET.

History of Marian Devotion in North America,
1866 — First and Only Book of Its Kind

sold it and settled at nearby Vaucluse. In 1849, when the question arose of selecting the seat of Pleasants County, he realized that his former holdings would be ideal in offering more room for expansion. He repurchased the land, had the town platted and named it St. Marys. It is one of fourteen communities named St. Marys (having post offices) in the country.

Ever moving southwest, Catholics found areas where their religion had established outposts hundreds of years previously. Such an area was at the junction of the Arkansas and Mississippi where Arkansas Post, oldest white settlement in Arkansas, had been founded in 1686 by Henri de Tonti, a lieutenant in one of La Salle's expeditions. As early as 1673 Father Marquette had visited here to minister to the Quapaws.

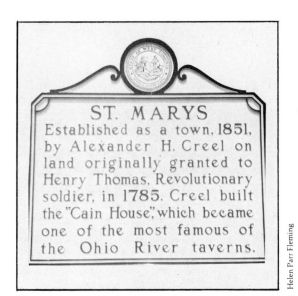

West Virginia State Marker for St. Marys, the Town Inspired by a Vision of the Virgin

When France ceded all land west of the Mississippi to Spain, Arkansas Post was renamed Fort Charles III, but reverted to its former name under the Louisiana Purchase. To serve fifty Catholic families living on the river, St. Mary's Church was begun about 1833 at nearby St. Mary's Landing. A double log cabin, half for priest's residence, and half for church, was erected on a gift of two acres of land.

Caving in of the riverbanks in 1869 threatened to destroy the church and its cemetery and they were moved inland to Plum Bayou. The original church was left intact but its walls, bearing shell marks from a Civil War skirmish, were encased in brick. The interior was plastered and trimmed with woodwork of polished walnut and cedar from trees growing on the church plot. Today this well-preserved structure is the object of much interest, being the oldest church building in Arkansas.

Settlers pushing to the Rio Grande would find abandoned missions but no priests. Being inured to frontier hardships,

this was but one more which had to be "waited out." Priests had come intermittently to Texas to serve Stephen Austin's twenty thousand colonists, but no formal church organization was effected until after their independence. Then Bishop Anthony Blanc of New Orleans appointed Father John Timon, C.M., as prefect apostolic, to investigate conditions.

Timon found Texan rulers interested, placing in his hands by special act of Congress the churches of San Antonio, Victoria, San José, San Juan, Espada, the Alamo, Goliad, Concepción and Refugio. (The latter three Marian churches, involved in battles for independence, are described in the section entitled "Virgin Militant.") In 1841 Timon appointed Father John Mary Odin, C.M., as vicar apostolic of the Diocese of Galveston, and now Mary's "new" history in Texas would begin.

Odin's first frame church was named

St. Mary's Church, Plum Bayou, is the oldest church building in Arkansas. It is now a mission of St. Joseph's, Pine Bluff.

St. Mary Star of the Sea Atop Her Cathedral in Galveston, Texas
The cathedral is the oldest religious building in the city. It is listed in the Historic
American Buildings Survey and has been designated a national historic landmark.

for Mary and soon proved "entirely too small to receive all. I have been obliged to have a little sacristy built, and I am getting some benches." The church was destroyed by a storm in 1843 and Odin began a large-scale campaign for raising funds for a cathedral, going even to his native Belgium where he was given a gift of one-half million bricks to be shipped free from Antwerp. With them the Cathedral of St. Mary Star of the Sea was built in 1847. In its tall steeple was placed the first bell ever cast in Texas.

Galveston suffered a severe flood in 1875 and, as a protection against storms from the sea, a fifteen-foot statue of Mary was placed on the steeple. Local legend has

it that while the statue stands, the island of Galveston will endure. That legend dates to September 1900 when a fierce wind, traveling one hundred twenty miles an hour, swept a six-foot tidal wave over the city, taking six thousand lives. Hundreds gathered in the cathedral to offer prayers of supplication. The two-ton bell crashed to the floor of the tower and the iron crosses on the front towers fell to the street. The destruction of the church seemed imminent and the bishop told his people to prepare for death. Gradually the wind decreased, the waters abated, and by morning the storm was over. A priest survivor wrote:

"The sun broke from behind the clouds

212

and we saw that Mary, Star of the Sea, had remained on high to continue her protection, while out through the south and southwest ends of the parish she was being invoked as the Mother of Sorrows to comfort the sore distressed. Everywhere I was greeted with 'Father, is the statue on the cathedral tower standing?' and when I answered 'Yes,' the response rang out 'Thank God!' And I believe the first note of confidence in the future greater Galveston was echoed in those fervent 'Thank God' responses."

The Rio Grande River is rich in song and story; where it touches Brownsville, Texas, the Oblates of Mary Immaculate would further add to its history. "Specialists in difficult missions," Pope Pius XI called them, and they had come by invitation from Bishop Odin who, in his desperate need of priests to serve the entire State of Texas, had gone even to Canada to plead his cause before the Oblate congregation.

Three priests and a Brother left their Arctic missions and discovered at Brownsville a tougher territory than the one they had left. The town was in a state of flux: thousands of California-bound gold seekers were mixing with rough cattlemen and fugitives from justice; lynchings and mob law prevailed. Against such odds, the heroic missionaries in but three days after arrival had converted a store into a chapel and offered the first Mass on the feast of the Immaculate Conception.

A wooden chapel built in 1850 was succeeded by a magnificent Gothic structure, erected from 1859-1862, dedicated to the Immaculate Conception. Its designer, Father Peter Keralum, had been an architect in France before ordination. He and a Brother supervised the baking of a quarter million bricks of local clay used in construction. Bells and chandeliers were donated by appreciative parishioners, but the church's first organ was procured by "an unwonted method." Father Pierre Parisot, assisted by four cowboys, traveled for fifteen days in visiting ranches outside of Brownsville to beg for donations of livestock. The party on return led a herd of sixty-five cattle, four horses and two colts, which were sold to provide the fourteen hundred dollars needed for the pipe organ.

The church's history contains the sad record of Father Keralum's death. In November of 1872 he left Brownsville to visit the seventy widely scattered ranches assigned to his care, made a scheduled stop north of Mercedes, then headed for Las Piedras, eighteen miles farther north. He was never heard from again. Ten years later two cowboys found some human bones, a chalice, Oblate cross, part of a rosary and a bell in a thicket. The priest had perhaps died of exhaustion and starvation, or by some accident. Paul Horgan, eminent Catholic historian of the Southwest, has dramatized the death in his *Devil in the Desert*.

Texas in the 1850s almost tripled her population, exceeding six hundred thousand. The state's fame had reached across the Atlantic to attract its share of immigrants. From one town in Poland alone, one hundred families with their priest, Father Leopold Moczygemba, came in 1854 bringing not only tools and plows but even the bell and the great cross from their village church. Reaching their destination on Christmas Eve, they attended Midnight Mass beneath a great oak tree. In gratitude for safe arrival they named the area Panna Maria (Virgin Mary in Polish). A state marker documents it as the oldest Polish settlement in the state.

Though all the original settlers did not remain at Panna Maria, wherever they moved they established parishes. Father Moczygemba founded a Polish seminary in Detroit to assure Polish-Americans of spiritual leadership. By 1870, there were twenty Polish settlements in ten parishes in Michigan, Wisconsin, Illinois, Indiana, Missouri and Pennsylvania.

Special Masses are still said today beneath the historic oak. On the feast of the Assumption flowers, plants and vines are brought to the church and blessed; the day is called Our Lady of the Greenery.

The European discovery of California had bequeathed to the land a Marian devotion unparalleled in any other state. The color and romance of the missions formed an enduring tribute to the Spiritual Mother motivating California's pioneers. In 1848 "color" of another kind, in the discovery of gold, created a new era of devotion which soon blended with the old. The intervening years are of importance in the state's history.

Father Serra's rosary of missions had been supported from a "Pious Fund" first established by the Jesuits in Lower California from private sources; upon suppression of the Society of Jesus this fund was taken over by the Mexican government, which gradually discontinued payment of interest on the fund, preliminary to secularizing the missions. This meant changing them to diocesan status, with missionaries being supplanted by diocesan priests. This was accomplished in 1840 at which time Father Diego García, O.F.M., was consecrated the first bishop of the newly created Diocese of the Californias, embracing both Upper and Lower. Bishop García proclaimed Mary patroness under the title Nuestra Señora Refugio de Los Pecadores (Our Lady Refuge of Sinners).

When the war with Mexico ended, the United States was ceded Upper California by the Treaty of Guadalupe Hidalgo. The religious condition of the area was deplorable; cut off from Mexico as it had been from Spain, no further supply of priests could be expected from either — and to add to the difficulty, a stampede of humanity was now descending in search of California's gold. Coarse, rough, brutal and mur-derous men were arriving, but coming also were self-reliant, stern and just men, aware of the need of religious organization.

Letters were sent to eastern bishops, who in turn appealed to Rome, and in 1850 a Dominican, Father Joseph Alemany, was appointed ordinary of California. He soon pleaded for a division of his vast diocese because its administration was complicated by the presence of two varying segments of population: prospectors and settlers in the north, earlier settlers with their own established customs in the south. After deliberation, the Sacred Congregation of Propaganda created the Archdiocese of San Francisco for the northern part of California, with Alemany as its archbishop, and named Thaddeus Amat, C.M., for the south. (The eastern and northern parts of Alemany's diocese would later become the Vicariate of Marysville.)

The war with Mexico had effected many changes. From New Mexico countless families moved northward (into present southwest Colorado) to land grants given to individuals by the Mexican government prior to 1846. A group of settlers chose the San Luis Valley near the Conejos River for locating. The land was almost wilderness but had the protection from Indian raids by nearby Fort Massachusetts. They brought with them a statue of Our Lady of Guadalupe, a devotion of their Mexican ancestors.

In planning their church, cedar posts and logs were plastered with adobe, the floor tamped earth; its bell was made of jewelry melted down. It was the first Catholic church in Colorado and was named, naturally, Our Lady of Guadalupe. A second structure was built around and over this, dedicated by Bishop John B. Lamy, first bishop of Santa Fe. Two large towers were added in 1879. Fire destroyed this church but a third was built in 1948. Its Lourdes Grotto honors parish beginnings in 1858, the year of the apparition of Mary

Historic American Buildings Survey, U.S. Department of the Interior

Country's First Permanent Establishment
of the Oblates of Mary Immaculate

Perfect in design and purity of style, the Immaculate Conception Cathedral in Brownsville, Texas, constructed during 1859-1862, is included in the Historic American Buildings Survey. In the Rio Grande Valley are fifty churches and chapels which the Oblates have dedicated to God under various Marian titles.

to Bernadette Soubirous at Lourdes, France.

In the frenzied search for gold, men moved in many directions to establish camps. And wherever they went, a priest soon followed. As the first flush of "get-rich-quick" faded into ordinary survival, the more stable miners decided to stay put. Churches were built, such as that at Downieville. The settlement had been named for "Major" William Downie who camped

in the Sierras along the Yuba River looking for gold and finding it. The area boomed into a supply depot for all the camps ten miles around. One street, four hundred feet in length, comprised the whole town, since the mountain's steep sides allowed no room for other thoroughfares.

Missionaries in the Vicariate of Marysville had come to Downieville as early as 1852, riding sixty miles on muleback along

215

Shown is the Immaculate Conception of the Blessed Virgin Mary Church, Panna Maria, Texas. Polish settlers attended the first Mass in their new homeland on Christmas Eve, 1854, under the oak tree at left.

narrow canyon trails. On one of the town's steep slopes a church was built in 1855 and named the Immaculate Conception. It is unchanged today, looking down on the Yuba River where gravel was once so rich that sixty square feet yielded $12,000. Some movies of gold-rush days include the church, for Downieville is often filmed as a typical boom-day town with its buildings, board sidewalks and dirt streets. A gallows may be seen with a memorial plaque stating that the last execution was on "Friday, November 27, 1885, by Sheriff Sam Stewart."

The church today is a mission of Immaculate Conception parish in North San Juan. The present pastor writes that the Downieville church is "still active and has been since its foundation in 1852, although as you might surmise not on the grand

216

scale to which it was once accustomed during the peak of the Gold Rush."

Archbishop Alemany's cathedral, dedicated to Mary in 1854, was constructed of materials coming from China and around the Horn. It was built on the eastern slope of Nob Hill several years before the railroad magnates chose the area for their pretentious mansions. The imposing Victorian Gothic structure served as the bishop's cathedral for forty years while around it grew a settlement made up of Chinese who had come to California when ships from around the world brought those eager to "share the wealth."

As Chinatown grew, the need for locating the cathedral in more imposing surroundings became apparent, but "old" St. Mary's was left untouched. It continued to hold its own even when the earthquake and fire of 1906 toppled buildings all around. The church's rebuilding took three years and retained as much as possible of the original structure. The sign below the clock cautions: "Son, observe the time and flee from evil," a reminder of Chinatown's early days when tong wars

State Marker Commemorating Panna Maria

TOWN OF
PANNA MARIA
OLDEST POLISH SETTLEMENT IN TEXAS.
ESTABLISHED DECEMBER 24, 1854 BY
THE REVEREND LEOPOLD MOCZYGEMBA
O. F. M., WHO WAS INSTRUMENTAL IN
BRINGING FROM POLAND ABOUT 100
POLISH PEASANT FAMILIES • WITHIN A
FEW MONTHS THE MAJORITY SOUGHT
HOMES IN OTHER LOCALITIES IN TEXAS

A.D. Spearman, S.J.

This painting of Nuestra Señora Refugio de los Pecadores (Our Lady Refuge of Sinners), named patroness of Upper and Lower California in 1840, was done on a piece of tin by Eulalio, a former Santa Clara Mission Indian.

and opium dens were part of the colorful history.

Old St. Mary's today is part of Chinatown's tourist business, where in an area of little more than twelve square blocks are crowded shops with Oriental goods, restaurants whose menus offer strange dishes, markets crammed with exotic foodstuffs, and a temple where Tin How is worshiped as Queen of Heaven and Goddess of the Seven Seas. A contemporary touch is the stainless steel statue of Sun Yat-sen, statesman and revolutionary leader, standing in St. Mary's Square. In addition to sharing the tourist atmosphere, the church is also the parish church for the luxury hotel district, the people of the ex-

pensive apartments of Nob Hill, the much more modest little flats and residence hotels down the sides of Nob Hill occupied by senior citizens, and also a weekday church for the business community.

Mention Indians and many people think of war cries, flaming arrows and bloody massacres. Forgotten is the red man's desire of living at peace with the ever-encroaching white population of his ancestral lands. While frontiersmen were striving to establish homes in the wilderness, Congress, in the name of national welfare, committed the government to a policy of removal of all eastern Indians to west of the Mississippi, with a view to so-called Indian consolidation, supposing that the unorganized territory between the Rocky Mountains and the Missouri River would long be left in Indian hands. In the process, treaties were violated and the Indians ended up on widely separated reservations.

The unhappy picture is brightened by the work of Franciscan, Benedictine and Jesuit missionaries among the tribes they

This structure, built over and around the first church of cedar logs and adobe, was destroyed by fire in 1926. The present Church of Our Lady of Guadalupe, Conejos, Colorado, is similar in design, with fifty-six-foot towers.

Denver Public Library Western Collection

served. A heroic chapter in that record is the Jesuit labors among the Great Plains Indians. Three men are outstanding: Peter de Smet, trusted and loved by red and white, Charles Van Quickenborne and Christian Hoecken. Father de Smet established a mission in 1838 with the Pottawatomie at Sugar Creek in eastern Kansas and Father Hoecken took over. He was a loyal friend to the tribe, advising them in their negotiations with the government. Fluent in their language, he wrote several catechisms, one in 1846, and also published *Le Chapelet de la Sainte Vierge Marie (The Rosary of the Blessed Virgin Mary),* which explained its mysteries in

Church of the Immaculate Conception in the Gold Rush Town of Downieville, California

was established. Since most of the inhabitants were Indians in care of the Jesuits of St. Louis, a member of the society, John Baptist Miege, was appointed "Bishop of the Indians."

Miege had been reluctant to accept the appointment, foreseeing the eventual dispersion of the Indians from this territory. The struggle began in 1854 with the enact-

In this view of much-photographed Downieville, boom town in Gold Rush days, the belfry of the Church of the Immaculate Conception is visible in center background.

This is the Yuba River at Downieville, where fortunes were made during the Gold Rush. Tourists still "try their luck" panning the river.

Pottawatomie and contained a hymn in Mary's honor.

In 1848 St. Mary's Mission moved to a more desirable location on the Kansas River and a town soon grew up around it and became St. Marys. It was a stopping place for settlers taking the Oregon Trail. In 1851 the Vicariate of Indian Territory

218

Historic American Buildings Survey, U.S. Department of the Interior

Shown is St. Mary's Church after the San Francisco earthquake of 1906. Formerly Archbishop Alemany's cathedral, it was dedicated to Mary in 1854.

West. The treaty ceded the present Douglas County of Nebraska to the United States and here Omaha was begun and named first capital of the territory.

Among the very first missionaries here was Father de Smet, whose work among the Pottawatomie in Council Bluffs in 1838 resulted in some of the earliest information on this area. During the period of his stay, he probably was on this side of the Missouri at times. With the groundwork thus laid, the settlers coming to Omaha soon planned for a church, St. Mary's. It would be the first church in Omaha.

Omaha's acting governor, Thomas B. Cuming, son of an Episcopalian minister, gave generously to a campaign for funds for building. Land had been donated by the Nebraska and Iowa Ferry Company and on it a twenty-four by forty-foot brick church, surmounted by a simple cross, was erected in 1856. The occasion was warmly heralded in *The Nebraskian*, whose slogan, "The Sovereignty of the People," is

ment of the Kansas-Nebraska Act which organized the Indian country, north of thirty-seven degrees north latitude and as far west as the Rocky Mountains, into two territories — Kansas and Nebraska. Settlers and immigrants now poured in from north and south, bitterly hostile to each other, divided on the question of slavery. This proved the State of Kansas fertile ground for John Brown's antislavery agitation. In 1865, with his approval, four of his sons and a few followers murdered five slavery adherents in what is now known as the Pottawatomie Massacre.

In the early 1850s, adventurers and settlers began congregating at Council Bluffs, Iowa, awaiting only final signing of a government treaty with the Omaha Indians before crossing the Missouri to where a plateau on the west bank offered a stopping place before striking out for the Far

Old St. Mary's Church, San Francisco

Old St. Mary's Church Archives

Pottawatomie Indians at St. Mary's Mission, Kansas, 1868

indicative of the times. The Kansas-Nebraska Act had provided that residents of the two territories were to put "popular sovereignty" into practice in deciding whether their state constitutions would prohibit or permit slavery. Both voted to prohibit.

"Eastward I go only by force, but westward I go free." Such was the magnetism of the Far West which fired men's imaginations and lured thousands into the wilderness. Knowledge of the Oregon country had been revealed by the explorers and traders and augmented by letters which missionaries sent home. The uncertainties and dangers of the so-called "Great Desert" could not dim the brilliant concept of manifest destiny, and into the area would go farmers, homebuilders, emigrants and men with families.

The premier history of the vast Northwest Territory had been written by Peter de Smet, the intrepid Belgian Jesuit. He had worked since 1838 at Council Bluffs, Iowa, and elsewhere in what was known as the Platte Purchase, and in 1840 began traveling through the Rocky Mountains in ministering to the Indian tribes of four states. His accurately kept records would later serve as guides for the safe routes which emigrants followed. Wherever he went he would leave Marian memorials on the land, notably St. Mary's Mission at present-day Stevensville, Montana, and St. Maries River in Idaho.

Back in St. Louis from one of his travels he wrote: "I was kneeling at the foot of St. Mary's altar in the Cathedral, offering up my thanksgiving to God. . . . I had descended and ascended the dangerous Columbia River. I had seen five of my companions perish in one of those life-destroying whirlpools, so justly dreaded by those who navigate that stream. I had traversed

220

This statue of Mary once occupied a shrine built by the Pottawatomie on the grounds of St. Mary's Mission. The story is told that the statue had become so weathered the Jesuit superior wished it restored because Mary appeared blind. The Indians pleaded for leaving it unchanged, the chief explaining, "We like her that way; she cannot see our faults, she can only hear our prayers." The statue is now on private property near the mission site.

the Wallamette, crossed the Rocky Mountains, passed through the country of the Black Feet, the desert of the Yellowstone, and descended the Missouri; and in all these journeys I had not received the slightest injury."

Father de Smet's first visit to the Flatheads of Montana was in 1840 when he baptized three hundred before returning to St. Louis. On his visit the following year

Shown is a Kansas historical marker of the early history of St. Marys. The college was closed in 1967, the land sold to a developer. Northeast of the site the remaining Pottawatomie occupy a reservation.

Pages From Pottawatomie Catechism Composed by Christian Hoecken, S.J., at St. Mary's Mission, Kansas, 1846

Morton: *Illustrated History of Nebraska*

St. Mary's, First Church at "Crossroads of the Nation," Omaha, Nebraska

he chose a site on the banks of the Bitter Root River where the Indians erected a simple log church. Of the occasion he wrote: "So many favors have induced us unanimously to proclaim Mary the pro-

tectress of our mission and give her name to our residence." Here the first white settlement in Montana began. The simple log chapel was succeeded in 1846 by a much more substantial structure. At St. Mary's

THE NEBRASKIAN.

THE SOVEREIGNTY OF THE PEOPLE.

OMAHA CITY, WEDNESDAY, JULY 16, 1856.

Masthead and Clipping From Omaha Newspaper on Building of St. Mary's Church, 1856

Library of Congress

It is somewhat significant that the first public house for worship now in progress of building in Omaha City, and perhaps in the territory, is a Catholic church;—a nice, fine brick building on park place. Whoever may be the first promoters and supporters of this enterprise, and to whatever denomination they may belong, it gives them much credit, and shows that there exists a true christian spirit of religious toleration among the population of this territory.

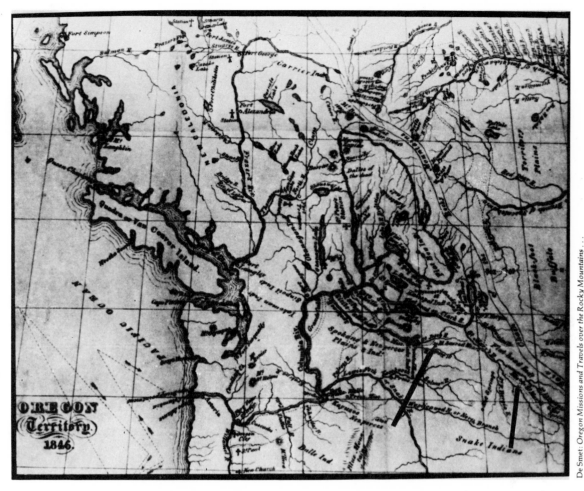

Father de Smet's Map of His Travels in Oregon Territory
Showing Mission and River Named for Mary

Left arrow points to present-day St. Maries, Idaho, which takes its name from the river Father de Smet designated in 1842. Right arrow indicates the Marian mission at what is now Stevensville, Montana.

the Jesuits taught the Indians how to plant, cultivate and harvest crops of wheat, oats and potatoes. Cattle, hogs and chickens were introduced. A water-powered gristmill, the first in Montana, was set up and later a sawmill which furnished the planks and posts for public and private buildings of the area's settlers.

De Smet's ministry in Idaho would result in naming two rivers — St. Maries and St. Joseph. At their confluence a settlement grew up and took the name St. Maries. A

peak on the Continental Divide would also be named in honor of the Virgin. De Smet's simple trust in her intercession became a legend. The tribes loved him as a brother and described him as the one white man they had ever known who did not speak to them "with a forked tongue." This high regard would be an important factor when Father de Smet negotiated with the warring Sioux in 1868 (see section entitled "Virgin Militant").

St. Mary's Church is listed in the His-

De Smet: Oregon Missions and Travels over the Rocky Mountains . . .

*Interior of Second Mission Church at St. Mary's,
Present-Day Stevensville, Montana*

Drawn in 1846 by Nicholas Point, S.J., the ceremony represents a baptism.

toric American Buildings Survey. The original structure, measuring nineteen by twenty-two feet, now has an enlargement which was completed in 1879. Also to be seen is an original pharmacy building, Flathead Chief Charlot's house, a cemetery and an Indian burial ground.

The Christianization of the northwest country would demand heroic sacrifices of its missionaries. Canadians working for the Hudson's Bay Company early in 1834 sent a plea for priests to the archbishop of Quebec. Two Sulpicians came in answer, Francis N. Blanchet and Modeste Demers, who soon realized their inadequacy to serve so vast a field and contacted Father de Smet who was working nearby. Through their combined efforts an appeal for more priests was sent to bishops in the east, who in turn relayed the request to Rome.

A vicariate was erected embracing all the territory from California to Alaska! Father Blanchet was named vicar apostolic. Included were two suffragen dioceses: Vancouver Island under Demers, and Walla Walla under A.M.A. Blanchet, brother of Francis. The vicariate included the "fifty-four forty or fight" area contested by Great Britain and the United States. Under the compromise of 1846 Vancouver came under British civil administration. An Indian massacre compelled Bishop Blanchet and his priests to move to the Columbia River. In 1850 the bishop was made the ordinary of the newly created Diocese of Nesqually.

Meanwhile the Oblates of Mary Immaculate were making history in Washington. Father Auguste Veyret, serving the Puget Sound Indians outside Steilacoom, built in 1848 a church, the Immaculate Concep-

224

General View of Fort Steilacoom, Washington Territory,
1858, Where Marian Church Was Erected
This U.S. Signal Corps photo is among the earliest taken in the
Washington Territory, evidently made during an inspection by
Colonel Joseph K. F. Mansfield and forwarded with his report.

tion, a significant name in that this was six years before the definition of that dogma. One year later the soldiers of nearby Fort Steilacoom built a larger church outside their parade grounds. The fort had been

established for the protection of settlers in the inter-tribal warring of the Squally and Snoqualmie.

With peace restored, the settlers returned to their farms on the prairies and

Church of the Immaculate Conception, Steilacoom — Oldest Catholic Church Building in Washington State

Depicted is the Lownsdale House, Portland, Oregon. It was to become St. Mary's Academy, a pioneer in Catholic education in the state.

valleys and the Catholic soldiers then built a shelter for missionary priests traveling up and down Puget Sound. The fort was abandoned in 1867, but the church was dismantled in three sections and drawn by teams and wagons to Steilacoom where Bishop Blanchet dedicated it as the Church of the Immaculate Conception. Today it is a mission of St. John Bosco Church in Tacoma. It attracts many visitors for its unique history as oldest Catholic church building in the State of Washington. At Fort Steilacoom a hospital and doctors' residences occupy part of the grounds.

The year 1859 which marked Oregon's admission to statehood also heralded the beginning of Catholic education in the state. In Portland, twelve Sisters of the Holy Names of Jesus and Mary opened St. Mary's Academy in an abandoned hotel. The school was the first chartered private school in the state, a fact which would be of importance in 1922 when the constitutionality of the Oregon School Bill was being decided (see section entitled "Mother of the Church").

226

A second St. Mary's was built at The Dalles; on its near-centennial celebration the city's newspaper praised "the pioneer spirit and courage" of its founding Sisters and their unselfish service to the community. Yet a third St. Mary's was begun at Jacksonville in 1865. This school's staff would render heroic service to the town's inhabitants in 1868 when a smallpox epidemic killed forty and left many sick and dying. The Sisters prepared the dead and cared for the survivors, returning at night to the little woodshed adjoining the school to change their clothing, bathe, and eat the food brought them. The public press praised "these self-sacrificing women who have wrestled with the king of terrors.... We must view with admiration the power and truth of a religion that bestows on the weakest and gentlest of humanity a courage so unfaltering, a faith so powerful and so everlasting."

The story of the nuns' service to our country in the Spanish-American War is told in the section entitled "Virgin Militant." The order today has four provinces: Oregon, California, New York and Washington.

The treasure-hunters of California were

St. Mary's Academy, Jacksonville, Oregon

Discovery of the Comstock Lode

This 1875 painting by Joseph A. Harrington shows Henry Comstock, seated at far left, looking anything but cheerful for having just discovered silver in the Washoe Range of Nevada in 1859.

ever on the move with each new report of strikes in the north. Oregon, Washington, the Fraser River country of Canada — all were explored in the hope of quick fortunes. When silver was discovered in the Comstock Lode in Nevada in 1859, "there was launched a human stampede that created the state of Nevada, transformed the financial structure of the Far West, and set the pattern of settlement for the vast basin between Great Salt Lake and the Sierra."

The Comstock Lode was the greatest single deposit of precious metal ever discovered in the United States. In a short time twenty thousand men swarmed into the wild country around Mount Davidson and established Virginia City. Mass had been said the previous August on the feast of the Assumption and the nucleus of a parish formed at that time; but, with the

miners' coming, a church was needed and St. Mary's of the Mountains was built in 1860.

The church was destroyed by tornadic winds, to be replaced two years later by another church which soon proved inadequate for its expanding parish. A third structure, seating eight hundred persons, was considered the "Jewel of the Comstock," but it had a short life. In 1875 when much of the community was destroyed by fire, St. Mary's was dynamited to provide a firebreak. In gratitude the mine owners financed a new and larger church, one of the most beautiful in the state. Its cross topping the main spire is one hundred seventy feet above the ground; eight minarets are sixty feet high; there are five entrance doors on two levels, two transepts and a gallery. The real glory is the interior with tall, slender clustered

227

redwood columns, carved redwood trusses and arches supporting a pale blue ceiling. The church's bell is of silver — Comstock, of course.

Since 1863 the area around and including Virginia City had been served by one of the West's most colorful personalities, Patrick Manogue, S.S. He shared the rough life of his people, arbitrated on their behalf with the mine owners when conflicts arose, comforted those afflicted when mine cave-ins and fires took their toll. He early saw the need for organized assistance of the miners and established St. Vincent de Paul Benevolent Society, first of its kind in the state, open to all regardless of creed.

This is the Nevada statehood commemorative stamp showing St. Mary's. St. Mary's in the Mountains enjoys the distinction of being the first Marian church to appear on a United States postage stamp.

Historic American Buildings Survey, U.S. Department of the Interior

St. Mary's in the Mountains, Virginia City, Nevada

U.S. Postal Service

Father Patrick Manogue Comforts the Afflicted at the Yellow Jacket Mine Fire, Nevada, April 7, 1869

Wright: The Big Bonanza

Father Manogue established an orphan asylum, hospital and schools. From Nevada he went on to become first bishop of the Diocese of Sacramento in 1886.

In the summer of 1976 an engineering professor discovered gold and silver in Virginia City. County officials were not enthused, preferring tourists to miners. The

228

Central City, Colorado, Once Called
"The Richest Square Mile on Earth"

Arrow points to St. Mary of the Assumption Church,
first Catholic church in the entire gold mining area.

district is a national historic landmark, preserving the flavor of the flamboyant days so aptly described by Mark Twain when he was on the staff of the *Enterprise*. He added his own share of local color by being exiled from Nevada over an abortive duel with a rival editor.

California's forty-niners became Colorado's fifty-niners, invading the state to dig the precious metal. How many made the trek is anyone's guess; one estimate is one hundred thousand. Central City absorbed a good portion of the adventurers, its population of eight thousand doubling in two months' time. Caring for the Catholics there was the saintly "Apostle of Colorado," Father Joseph Projectus Machebeuf.

Machebeuf had come from France in 1839 with his priest-friend of seminary days, John Baptiste Lamy, who one day would be the first archbishop of Santa Fe. Before coming to Colorado Machebeuf had served an "apprenticeship" of eleven years on the Ohio frontier and nine — half across the country — in Arizona and New Mexico. His short, slender body had been toughened by the rigors of travel and

229

crude accommodations, conditions to which he was apparently impervious. He seemed to lend a glow to whatever kind of human society he encountered.

When Bishop Lamy learned in 1860 that the whole districts of present-day Colorado and Utah were to be added to his already huge ecclesiastical district, he sent Machebeuf, his *vicario andante* (wandering vicar) as he affectionately called him, to see what could be done for the Catholics coming in great numbers into the vicinity of the Front Range of Colorado. Working out of Denver, Machebeuf had visited Central City at uneven intervals up to 1861, saying Mass in stores, a theater, a vacant billiard room — whatever availed — and, when space was lacking, even the back of his buggy was transformed into an altar.

To all his pleas for a church in Central City the miners remained indifferent until Machebeuf resorted to "holdup" tactics. One Sunday after Mass he had the hall doors locked and the keys brought to him at the altar. He informed the congregation they could leave *only* when the question of a church had been settled. His daring did the trick; donations poured in, a house was purchased and remodeled into a church complete with bell tower, the first Catholic church in the entire mining area. Machebeuf named it St. Mary of the Assumption.

In 1868 Machebeuf became the first vicar apostolic of Colorado, a jurisdiction which then included Utah and Wyoming territories; the vicariate became a diocese in 1887 with Denver the see city and Machebeuf the first bishop. In a diocese that embraced the entire State of Colorado he established one hundred two churches and chapels, sixteen parish schools, nine academies, brought to Colorado the first teaching and charitable orders, and established the Catholic educational system in the state. He founded St. Joseph's Hospital, the first permanent hospital in Denver,

Wax Museum, Denver

Shown here is Father Machebeuf with his familiar buggy in the Wax Museum, Denver, Colorado. The museum is devoted to displays of interesting scenes and personages in the history of Colorado and the nation. Father Machebeuf is depicted offering Mass on the back of his buggy when no building was available. The altar was enclosed in a trunk-like box which he had fitted on the rear. He would hear confessions in the front seat.

and in 1888 Colorado's first Catholic college for men, as well as St. Vincent's Orphanage and the Good Shepherd's Home, the state's first Catholic charitable institutions.

By the time of his death in 1889 he had established his place in Colorado's history. To preserve his memory, a Denver co-worker, Father William Joseph Howlett, gathered material on his life, even going to France to the bishop's sister for letters she

230

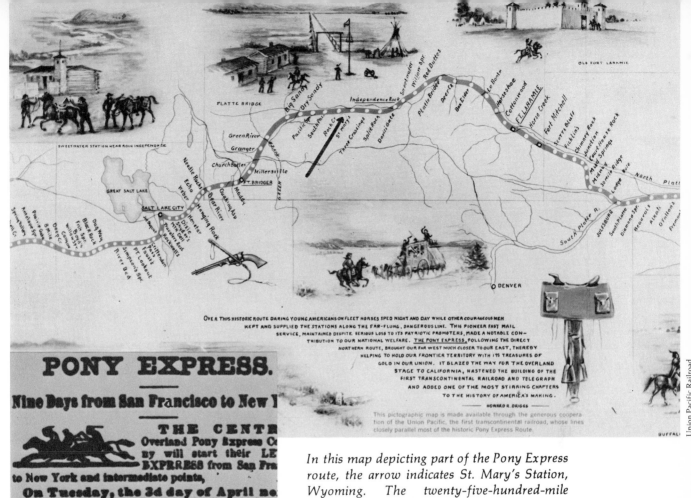

PONY EXPRESS.

Nine Days from San Francisco to New Y

THE CENTR
Overland Pony Express C
ny will start their LE
EXPRESS from San Fra
to New York and intermediate points,

On Tuesday, the 3d day of April ne

And upon every Tuesday thereafter, at 4 o'clock P. M
Letters will be received at San Francisco unt
o'clock each day of departure.

OFFICE—
Alta Telegraph Office, Montgomery

Telegraphic Dispatches will be received at Carso
until 6 o'clock P. M., every Wednesday.

SCHEDULE TIME FROM SAN FRANCISCO TO NEW YOR

For Telegraphic Dispatches...........................Nine
For Letters..Thirteen

Letters will be charged, between San Francisco an
Lake City, $3 per half ounce and under, and at that
according to weight.
To all points beyond Salt Lake City, $5 per half
and under, and at that rate according to weight.
Telegraphic Dispatches will be subject to the
charges as letters.
All letters must be inclosed in stamped envelopes.
WM. W. FINNEY,
m18 Agent C. O. R. E.

*Broadside Advertising Rates and Conditions of
Pony Express Service*

*In this map depicting part of the Pony Express
route, the arrow indicates St. Mary's Station,
Wyoming. The twenty-five-hundred-mile
route had one hundred ninety stations set at
ten-mile intervals, manned by four hundred
station men.*

*This photograph of a painting by George M.
Ottinger shows a Pony Express rider hailing
workmen putting up the transcontinental telegraph line. Ironically, the line put the Pony
Express out of business.*

National Park Service, U.S. Department of the Interior

Merced River, Yosemite National Park, California
Awe-inspiring Half Dome is reflected in the placid-looking waters of the Merced River.

had received from America. In 1908 he published *Life of the Rt. Reverend Joseph P. Machebeuf, D.D.* A copy of this book came into the hands of Willa Cather, Pulitzer prize winner in literature. She was then (1925) researching the southwest for a planned tribute to Archbishop Lamy, *Death Comes for the Archbishop.* After reading Howlett's book with its wealth of

Machebeuf's own letters, she publicly stated: "Without those letters to guide me, I would certainly never have dared to write my book." Lamy was characterized as Jean Marie Latour, Machebeuf as Father Joseph Vaillant. For Machebeuf she devoted a section of the book, "The Month of Mary," revealing the childhood devotion he had for May which to him was the holy month

232

of the year, dedicated to contemplation of his Gracious Patroness.

Central City today attracts large numbers — not gold seekers, but historians studying this quaint sample of the Old West. One can see the miners' double-decked bunks which gave George Pullman the idea for his Pullman cars. In all Colorado the name of Machebeuf is known and honored. In Denver his monument bears an inscription from the Cather book: "Without fear, and without shame, a great harvester of souls."

The opening of the West required long-range transportation and communication facilities; the former was supplied by Butterfield's stagecoach service, the latter by the Pony Express and the transcontinental telegraph. Each was served in its time by St. Mary's Station in Wyoming. The station took its name from the peak on the Continental Divide named in the 1840s by Father de Smet.

The station, built in 1859, served as one of the one hundred ninety stops on the Pony Express route from St. Joseph, Missouri, to San Francisco. Eighty riders, "young, skinny . . . willing to face death," carried the mail twenty-five hundred miles in the incredible time of ten days. The Pony Express operated for the short but exciting period of April 1860 to October 1861.

When the transcontinental telegraph line was established, St. Mary's was made a depot and at it a trading post maintained. In May of 1865, while its five-man garrison took refuge in an abandoned well, one hundred fifty Cheyenne and Arapaho burned the station and cut four hundred yards of telegraph wire, leaving only when ammunition in the station exploded. Besides Indian attacks, the station was the target of white marauders preying on wagon trains. Today a simple marker is all that remains to recall the station's service to the nation.

The grandeur and majesty of the scenic West include many beautiful tributes to Mary. One is the Merced River, which me-

The Virgin River Flowing Through Zion National Park, Utah

The view is from Observation Point, twenty-six hundred feet above the park's headquarters.

anders through Yosemite National Park, California. The river was named Río de Nuestra Señora de la Merced (River of Our Lady of Mercy) by Gabriel Moraga in 1806, expressing his joy and gratitude at the sight of its sparkling waters after his forty-mile exhausting journey through waterless country. From the river a town and county in California were also named Merced.

Father Silvestre Vélez de Escalante, O.F.M., coming upon a river in exploring the Utah Valley in 1776 named it Río Sulfureo because of its hot and sulphurous water. The Indians knew the river as Mukuntuweap, meaning "straight canyon." Around 1813, Spanish traders — attempting to bridge the two Mexican provinces of New Mexico and Alta California — named it Río de Virgen (River of the Virgin). Antonio Armijo, commander of the first trading expedition, records his presence on the Río Virgen, imprinting the name on the land.

Today Zion National Park comprises the upper part of the valley of the Virgin River, which here flows for eight miles in a narrow canyon, falling from fifty to seventy feet per mile, with walls in places twenty-five hundred feet high, of brilliant colors and with great variety of cliffs, towers and pinnacles, often blotting out the sky. From Observation Point, twenty-six hundred feet above the park's headquarters, one has a fine view of the massive vertical walls. Angel's Landing is in the right foreground; the edge of the Great White Throne butts in on the left. The river flows across the extreme northwest tip of Arizona to empty into Lake Mead in Nevada.

St. Marys Lake in northwestern Montana is the "queen among queens of mountain lakes." According to legend it was named by a half-breed, Rising Wolf, who had a vision of the Virgin while camping by the lake. The Indians believed that the

Wind Maker, their underwater god, lived in St. Marys and spoke to them when his waters were ruffled. The lake is the source of St. Marys River which flows through the Waterton-Glacier International Peace Park in Montana and Canada. The park was dedicated in 1932 by Rotarians of the United States and Canada to commemorate the peace and goodwill existing between their countries.

New Mexican traders in Colorado found a river rushing through narrow gorges between high and unscalable cliffs and aptly named it for Our Lady of Sorrows. A main tributary of the Colorado, the river flows for two hundred thirty miles through eastern Utah and southwest Colorado, coursing through Dolores County and then flowing due south through neighboring Montezuma County, where in 1892 a town at the big bend in the river was named Dolores.

St. Marys Lake and St. Marys Glacier in Colorado were probably named as early as 1765 by Spanish explorers in the Rocky Mountains. The glacier lies in a great cirque on the southern shoulder of Kingston Peak (12,135 feet) near Idaho Springs, and feeds St. Marys Lake by a small stream which at its point of emergence has hollowed out weirdly beautiful ice caverns. St. Marys is the most accessible of all Colorado glaciers, affording year-round skiing and has been used as a training ground for the U.S. Olympic Team.

Certain events occurring across the land in this century would give graphic proof of Mary's intercession for her children. One such event occurred in the city of St. Louis, Missouri, in 1849. A cholera epidemic struck in May and by June the deaths had reached such proportions that the daily interments at the city's cemeteries were reported by total numbers, not by names. In less than two months six thousand of the city's seventy thousand inhabitants had died.

The Jesuit officials at the University of St. Louis were apprehensive for the well-being of more than two hundred resident students. Priests were going out to minister to the sick and dying and it was feared they would become infected or transmit the disease to the students.

Father Isadore J. Boudreaux, moderator of the Sodality of the Blessed Virgin, urged faculty and students to petition divine protection through Mary's intercession. The efficacy of their prayers is evidenced in a plaque which may be seen today beneath a statue of Mary in the new College Church of the university. The plaque, translated from the Latin, reads:

HOLY MARY PRAY FOR US

In memory of the signal favor conferred through the intercession of Mary, A.D. 1849, while the pestilence was raging in this city, whereby, in the space of a few months six thousand citizens perished, the Rector, Professors and Students of this University, finding themselves in imminent danger of death, had recourse to Mary, Mother of God and of men, and by vow bound themselves to place a silver crown upon her statue, if every member of the University was preserved from infection. This great confidence in the Mother of God pleased Her Divine Son, for the devastating scourge through the intercession of Mary was not allowed to enter within the walls of the University; and to the admiration of the entire city, not even one of two hundred and more resident students was affected by the plague.

The Grateful Sons of Mary

In fulfillment of the above vow, each May the original silver crown was taken from its vault and placed on Mary's statue. (The practice ended in 1969.)

When the three-month plague had ended, St. Louis observed a special fast day of thanksgiving. The *St. Louis Daily New Era* reported:

"Yesterday was very generally observed through our city as a day of fasting, humiliation and prayer by all denominations of Christians and by all classes in community. The churches of each different sect were thrown open to public worship and the attendance upon them greater than upon any similar previous occasion. All seemed to feel the great propriety of the religious observance of this day, and of the cause that existed for praise and thanksgiving to the Father of Lights that in his own appointed time he had removed the chastening rod which so long has been held over us."

Grasshoppers bowing to Mary? Incredible! But how else describe what happened in 1877 in the area of Cold Spring, Minnesota? For five years grasshoppers had been ravaging thirteen counties of southwestern Minnesota, leaving twelve hundred to fifteen hundred farmers and their families utterly impoverished. In the summer of 1877 Father Leo Winter, O.S.B., suggested that the farmers of the parishes of Jacob's Prairie and St. Nicholas bind themselves by a vow to erect a chapel in honor of the Assumption of the Blessed Virgin and to offer a Mass frequently for a period of fifteen years if Mary would intercede and protect them against the grasshopper plague. The vow was made, and the grasshoppers disappeared!

True to their promise the farmers chose a site on a hill on the east outskirts of Cold Spring and erected there a frame chapel. In it they enshrined a statue of Mary carved by one of their number, J. Ambroziz, a descendant of skilled Bavarian woodcarvers. The chapel was destroyed by a tornado in 1894, but the statue was saved. The site remained a place of respectful homage through the years, but no attempt was made to build a new chapel until 1951 when a beautiful stone chapel was erected.

The chapel sits on a hill among oak, ash and basswood trees. The exterior is rough pink granite; the steeple's top is thirty-five feet from the ground. The interior — altar, walls, floor — is of polished granite in col-

National Park Service, U.S. Department of the Interior

St. Marys Lake, Glacier National Park, Montana
This lake is bordered by the highway known as "Going to the Sun."

ors of pink, agate, carnelian, diamond gray and greenish-black. The imported stained-glass windows represent titles of Mary. The entire chapel is a labor of love, made possible by donations of material and man-power. Each year, Mass is celebrated by the bishop on August 15. Not once has the Mass been canceled because of inclement weather — or grasshoppers.

CAUSE FOR WONDER could well be the

Dolores River, Colorado
The name has been shortened from Río de Nuestra Señora de los Dolores (River of Our Lady of Sorrows).

Otis Marston

St. Marys Lake and St. Marys Glacier, Colorado

caption for a statue of Mary in the Johnstown Flood of 1889. On May 31 of that year the worst flood in United States history occurred in western Pennsylvania when a dam across a tributary of the Conemaugh River gave way under the pressure of the rain-swollen waters of the three-mile-long Lake Conemaugh, a private hunting and fishing preserve of wealthy Pennsylvanians. Millions of tons of water, mount-ing to a height of fifty feet, poured with express-train speed down the narrow valley of the Little Conemaugh River, gathering mud, rocks, trees, trains, houses and people in a juggernaut of destruction. When the flood was spent, twenty-two hundred people were dead and ten million dollars' worth of property destroyed.

Adjoining Johnstown, in the church of St. Mary's in Cambria City, parishioners

237

were attending closing Month of May devotions. The roar of the coming flood alerted their evacuation. As the waters inundated the empty church, the statue of Mary on its wooden pedestal rose to a height of fifteen feet; as the waters receded, the statue slowly came down into place. The church was a shambles: furnishings destroyed, the sacristy torn away, and mud everywhere. The statue had only water staining at the bottom of its satin canopy.

The tragedy found a nation instantly responding, with Clara Barton supervising a monumental relief program for the victims. Today the dead are remembered in the Johnstown Flood National Memorial, a fifty-five-acre park established by the National Park Service. Mary's statue is now in the Immaculate Conception Church in Johnstown. It survived a second flood in 1936 when it was lifted off its brackets high on a wall and later found standing on the church floor, unharmed.

In Lourdes, France, from February 11 to July 16, 1858, there occurred eighteen manifestations of Mary to a fourteen-year-old girl, Bernadette Soubirous. These occurred in a cave at Massabielle, west of Lourdes. A spring of water began to flow at the site and Bernadette was instructed to drink at the spring and wash in it.

Less than two weeks after the last appearance, Bishop Sévère Laurence, bishop of Tarbes, France, appointed a commission to investigate the authenticity of these apparitions. Not until three and a half years later, on May 31, 1863, did he declare that the apparitions had occurred.

On one of Mary's appearances, on the feast of the Annunciation, March 25, she told Bernadette, "I am the Immaculate Conception." For Americans these words were Mary's own confirmation of their already existing devotion under this title. The Sixth Provincial Council, meeting in Baltimore in 1846, had asked Rome for the privilege of inserting in the Office and

238

This statue and plaque commemorating Mary's intercession in the plague of 1849, St. Louis, Missouri, is located in the College Church of St. Louis University.

The Assumption Chapel, Cold Spring, Minnesota, was erected in 1951 and replaces its frame predecessor built in thanksgiving for Mary's intercession during the grasshopper plague of 1877.

Recalling Mary's intercession in the grasshopper plague of 1877, this carving graces the entrance of the Assumption Chapel in Cold Spring, Minnesota.

Mass of December 8 the word *Immaculata.* This request was made eight years before the dogma of the Immaculate Conception was defined by Pope Pius IX.

Churches, shrines and congregations, in commemorating Lourdes today, reflect the message which Mary gave to the world: prayer, poverty and conversion of heart. Thousands of sick who go each year to Lourdes, to the site of the apparitions, come home with no change in the clinical picture but with a complete change occurring in the whole experience of their sickness.

Wagon trains rolling westward through Minnesota made overnight camp at Rochester. To this sparsely settled frontier town in 1877 came the dynamic Mother Alfred and twenty companions to build their first

This statue was saved from the original Chapel of the Assumption which was destroyed by a tornado in 1894. The work of J. Ambroziz, a descendant of Bavarian woodcarvers, the statue is now in the Assumption Chapel, Cold Spring, Minnesota.

239

Escapes Ravages of Flood

This is the interior of St. Mary's Church in Cambria City, Pennsylvania, showing the statue of Mary preserved from the disastrous Johnstown Flood of 1889.

convent and academy in founding the Sisters of the Third Order Regular of St. Francis of the Congregation of Our Lady of Lourdes. Its dual purpose: education of youth and care of the sick.

When the call came, they were ready. On August 21, 1883, a tornado struck Rochester, leveling hundreds of homes, leaving thirty-five dead and ninety-seven injured. The Sisters immediately converted a part of the academy to care for the victims.

The great lack of hospital facilities precipitated Mother Alfred to action. Approaching Dr. William W. Mayo, she proposed that a hospital be built. He did not approve: The city was too small, the cost too high, with little likelihood of the project succeeding. Overruling his objections Mother Alfred promised that if he would take charge of the hospital the Sisters would finance it. Still hesitating, he cautioned that forty thousand dollars would be needed. Undaunted, Mother Alfred offered to raise that and more. In the face of such determination Dr. Mayo had to yield and the nuns began campaigning.

By hard work and frugal living the Sisters accumulated funds. Every cent their missions could save went to the motherhouse; to send more they encouraged donations of food and clothing, took in extra

240

Our Lady of Lourdes

This hand-colored Currier and Ives lithograph (circa 1872-1874) shows Mary in one of eighteen apparitions at Massabielle, west of Lourdes, France. Over Mary's head are the words (translated from the French): "I am the Immaculate Conception," words spoken to Bernadette Soubirous on March 25, 1858.

work for pay and spent their scant leisure time in giving music lessons, or crocheting and embroidering linens to be sold. With the money in hand, Dr. Mayo and his two sons planned the hospital and supervised its construction, but it was Mother Alfred who chose its name — St. Mary's.

A bigoted minority of the American Protective Association living in Rochester vowed the hospital would never take root in the community. Dr. Mayo shrewdly silenced them by engaging a leading Presbyterian to be the hospital's nominal superintendent. The hospital opened with five nursing Sisters and a twenty-seven-bed capacity. Though the Mayos were not Cath-

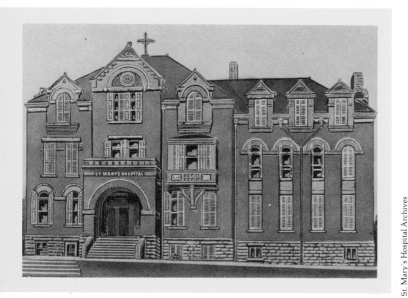

The first St. Mary's Hospital, Rochester, Minnesota, was established in 1889. It started the Doctors Mayo on the road to fame.

St. Mary's Hospital Archives

St. Mary's Hospital Archives

St. Mary's Hospital and Mayo Clinic Today

olic, they respected the faith of the Sisters. One time, on leaving a seemingly hopeless surgical case, Dr. Mayo said to a nun, "I know she can't live, but you burn the candles and I'll pay for them." The patient lived.

From their work in Rochester the Mayos were started on the road to world fame. In a testimonial given Dr. William Mayo in 1904 he publicly acknowledged in the Rochester *Post and Record* that "the Sisters of St. Francis are to be credited with the inception and the funds for its building. . . . To me they have always been true and good Sisters. In all matters they have trusted and confided in me without question; sympathized in my defeats, and urged me on to higher planes of effort for the progress not only of the hospital but the whole city."

The Sisters today still sponsor St. Mary's Hospital. The Mayo Clinic and the Mayo Hospital are two entirely separate corporations but work very closely to-

gether. The medical staff of the clinic is the medical staff of the hospital.

It would be a monumental task to list all the agencies of charity which came into existence in the second half of the nineteenth century to care for the large numbers of infirm, aged and orphans, many of the latter from immigrant parents who did not long survive the transition from their homeland. A choice has been made here of those agencies that are representative of the heroic efforts of priests and religious who,

242

This is St. Mary's Industrial School, Baltimore, Maryland, as it looked in 1866. It was staffed by Xaverian Brothers whose order was inspired by an American need.

in honoring Mary as comforter of the afflicted, contributed so greatly to the American story.

In 1832 Theodore James Ryken, a Belgian, visited the United States and first recognized the need of having Brothers for instructing Indian boys. He made a second visit five years later for the purpose of consulting with some bishops on the feasibility of founding a religious society of Brothers to carry out his plan. Though seven bishops approved, they advised that foundations be laid in Belgium where vocations could more easily be obtained, and suggested that the instruction of boys should not be confined to Indians alone. From Ryken's efforts the Brothers of St. Francis Xavier (commonly called Xaverian Brothers) came into being. Not until 1854 did members of the society come to the United States, when seven Brothers went to Louisville, Kentucky, at the invitation of Bishop Martin Spalding.

When Bishop Spalding was transferred to the See of Baltimore, he invited a group

Shown is the second St. Mary's Industrial School, Baltimore, before the fire of 1919. This building replaced an 1816 frame building. Rebuilt after the fire of 1919, it continued operation until 1950. It was here that George Herman Ruth, better known as Babe Ruth, was educated.

of Xaverians to go there and they established St. Mary's Industrial School in 1866. At that time it was the second school of its kind in the country for homeless, neglected and wayward boys. Later, orphans and sons of widows and widowers were also enrolled. Thousands of young men were prepared for the future, notably George Herman Ruth, better known as Babe Ruth, who first learned how to play baseball at St. Mary's.

243

Basilica of Our Lady of Victory, Lackawanna, New York

Lepanto, Paris, Lackawanna — three cities and a span of three hundred years' devotion to Mary concern the Basilica of Our Lady of Victory. It was at Lepanto in Greece that the Turkish fleet was destroyed in the concluding battle of the Crusades in 1571. During the battle Pope Pius V had been favored with a heavenly vision and exclaimed: "Victoria, Victoria." In honor of Mary's intercession in this crucial encounter he established the feast of Our Lady of Victory. A famous shrine under this title is in Paris and there in 1874 an American seminarian, Nelson Baker, went to pay homage. He promised Mary that he would build her a church, but "she would have to do the work; he would be the silent partner, her clerk down here."

Newly ordained Father Baker was sent to Lackawanna, New York, in charge of St. John's Protectory. Desperate for finances, he began his Association of Our Lady of Victory to solicit funds from all over the nation. He later established St. Joseph's Orphanage, Our Lady of Victory Infant Home for unwed mothers and their babies, and Our Lady of Victory Hospital. At one phase of his work he faced enormous bills for heating and lighting his institutions. Natural gas had been developed in the Buffalo area and Father Baker was confident that if he drilled for gas Mary would find it.

Drilling was begun in 1891 at a spot he designated, and where he had placed a small statue of Mary. After a month and a half's drilling to a depth of a thousand feet gas was discovered on August 22 — a date

244

Marble Statue of Mary, Basilica of Our Lady of Victory, Lackawanna

which in 1944 Pius XII named "Feast day of the Immaculate Heart of Mary." The well provided all the gas Father Baker needed and since that day the institutions have never had to purchase any.

Father Baker, at age eighty, began construction of the National Shrine of Our Lady of Victory; it was completed at a cost of over three and a half million dollars. The Homes of Charity today provide medical and residential services for children, counseling and maternity care for unwed mothers, medical care and therapy for handicapped children, education counseling and residential care for disturbed teenage boys, as well as planning services.

One section of New York perpetuates the history not only of the city, but of the nation, the Catholic Church, and Marian devotion as well.

New York's famed Battery takes its name from West Battery Fort built at the tip of the island as one of the city's main defenses in the War of 1812. With the addition of a roof the fort was converted to Castle Garden, to serve as a reception place, theater, music hall, opera house and exhibition and fair palace. Here P.T. Barnum arranged the American debut of Jenny Lind, the "Swedish nightingale."

This is an 1859 view of New York's famed Battery. Castle Garden is located at far right. At right (by men at fence) is 7 State Street, future Mission of Our Lady of the Rosary. To its left is the Seton residence.

In 1855 Castle Garden was made a landing depot for thousands of immigrants. Many had no friend or relative awaiting them and became victims of the unscrupulous. Others, though, found a friend in a young Protestant woman, Charlotte Grace O'Brien, daughter of the Irish Nationalist leader, William Smith O'Brien.

In appealing for assistance to the Archdiocese of New York a house at 7 State Street was made available. The house had been built around 1800 as a federal-style residence for John Watson, presumably on the designs of John McComb, Jr., co-architect of City Hall. Miss O'Brien had the spacious ballroom in the rectangular section of the house converted into a chapel and here on October 5, 1887, the Mission of Our Lady of the Rosary was incorporated. All immigrants, irrespective of religion or national origin, were welcomed. The number helped is unknown, but a conservative estimate is one hundred thousand.

One event in the mission's history was a fair at which Mrs. Grover Cleveland, wife of the President, raised fourteen thousand dollars by selling roses at twenty-five dollars each.

New York City would be the natural location for the Shrine of St. Elizabeth Ann Seton. Born and raised in the city, she enjoyed the privileges of a family of means and prominence. Her father, Dr. Richard Bayley, was New York's first health officer. In his care of the sick poor he contracted yellow fever from Irish immigrants which resulted in his death. Her grandfather, Father Richard Charlton, as a young curate of Trinity Episcopal Church, had been catechist to the black slaves of the city and instructed both white and black side by side.

Elizabeth Bayley married William Seton

Shown is St. Elizabeth Ann Seton, our country's first native-born saint. This, her most famous portrait, shows her widow's cap, small white collar and well-fingered rosary.

Shrine of St. Elizabeth Ann Seton, New York City

in 1794 and had five children by him before his death in 1803. Prior to that time, ever imbued with a spirit of social compassion, she had founded along with other charitable Protestant matrons the Widows' Society, to sew for and feed and nurse poor widows and orphans. After her husband's death she lived several months in Italy with the Filicchi family whose Catholicity so inspired her that she considered joining the Catholic Church. She was received on Ash Wednesday, March 14, 1805, and on the feast of the Annunciation received First Communion.

Following her conversion, cut off from family assistance and mindful of the ostracism of former friends, she began supporting herself and family by starting a school in New York. This led to her moving to Baltimore where in 1808 she established a school for girls on Paca Street, in a building which still exists today. The year following she went to Emmitsburg where she would make her greatest contributions in establishing the first free parochial school in the United States and in founding the religious community of the Sisters of Charity. Six religious congregations in this country and Canada trace their foundation to this first order.

Mother Seton was beatified by Pope John XXIII on March 17, 1963, and canonized by Pope Paul on September 14, 1975, as America's first native-born saint. This momentous and historic occasion prompted one biographer to write: "America has

247

Our Lady of Knock
This Currier and Ives hand-colored lithograph was published in 1880, within the year after the apparition at Knock, Ireland.

never produced a greater woman, and few as great. And no other country but America could have produced anybody just like her."

Her shrine occupies the site of 8 State Street where the Setons lived from 1801-1803. Adjoining is the rectory, the former Church of Our Lady of the Rosary. Its curved facade remains as the city's best surviving example of a federal-style residence.

Currier and Ives, "printmakers to the public," recognized the popularity a print of Our Lady of Knock would have for the thousands of Irish who had come to America. The lithograph represented the apparition of Mary on August 21, 1879, in Knock, County Mayo, Ireland. Below the picture was printed a precise description of the occasion:

"On the evening of August 21st 1879 on the outer gable wall of the Sacristy of the

248

Catholic Church in the village of Knock, County Mayo, Ireland, was seen an extraordinary light, in the midst of which appeared the Blessed Virgin, St. Joseph and St. John the Evangelist. Behind them an Altar on which stood a Lamb, and above it the Crucifix, with the figure of our Lord upon it. The people soon gathered at the spot gazing rapturously on the Heavenly Vision. And crowds now visit the scene of the wonderful apparition bringing many lame and blind, who by touching the structure have been miraculously cured and restored to sight.''

Sailing at night in New York's Lower Bay, looking toward Princess Bay of Staten Island, there is visible an illuminated statue of Mary on top of a lighthouse. She keeps vigil over the grounds of the Mission of the Immaculate Virgin, a reality which grew out of a dream of Father John Drumgoole.

This saintly priest spent a lifetime caring for newsboys, bootblacks, every helpless child in New York City he found. In the middle of the eighteenth century there were no laws protecting working children; many had no place to sleep and often went hungry, but in Father Drumgoole's house there was "always room for one more." As a young man, serving as sexton of St. Mary's Church in the city, he carefully saved what he could to eventually enter the Seminary of Our Lady of the Angels at Niagara Falls; when ordained in 1869 he was fifty-three!

Statistics on children in New York City at that time were appalling: forty thousand homeless, hundreds from ages four to fourteen found drunk, forty-six hundred girls and boys from ten to fifteen arrested for drunkenness and petty crimes. Father Drumgoole made such children his private concern. He established St. Vincent's Home for Homeless Boys, and to support his work organized St. Joseph's Union. The membership included Pope Pius IX,

This statue, located at Mount Loretto, Staten Island, New York, shows Father John Drumgoole and his constant companions: a huge black rosary and homeless children.

Pope Leo XIII, Father Damien and St. John Bosco, as well as thousands of men and women who caught some of the fire of this remarkable man.

As his work progressed he established the Mission of the Immaculate Virgin to whom he was devoted. The mission occupied a portion of a mile-square property in Tottenville, Staten Island, replete with a lighthouse. This had been known as Red Bank Lighthouse, for nearly a hundred years guiding the ships that passed on Princess and Raritan Bays. At the lighthouse top, Father Drumgoole placed a statue of Mary taken from one of the houses he had established in the city.

Father Drumgoole was ahead of his time

in insisting on the importance of vocational training for his youngsters. When he died in 1888 he had the joy of knowing that nineteen thousand young people had been able to take their places in society because he had cared enough.

Today the Mission of the Immaculate Virgin is popularly called Mount Loretto. Its former publication, *The Homeless Child*, has been succeeded by *The Mount Loretto Review*. Dedicated priests and Sisters provide loving care for the mission's four hundred fifty-six boys and one hundred eleven girls.

A kind of auxiliary staff is composed of groups of supporters who provide enriching experiences to supplement the mission's work. Anchor Clubs of New York City, comprising chapters drawn from the fire department, the newsdealers, the transportation industry, shipbuilders, department stores and U.S. Postal Service workers give of their time and financial as-

Shown at left is the Dearborn Mansion of American Revolution fame. Adjoining it is the first frame church of Our Lady of Perpetual Help. The brick church, far right, was constructed in 1877.

sistance. The Staten Island Kiwanis Club sponsors parties and a Boy Scout troop, and the Ladies of Charity of Staten Island implement the aims and purposes which Father Drumgoole envisioned a century ago. The work never ceases.

MARVELLOUS CURES SAID TO HAVE
BEEN EFFECTED MILES AWAY BY
ROXBURY'S WONDER WORKING SHRINE

With this heading the *New York Herald* of Sunday, March 24, 1901, prefaced a full-page description of the Shrine of Our Lady of Perpetual Help in a Boston suburb. Pictures of the church and of Miss Grace Hanley spread across the width of the paper. In a subhead — "A Lourdes in the Land of the Puritans" — there was reported the miraculous cure of Miss Hanley, sixteen-year-old daughter of P.T. Hanley, former colonel under General Ulysses S. Grant.

Bostonian Catholics were not the least surprised at the publicity. They had been faithfully attending services at the Re-

This is the Basilica of Our Lady of Perpetual Help, Roxbury, Massachusetts. The twin spires were added in 1910. Pope Pius XII raised the church to the rank of basilica in 1954.

demptorist church first established in 1869, next door to the famous Dearborn Mansion. The mansion once was headquarters for General Artemus Ward in the days of the Revolution, visited by Washington to discuss battle strategy. The mansion passed into the hands of General Henry Alexander Dearborn, secretary of war under President Jefferson, and finally came into the possession of the Redemptorist Fathers who in 1869 attached to it a modest frame church. A magnificent brick church was added in 1877 to become the shrine of the miraculous image of Our Lady of Perpetual Help.

The miraculous cure of Miss Hanley reported by the *New York Herald* is but one of the hundreds documented at the shrine. Miss Hanley had been thrown from a carriage at the age of four, with injuries resulting in permanent deformity of the back and lameness of the legs. For twelve years she wore a heavy leather-covered steel corset and hobbled on crutches. Specialists as well as hospitalization and medication offered no relief. Her parents began making novenas at the shrine and on August 18, 1883, on the last day of a novena, as Grace prayed with them, she suddenly laid aside her crutches and walked to the altar, cured. Soon after the cure she went to the Convent of Jesus-Mary at Fall River to complete her education and then joined the order. The *Herald* reporter had investigated the cure from a book of records, with names, addresses and details of cures all listed.

In the shrine at Roxbury, Massachusetts, is a copy of the miraculous image of Our Lady of Perpetual Help. The original is in Rome, its age and artist unknown. It had been venerated in the isle of Crete and from there removed to Rome, retained by a private family until Mary herself appeared to a daughter of the family and told her she wished her picture placed in a church "between my beloved Church

Basilica of Our Lady of Perpetual Help

Miraculous Image of Our Lady of Perpetual Help at the Basilica, Roxbury

of St. Mary Major's and that of my beloved son, St. John of Lateran."

On March 27, 1499, the picture was exposed for veneration in the Church of St. Matthew as Mary ordered, remaining there for three centuries, drawing pilgrims from all over the world. In 1798, war demolished the church; fortunately the picture was saved by the Augustinian Fathers who had charge of St. Matthew's. They removed the picture to the new monastery granted them by Pope Pius VII in another part of the city.

The very last member of their order professed in old St. Matthew's was Brother Augustine Orsetti. In his new location he was frequently visited by a young man, Michael Marchi (later to become a Re-

251

Mother Katharine Drexel, Foundress of the Sisters of the Blessed Sacrament for Indians and Colored People

demptorist). Michael had often been told the picture in the new St. Matthew's was that from the old church and was a miraculous picture.

The Redemptorists came to Rome in 1855 and built a church in honor of their founder, St. Alphonsus, on the site of old St. Matthew's. Father Marchi told his superior of the miraculous picture in the Augustinian monastery and the Redemptorists petitioned Pope Pius IX to have the picture placed in their church on the spot chosen by Mary herself. In granting the request the Pope commanded the Redemptorists to "make her known" all over the world.

The first group of the order to come to America in 1832 consisted of three priests

and three lay Brothers, answering an appeal from the Diocese of Cincinnati. Since they were German-speaking missionaries, they were in great demand for serving the thousands of German immigrants coming at this time.

They labored for seven years without a foundation. Finally one was made in Pittsburgh to be followed by others in Baltimore, Rochester, and Norwalk, Ohio. The first novice to join them in America was John Neumann, who would become America's first male saint.

A biographer has described Neumann's novitiate as consisting of "changing his abode eight times in a year, baptising constantly, preaching incessantly and travelling 3,000 miles through New York, Pennsylvania and Maryland, on horseback, on bumpy stagecoaches, on single track railroads or small steamers and canal boats crowded with raucous immigrants going west."

Neumann enumerated the temptations of the soul attendant on this novitiate, advising "but to remain steadfast and to persevere in all this turmoil of spirit, there is no better remedy than prayer to the Blessed Virgin for the grace of persever-

This is St. Mary of the Quapaws, Indian Territory, Oklahoma. The frame building at left was erected in 1894; the stone dormitory, right, was built by Mother Katharine Drexel in 1915.

ance." He made his profession on January 16, 1842. (A summation of his life will be found in the next chapter; it constitutes the closing entry of the book.)

This record of the nineteenth century closes with the story of a debt still to be paid, a problem as yet unsolved. The plight of the Indian and the unjust treatment accorded him have been referred to elsewhere in this book. Here the history of one tribe, the Quapaw, is given to pay tribute to a saintly woman who gave her life and her fortune for the brotherhood of man.

The Quapaws' Catholicity traces to Arkansas, near the mouth of the Arkansas River, where Father Marquette visited in 1673 and instilled a lasting devotion to the Mother of God. When Henri de Tonti founded Arkansas Post, missionaries came at regular intervals to instruct them. Through the years the Jesuits ministered and deepened the faith that would sustain them through the hardship of being forced from their lands to move into northern Oklahoma, in the area of present-day Douthitt. Benedictine missionaries established a station here and dedicated a chapel to St. Mary of the Quapaws.

When the land was finally allotted them by the government in 1893, Leander (Jack) Fish, a Quapaw, took up residence in a house attached to the chapel, thereby guaranteeing that the forty-acre tract surrounding it would be set apart for the use of Catholics. On the eve of the Assumption of that year the tribal council of the Quapaw reservation petitioned the Honorable Commission of Indian Affairs to establish a Catholic school, stating: "Nearly all those who are members of our tribe by blood are Catholics." First to staff the school was Sister M. Virginia, a diocesan Sister of St. Joseph of Long Island, New York. She was a convert, the niece of Henry Ward Beecher. With her came some Sisters of St. Joseph of Concordia, Kansas, to be followed by Sisters of Divine Providence of San Antonio, Texas.

To St. Mary's uneven history would be added the name of the saintly Mother Katharine Drexel, foundress of the Sisters of the Blessed Sacrament for Indians and Colored People. A Philadelphia heiress, she gave her entire fortune and herself in establishing missions for her red and black brothers. Through her assistance a stone dormitory was built for not only Quapaw children but for Miami, Peoria, Osage and Ottawa as well. In 1927 the school closed for lack of students.

In Santa Fe, St. Catherine's Indian School educates Pueblo, Navajo, Pima and Papago children. Another beneficiary is St. Michael's, west of Window Rock, Arizona, one of the largest Indian boarding schools in the country with an attendance of nearly four hundred Navajo, Hopi, Apache and Pueblo. Elsewhere in this book is the history of Holy Rosary Mission, Pine Ridge, South Dakota, named by Mother Drexel in memory of her stepmother, Emma Bouvier Drexel, who had instilled in her and in her two sisters a deep love of the rosary.

Mother of the Church

THE GOAL — UNITY

TWENTIETH CENTURY

Franciscan Sisters of the Atoner

Our Lady of the Atonement, Graymoor, Garrison, New York

First statue with this uniquely American title, it was so named by Lewis Thomas Wattson, an Episcopalian minister, who founded the Society of the Atonement. Less than a decade later the society was received into the Catholic Church.

Mother
of the
Church

The bright light of modern history shines on this chapter which closed with Bicentennial celebrations. Recorded within this century will be the wars involving our nation and the world, the memory of which is ever present. On the credit side will be the heroic, positive attempts to secure "a just and lasting" peace for all nations.

It was prophetic that as the twentieth century opened, an Episcopalian minister entrusted to Mary his great dream of Christian unity. Lewis Thomas Wattson founded the Society of the Atonement and issued a simple publication, *Rose Leaves from Our Lady's Garden*. To Wattson and his society is traceable every ecumenical endeavor this country has known or will know.

Within the second decade Fathers Thomas F. Price and James A. Walsh founded Maryknoll; its missionaries today serve in most areas of the globe. To read of Mary's intercession in preserving the young Price from drowning is to acquire new and deeper realization of the place she occupies in the fulfillment of God's plans.

Public acknowledgment of Mary's intercession has been provided by Father Patrick Peyton, C.S.C., and Father Harold Colgan. Father Peyton, stricken with tuberculosis, promised if restored to health to work for Mary. His gratitude inspired the Rosary Crusade with its eventual worldwide influence. Father Colgan's recovery from a severe heart attack initiated Mary's Blue Army, in contradistinction to the Red Army of communism. Father Stanley Matuszewski, M.S., began a publication, *Our Lady's Digest*, a compendium of Mariology, history and devotion. He acknowledged Mary's intercession when as a young boy he was saved from drowning "one sunny Sunday summer afternoon, the Feast of the Assumption."

The time-honored Marian titles, inherited from many races, were joined by American companions: Our Lady of Kansas, the Ozarks, the Hudson, the Prairies, and many more. If the great number of titles often puzzles those who do not know Mary, the late Monsignor Ronald Knox said the case is much worse than it appears! Each person has a particular title which makes Mary intimate, individual.

With the admission of Alaska and Hawaii to statehood, Marian history was further enriched by the sacrifices and dedication of pioneer churchmen in these states, particularly Archbishop Charles Seghers, murdered during his ministry in Alaska, and Damien de Veuster's work with the lepers of Molokai and Our Lady of Sorrows. The latter's record is of such heroic proportions as to be the basis for instituting candidacy for beatification.

Students of history will not find in print a dovetailing of events which occurred during World War I. Leon Trotsky and V.I. Lenin met on April 16, 1917, to plan the Russian Revolution which occurred on November 7. *Within that seven-month interval* Mary appeared six times to three shepherd children in Fatima, Portugal, pleading for prayers of reparation for Russia's conversion to her Immaculate Heart to prevent communism from engulfing the world. The miracles at Fatima evoked positive results in the United States with the inception of Block Rosary groups, the Rosary Crusade, the Blue Army and the Reparation Society of the Immaculate Heart of Mary, the latter begun in Baltimore by John Ryan, S.J. These national organizations expanded to worldwide influence, bringing men closer to God through Mary.

The proclamation of the dogma of the Assumption by Pope Pius XII in 1950 was the dawn of a new day for the Church, "the beginning of that great growth of Marian devotion which was to accompany the Christian revival — a revival which Divine Providence had seen fit to initiate even in the darkest hours of the world's materialism."

This proclamation would be followed four years later by the great celebration of the Marian Year which extended the knowledge of the true personality and dignity of the Mother of God. Pope John XXIII stated: "Unquestionably signs seem to point to the fact that ours is a Marian Age; and it likewise becomes clearer day by day that the way for men to return to God is assured by Mary."

In this century new shrines, new Sisterhoods, awards, publications, plays, songs — publicized by press, radio and television — guaranteed increasingly broad approaches in the general public's education of Mary's place in the Church. Pope John, in his inaugural address of Vatican Council II, emphasized: "Divine Providence is leading us to a new order of human relations. By man's efforts and beyond the greatest expectations, we are being directed towards the fulfillment of God's higher and inscrutable designs. Everything, even human differences, leads to the greater good of the Church."

One of the "human differences" proved

to be an outward lessening of Marian devotion — given the full treatment by a news-hungry press. This produced in the 1960s what one Methodist minister termed "a conspiracy of silence" where Mary was concerned. The silent treatment, engendered by the "piety void," permitted but minimum Marian recognition. However, the resulting climate of indifference served only to deepen the loyalty of those who love her.

In the mid-1970s a gradual change occurred, reflected in ecumenical dialogue both stimulating and rewarding, breaching somewhat the gap of ignorance and division on things Marian. Theodore A. Koehler, S.M., director-curator of the University of Dayton's Marian Library, believes Marian devotion is now on the upswing: "Roots are replacing routine. Devotion is more related to the Bible, revelation and liturgy, and this is a sign of spiritual progress." The title of an article by Colman Barry, O.S.B., contributes a consoling thought: "Spiritual Renewal: Best-Kept Secret of the Seventies."

Two hundred years ago Patrick Henry said "he knew of no way of judging the future but by the past." Five centuries of Marian devotion is sure ground for future recognition of the singular dignity of Mary and the place she occupies in the economy of salvation.

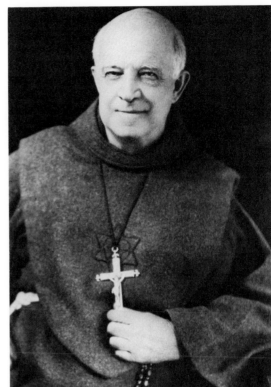

While an Episcopalian minister, Father James Paul Wattson founded the Society of the Atonement which effected the conversion to Catholicity of an entire community of men and women.

Cover and Pages of Episcopalian Publication, First Issued in 1901 by the Society of the Atonement

ROSE LEAVES

——FROM——

OUR LADY'S GARDEN

Vol. I. Graymoor (Garrison P. O.) No. 1
OCTOBER, 1901..

THE MONTHLY MESSENGER

OF THE

ROSARY LEAGUE

OF

OUR LADY OF THE ATONEMENT.

AN ASSOCIATION FORMED TO PRAY
AND WORK FOR THE RESTORATION OF

"MARY'S DOWRY"

TO OUR VIRGIN QUEEN, THE HOLY MOTHER
OF GOD.

Subscription price—10 cents a year.

Our Lady of the Atonement.

The Blessed Virgin is known among Catholics by many names and is invoked under many different titles. Famous among these are the following: Our Lady of Loretto, Our Lady of Lourdes, Our Lady of Grace, Our Lady of Victory, Our Lady of Good Counsel, Our Lady of Sorrows and Our Lady of Mercy. In her wonderful condescension and love the Mother of God has been pleased to reveal herself to the Children of the Atonement under a new name. In the Chapel of our Lady of the Angels, at Graymoor, since All Saints Day, a year ago, the Blessed Virgin has on three different occasions, to three different witnesses, distinctly appeared, thus giving remarkable evidence that the honor, love and prayers addressed to her as OUR LADY OF THE ATONEMENT she is graciously pleased to accept. We have every reason to believe that the Blessed Virgin specially loves this title that links her name with that of JESUS in the glorious work of the Atonement wrought upon the Cross. It must bring to her remembrance that blessed Atonement Day when she stood by the Cross of Jesus and heard Him say

(3)

Rose Leaves

from   our

Lady's Garden

at

Graymoor

The Beulah=Land of the Atonement.

——

Subscription Price—10 cents a year.

Divine providence chose one man to open the twentieth century with a mission which would reach the hearts and minds of millions. That man was Lewis Thomas Wattson. From early childhood he thought of unification of all Christians, a desire instilled by his father, an Episcopalian minister. On graduation from the General Theological Seminary in New York, Wattson worked in Kingston, New York, and Omaha, Nebraska, always with the conviction that he would one day "found a preaching order like the Paulists."

In July 1893, he opened his King James Bible three times to seek divine guidance about his future religious community. The second time his eye fell on the text: "And not only so, but we also joy in God, through our Lord Jesus Christ, by whom we have now received the atonement" (Romans 5:11). The word "atonement" became the guide in planning his future society.

In 1896 he communicated with Lurana Mary White, an Episcopalian Sister in Albany, who shared his convictions and was searching for an Episcopal community of religious which was vowed to corporate poverty. After correspondence and meetings they agreed to found the Societas Adunationis (in translation, At-one-ment), for the union of all Christians under one single authority. In an abandoned chapel on a large tract of mountain woodland in Garrison, New York, they began their work.

The chapel was named Graymoor, honoring Dr. Gray, a minister who had erected it, and Professor Moore of Columbia who had been its early benefactor. In this completely Protestant society, Mary was invoked as Our Lady of the Atonement and her statue installed (see page 257). A rosary league was formed "to pray and work for the restoration of 'Mary's Dowry' [England's] to our Virgin Queen, the Holy Mother of God." Its publication

was entitled *Rose Leaves from Our Lady's Garden.* The young society struggled against prejudice and bigotry, one newspaper labeling the group "ecclesiastical squatters." Nine years after inception the society was received into the Catholic Church. The *New York Times* headlined the event THE CONVENT THAT CHANGED ITS FAITH, and described the conversion as "unprecedented in church annals."

To publicize its objectives the society issued the periodicals *The Lamp* and *The Antidote*, and originated a radio program called *Ave Maria Hour.* From the first it promoted the Church Unity Octave, an eight-day period of prayer. While the octave was at first strongly papal and Roman in its orientation, it gradually evolved into what is known today as the Week of Prayer for Christian Unity. Each year also, laymen and clergy from Anglican, Catholic and Protestant churches meet for National Workshops on Christian Unity.

The society initiated the Union That Nothing Be Lost, a fund-raising organization for overseas and home missions, and engaged in pastoral activity among blacks and Chicanos. At Graymoor it maintains St. Christopher's Inn, open twenty-four hours a day, summer and winter. Any man who knocks at the door, any time of the day or night, is welcomed — no questions asked. In 1975 the inn provided a temporary home for over thirty-eight hundred homeless men and served one hundred seventy-three thousand hot meals. "It's the INN for men who are OUT — out of money, out of a job, out of luck, out of life." The society also maintains New Hope Manor, a live-in therapeutic community for the rehabilitation of female drug addicts. New hopes, with God's help, are given and returned by girls joined in a common fight and coached by Father Dan Egan, "The Junkie Priest," and friars and Sisters.

That the Church in the United States had come of age was formally acknowl-

DOMINA + NOSTRA   ADVNATIONIS

Our Lady of the Atonement, Garrison, New York

*This representation succeeded the earlier one shown in
this section's frontispiece. Here Mary wears a red mantle
to symbolize the Precious Blood of the Atonement.*

edged in 1908 when Pope Pius X removed it from mission status, under the jurisdiction of the Sacred Congregation of Propaganda, and placed it on an equal basis with such ancient churches as those of Italy, France and Germany. In the preceding century, American Catholics had received immense assistance from missionary societies of France, Bavaria and Austria; now it was America's turn to begin repaying its debt in aiding the world's needy. Two priests, unknown to each other, were being shaped for this work; the life of one had previously been spared by Mary's intercession.

Thomas Frederick Price, sixteen, left his Wilmington, North Carolina, home on September 12, 1876, sailing on the *Rebecca*

Clyde to Baltimore to enter the seminary. Five days out a gale came up, sinking dozens of vessels and stranding hundreds more. The *Rebecca Clyde,* disabled twenty miles south of Hatteras, ordered its passengers to put on life preservers. Two seamen were washed overboard and instantly drowned. Two crewmen, trying to clear the propeller, were thrown into the water and disappeared.

At the mercy of wind and waves the boat swamped and keeled over, drowning its captain, some passengers and crew. Young Price, fighting to keep his head above the waters, cried out to Christ to save him. He later recorded:

"Like a flash the sky seemed to open and out of a speck of blue came the clearest possible vision of the Mother of Christ. Upon her face was a smile and stretching forth her hand she pointed to a great floating plank which had been washed overboard from the sinking ship. I gained the plank, pulled myself upon it, and grasped a great ring on its upper surface. I began the Litany of the Blessed Virgin and in my joy I almost sang it."

Young Price was washed up on Portsmouth Island, one of North Carolina's Outer Banks. The *New York Times* of September 21 listed his name among the survivors.

Fever, exposure and exhaustion delayed for a year his entering the seminary. On ordination in 1886 he became North Carolina's first native priest, assigned to Asheville, laboring against poverty, hardship and prejudice, serving remote districts of the state, establishing a home for orphan boys near Raleigh and a seminary to train priests for his southland mission, and finding the time to publish a magazine, *Truth,* to throw light on Catholic doctrine.

As a seminarian his imagination had been fired by the Third Plenary Council's urging that an American branch of the Propagation of the Faith be established in

every diocese; the work of his priesthood had heightened this zeal. Divine providence now brought him in contact with Father James A. Walsh. Together in 1911 they founded the Catholic Foreign Mission Society of America, known as the Maryknoll Fathers.

Large numbers of Eastern Catholics came to America in the early twentieth century and the Russian Orthodox Church spared neither effort nor expense in attracting them to her schismatic fold. To keep them in the Catholic Church, the Holy See appointed a special ecclesiastical superior of their own rite, establishing in 1913 the diocese of the Byzantine rite at Philadelphia, its newly consecrated bishop becoming the ordinary for the more than three hundred thousand Ukrainian-Greek Catholics then in the United States. In 1924 the same was done for about an equal number of Greek Catholics of Russian, Magyar and Croatian nationality, by the appointment of a bishop for them at Pittsburgh.

Today Catholics of the Byzantine rites are ecclesiastically organized into two Metropolitan provinces — the Ukrainian Catholic Archeparchy of Philadelphia, and the Ruthenian (Byzantine) Catholic Archeparchy of Munhall-Pittsburgh. The former serves eight states and the District of Columbia with two suffragan eparchies of Stamford, Connecticut (five states), and St. Nicholas in Chicago (fourteen states). The Munhall-Pittsburgh Archeparchy serves three states, with two suffragan eparchies — Passaic, New Jersey (eight states), and Parma, Ohio (ten states); also one Melkite Catholic Eparchy of West Newton, Massachusetts, serving seventeen states. The combined membership in the above is over half a million.

Catholics of the Maronite rite are organized in the Diocese of St. Maron, Detroit (twenty-two states and the District of Columbia), thirty thousand members.

Catholics of the Armenian rite are organized in six parishes in six states, while Chaldean-rite Catholics have three parishes in the United States.

In the Eastern Church, Mary is called Theotokos (Greek *theos* for God, plus the root of *tiktein*, to bear). Devotion is primarily laudatory and only secondarily supplicatory. One Eastern-rite historian explains: "If we ceaselessly and generous-

State Marker (Wilmington, North Carolina) Honoring Co-Founder of Maryknoll Fathers

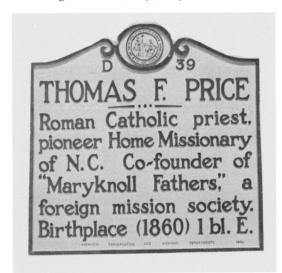

ly sing the glories of Mary as contrasted with our own misery, her own greatness — not to mention her boundless motherly love — will compel her to take into account our lowliness, our misery, our needs, without our directly pointing at any particular need."

The onset of World War I ushered in the pontificate of Benedict XV whose entire reign was filled with the sorrows of the war and its aftermath. Five days after his election on Mary's Nativity, 1914, he addressed the Catholics of the world, expressing his confidence in the help of God, begging the prayers of the faithful in the impending conflict. He concluded: "We pray that our united prayers may be aided by the intercession of the Virgin Mother of God whose blessed birth . . . shone upon struggling humanity as a dawn of peace." When the war ended he ordered the words "Queen of Peace" added as the last invocation to the Litany of the Blessed Virgin.

In that same year in North Arlington, New Jersey, Father John A. Westman, celebrating the first Mass in the area, announced that plans would be drawn up for

Motherhouse, Catholic Foreign Mission Society of America, Maryknoll, New York

World War I, set into motion anti-German feelings in this country which found varied expressions. Bordering on the ridiculous was the substitution of "liberty cabbage" for sauerkraut. Town names were changed: Potsdam to Pershing, Brandenburg to Old Glory, Kiel to Loyal. One name, however, rode out the storm. Its history dated to 1682 when Germans coming to Penn's colony settled on the outskirts of

Shown is a stained-glass window in Our Lady of Purgatory Church, New Bedford, Massachusetts. The only church of this name in the United States, it was built in 1914 for Eastern Catholics of the Maronite rite. The window was designed by Guido Nincheri and installed on Mother's Day, 1954.

This is the mother church of the Ukrainian Archeparchy of Philadelphia. Located in the heart of Philadelphia, the Cathedral of the Immaculate Conception was designed by Julian K. Jastremsky, A.I.A., and dedicated in October 1966. It is the largest church of the Byzantine Catholic rite in the world. A need for icons to adorn it, inspired the formation of the Byzantine Slavic Arts Foundation in Washington, D.C., to encourage the study of painting icons and the collecting of masterpieces from all over the world.

a church to be named Our Lady Queen of Peace. A temporary church had to suffice while elementary and high schools were built, and only later did the beautiful church planned become a reality. Its design is significantly American: The colonial spire, one hundred sixty-five feet above ground level, is visible for a mile on busy State Highway 17. The church's twelve great windows show the contributions which Catholics have made to the foundation of liberty on this continent and to the history of our nation in particular.

The German sinking of the *Lusitania* in 1915, which foreshadowed our entry into

266

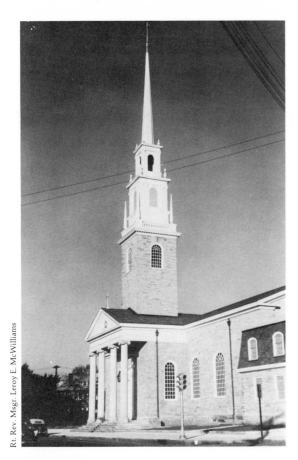

Rt. Rev. Msgr. Leroy E. McWilliams

Pictured is Queen of Peace Church, North Arlington, New Jersey, so named to commemorate the addition of the last invocation to the Litany of the Blessed Virgin by Pope Benedict XV at the close of World War I.

Philadelphia and called their settlement Germantown.

In this Germantown in 1915 a priest was thanking Mary for assisting him. Joseph A. Skelly of the Congregation of the Mission of St. Vincent de Paul (Vincentians) formerly had been prefect of the Apostolic School in Germantown where future Vincentians trained. He had been released from this duty in 1912 to raise funds for building St. Joseph's College in Princeton, New Jersey.

In each letter of appeal he enclosed a Miraculous Medal. So generous was the response through Mary's intercession that

he felt some expression of gratitude was due her. Accordingly he formed in 1915 the Central Association of the Miraculous Medal to promote through this medal devotion to Mary Immaculate.

"Mary's Fortress" was the name given the association's first quarters. Soon larger quarters were required and in 1927 a magnificent shrine was built in the Immaculate Conception Chapel attached to St. Vincent's Seminary in Germantown. A per-

Washington's recognition of patriotism and assistance of Catholics in the Revolution and in the establishment of our government is the theme of this window in Queen of Peace Church, North Arlington, New Jersey.

Rambusch

petual novena is held here every Monday; its twelve services are attended by about four thousand weekly. Similar weekly novenas are held across the country and overseas, with weekly services in more than thirty-four hundred churches and chapels here and abroad — even in the Church of St. Louis in Moscow. Millions of medals, and more than seventeen million novena booklets, have been distributed here and throughout the world.

An American artist, Lauren Ford, has painted an incident in the life of little Catherine Labouré which is part of the medal's history. Nine-year-old Catherine, third youngest of eleven, was left motherless in 1815. For consolation she climbed on a chair and took down from the kitchen

This painting by Lauren Ford, entitled "The Celestial Mother," portrays an incident in the life of Catherine Labouré, to whom Mary entrusted the Miraculous Medal devotion.

Design of Miraculous Medal Entrusted to Catherine Labouré by Mary in 1830

shelf a statue of Mary. Hugging it close to her breast she said, "Now you will be my Mother." As older brothers and sisters left home she remained to care for her father, until at twenty-two she joined the Daughters of Charity of St. Vincent de Paul.

Her novitiate was spent at the order's motherhouse at 140 Rue de Bac in Paris. There on the evening of July 18, 1830, Mary appeared to her and told of a mission she wished undertaken, though not disclosing its nature, and then disappeared. Mary appeared again on November 27, resplendent in a white silk robe and veil, her hands outstretched; framing the apparition were the words, "O Mary, conceived without sin, pray for us who have recourse to thee." Mary directed that such a medal be struck, promising that its wearers would receive great graces. The apparition then turned and Catherine beheld the medal's reverse.

The vision of November 27 was repeated on several later occasions, imprinting the medal's design indelibly on Catherine's mind. Her spiritual advisor informed the archbishop of Paris of the apparitions and he directed that the medal be struck.

Within four years more than four million of these medals were distributed. Catherine had also told her advisor, Father Aladel, of a mission which the Virgin had entrusted to him — that of establishing an order, a confraternity of Children of Mary, of which he would be founder and director. Through it many graces and indulgences would be granted, the month of May would be celebrated with great solemnity, and its observances rewarded with abundant graces. The first group of Children of Mary came into existence in 1838 at Beune, France, in the district where Catherine had been born. Membership today is in the millions. The association's primary aim is veneration of Mary in her Immaculate Conception and the personal sanctification of its members, coupled with a true social apostolate.

The pending trial of John T. Scopes for teaching Darwin's theory of evolution to high-school students wasn't the only issue occupying the attention of the nation's educators in June of 1925. Eagerly awaited was the Supreme Court decision on a bill passed in Oregon ordering parents and guardians to send children between the ages of eight and sixteen to the public schools.

When the bill had first passed, leading the protest were the Sisters of the Holy Names of Jesus and Mary, pioneers of Catholic education in the state. Their St. Mary's Academy in Portland had become in 1859 the first chartered private school in Oregon. The Sisters brought suit in the case known as *Pierce vs. Society of Sisters of the Holy Names of Jesus and Mary.*

The United States District Court declared the law unconstitutional on the grounds that it unjustly repudiated the binding contract which the state had entered with the school on its legal incorporation. Enforcement of the law was thus restrained and the state now appealed to the Supreme Court.

That body on June 1, 1925, upheld the lower court's decision stating that the Oregon law violated the Constitution's Fourteenth Amendment, unreasonably interfering "with the liberty of parents and guardians to direct the upbringing and education of children under their control. As often heretofore pointed out, rights guaranteed by the constitution may not be abridged by legislation which has no reasonable relation to some purpose within the competency of the state. The fundamental theory of liberty upon which all governments in this union repose excludes any general power of the state to standardize its children by forcing them to accept instruction from public teachers only. The child is not the mere creature of the state; those who nurture him and direct his destiny have the right, coupled with the high duty, to recognize and prepare him for additional obligations."

In the aftermath of World War I, spiritual values would be reassessed; good men would seek broader avenues for spreading the faith, for promoting peace and unity. In Dublin, Ireland, Frank Duff, a member of the lay Society of St. Vincent de Paul, conceived the idea of an organization which through prayer and apostolic works could bring Christ into the world through Mary's all-powerful mediation.

He met with Father Michael Toher and fifteen young working women, and after addressing the Holy Spirit for guidance they began the association called Our Lady of Mercy. Its first assignment was visiting the sick in Dublin hospitals. Gradually their work expanded and their numbers increased as others recognized the importance of this apostolate. Here laymen were filling a need in making personal contacts preliminary to the essential, sanctifying work of the priest.

By 1921 the organization had only nine branches, but now a more solid structure was being planned. The members would be called the Legion of Mary, thinking of themselves as an army like the Roman Legion, but an army for service in the Church's spiritual warfare against the forces of evil. They borrowed the military vocabulary of the early legion for the basis on which they would function.

Under a *concilium* (the international governing authority of the legion) would be a *senatus*, set up on a national or regional basis, under which would be a local *curia*, which in turn would preside over separate *praesidia*. The word *praesidium* in the ancient legion was given to a detachment, a frontier guard, which was a beachhead for conquests or a bulwark for defense; in the modern Legion of Mary it would become a symbol of loyal courage and military solidarity. After several years' progress in Ireland the legion spread into Scotland, gradually over Europe, and eventually over the world.

In 1931 Joseph P. Donovan, a Vincentian priest, visited the famous convent of the Daughters of Charity of St. Vincent de Paul on the Rue de Bac in Paris. It was here that Mary had appeared a century earlier to Catherine Labouré, to initiate devotion to her Immaculate Conception through the Miraculous Medal. A nun at the convent placed a Legion of Mary handbook in Father Donovan's hands and its reading so impressed him that on returning to the States he acquainted the readers of the *American Ecclesiastical Review* with the legion's work in an article entitled: "Is This the Long-Awaited Parish Organization?" Father Nicholas Schaal, pastor of St. Patrick's Church in Raton, New Mex-

Rev. Eugene E. Geiger

Depicted are the objectives of the Legion of Mary, an international organization begun in Ireland. In this picturization, Mary is crushing the serpent (Satan). Soldiers symbolize the legion's armies. Their banner, with the inscription "Legio Mariae" (Legion of Mary), is displayed proudly, while their standard (at right) signifies the predominance of the Holy Spirit guiding the members in bringing Christ into the world.

ico, read the article and set up the first American praesidium among the mining men of his parish. A second praesidium was begun at a Midwest Catholic women's college and before long the legion had taken root in this country.

Today the Legion of Mary is the largest apostolic organization of lay people in the

Catholic Church, with well over a million and a half active members in every country of the world. In the United States its members strive to become better Christians by a balanced program of prayer and action, which gives Catholics of all ages an opportunity to do something positive for Church and community while at the same time deepening their spiritual life. Members meet together once a week for prayer and discussion, and spend a couple of hours doing a definite work, always done in pairs and geared to the individual's capabilities.

The legion's handbook has been translated into some thirty languages and legion prayers are recited in over one hundred languages and dialects in eighteen hundred dioceses throughout the world. (For accounts of the legion's activities, read of Missouri's "Lady of the Rivers" and the

Page From First Issue of The Queen's Work, *Organ of Sodalities of Our Lady*

THE

QUEEN'S

WORK

MAY, 1914

VOLUME 1   NUMBER 1

The Queen's Work

IT IS pleasant to think how many friendly eyes will read these first lines of Our Lady's new magazine. Not every new monthly, indeed, very, very few of them, can count upon such a host of well-wishers and lovers. The Sodalists of the Blessed Virgin, by thousands upon thousands, will welcome it into their homes for its Mistress' sake, and many of the faithful besides, who are not yet Sodalists will be its readers too.

Yet there are certain questions, such as arise upon the ushering in of every new magazine, which it will be worth our while to dwell upon at the beginning. The answers to them will bring out more and more clearly just what the new monthly means and does not mean to do.

First of all, what does the name THE QUEEN'S WORK signify?

THE QUEEN'S WORK is to be the expression here in America, of a great, international movement, which is making itself felt throughout the world-wide Sodality of the Blessed Virgin. This movement aims at bringing all the Sodalists closer together, and at giving them new zeal and courage to work for their own greater holiness, the help of others, and the defense of the Church. THE QUEEN'S WORK is this work which the sons and daughters of the Blessed Virgin throughout America are to do for the love and honor of their Heavenly Queen. The new magazine will do its utmost to encourage, help and inspire the Sodalists

of every age and state of life, to realize the true ideal of the Sodality; it will strive to inspire them with an active and apostolic spirit, and thus do for our Sodality here in America what other Sodality magazines are doing in England, Austria and Holland, in Ireland and in Germany, in Italy, Hungary, Bohemia, Croatia, Brazil, Colombia and even in far away India.

A great many good Catholic folk begin to wonder when they hear this explanation of the name, THE QUEEN'S WORK.

"I didn't know that Sodalities were meant to do apostolic work," they say, "I thought they were only for the Sunday meeting and office, and for the monthly Communion." This is a very serious misapprehension. The first rule of the Sodality (Rules of 1910) clearly contradicts it, and gives us at once, the scope and purpose of the new magazine:

"The Sodality of Our Lady * * * *," says this rule, "aims at fostering in its members an ardent devotion, reverence, and filial love towards the Blessed Virgin Mary. Through this devotion * * * * it seeks to make the faithful gathered together under Her name, good Catholics sincerely bent on sanctifying themselves * * * and zealous * * * * to save and sanctify their neighbor, and to defend the Church of Jesus Christ against the attacks of the wicked."

Here we have in brief, the program of THE QUEEN'S WORK. To promote a

The Annunciation

"Hail Mary, full of grace," the Angel saith.
　　Our Lady bows her head, and is ashamed;
She has a Bridegroom who may not be named,
Her mortal flesh bears Him who conquers death.

Now in the dust her spirit grovelleth;
　　Too bright a Sun before her eyes has flamed,
　　Too fair a herald joy too high proclaimed,
And human lips have trembled in God's breath.

O Mother-Maid, thou art ashamed to cover
　　With thy white self, whereon no stain can be,
Thy God, who came from Heaven to be thy Lover,
　　Thy God who came from Heaven to dwell in thee.
About thy head celestial legions hover,
　　Chanting the praise of thy humility.

This is the winning poem in The Queen's Work, *1917 Marian poetry contest. Kilmer wrote the poem before enlisting for service in World War I; he was killed in action the following year.*

Forty-first Eucharistic Congress later in this section.)

Signal honor must be shown to the efforts of the Jesuits — Edward Garesche and Daniel A. Lord. To them is traceable the great impetus which the Sodality of the Blessed Virgin movement received in the United States. Their work followed in the Jesuit tradition, begun in the eighteenth century. (See section entitled "Mother of Good Counsel.")

Father Garesche, appointed national promoter of sodalities in 1913, had as his assistant Father Lord, then still a scholastic. They began *The Queen's Work* to give the sons and daughters of the Blessed Virgin throughout America "new zeal and courage to work for their own greater holiness, the help of others, and the defense of the Church." The publication included the writings of many notables. Joyce Kilmer

271

won first place in the magazine's 1917 Marian contest for poetry with "Annunciation." *The Queen's Work* was succeeded by *Direction* (for sodality directors, moderators and officers) and *The Junior Sodalist* and *The Children's Moderator* for those working on the elementary level.

After 1971 the sodalities became known as Christian Life Communities, formed of groups of men and women, adults and youth, joined with other people involved in living their full Christian vocation and commitment in the world. The governing principles and operating norms of sodalities, revised in the spirit of the Second Vatican Council documents, were promulgated and approved by Pope Paul VI. The Spiritual Exercises of St. Ignatius remain a specific source and characteristic of the spirituality of the movement. Christian Life Communities are located in forty-two countries; in the United States there are approximately one hundred fifty.

Each decade of the century pointed up the need for establishing a depository for the rapidly accumulating output of published Marian material. In 1943 Father Lawrence Monheim of the Society of Mary (Marianists) began at the University of Dayton, Ohio, a Marian library, to help commemorate by 1950 the centenary of the society's arrival in America. The aim of the library was to be "a new apostolic weapon to help the Marianists carry on in this Marian era Our Lady's dynamic mission as the spiritual mother of all men."

Scholars and professional people turn to this library for literary ammunition with which to defend basic Marian truths and justify Marian devotion. The library contains nearly forty-eight thousand Marian books and pamphlets and the better-known Marian periodicals. Thirty-seven thousand mounted and indexed clippings from non-Marian magazines and newspapers are available. Marian records, filmstrips and slides are loaned free; Marian

Marian Library, Dayton

Our Lady of the Marian Library, University of Dayton, is the home of this wood carving, the work of Xavier Hochenleitner, Oberammergau.

art pieces on display supply atmosphere and stimulate visitors in choosing artistic devotional art for their homes.

Here Marian authors can find complete source material on the Immaculate Conception, the rosary, music, poetry, art, selected material on Marian shrines or liturgical Marian anthems. The library's international research center collects and indexes all available Marian printed material in books, pamphlets and periodicals, with special emphasis on the major research languages of Latin, French, German, Spanish, Italian and English.

Marian Library Studies is published eight times a year and contains official

272

Marian documents, articles or important addresses. Special awards, made yearly, are considered elsewhere in this section.

To promote the renewal of religious studies called for in the postconciliar era according to the guidelines of Vatican II, the Marian Library has created the Marian Library Institute. It is an American branch of the Pontifical Faculty of the Marianum of Rome, and offers a pontifical doctoral degree in sacred theology, with specialization in Marian studies. The first person receiving the degree was Marion Zalecki, of the Pauline Fathers, for his work entitled "The Theology of a Marian Shrine: Czestochowa."

An important Marian library was begun by Juniper B. Carol, O.F.M., at the Franciscan monastery in New York City. The

Shrine of Our Lady of La Salette, Attleboro, Massachusetts

To commemorate the centennial in 1946 of our nation's dedication to the Immaculate Conception, Stanley Matuszewski, M.S., published Our Lady's Digest. Pictured is the first edition.

collection comprised over twelve thousand items (books, pamphlets, articles) including photostatic copies and microfilms of hundreds of out-of-print pieces. It is estimated that Father Carol has virtually everything written on the co-redemption in any language. The collection has recently been divided, half housed in Tampa, Florida, the other half in Washington, D.C.

At Poughkeepsie, New York, the Marist Brothers maintain an extensive library, begun in 1950 by Brother Cyril Roberts. Still another library, started around 1922, is at the National Shrine of the Immaculate Conception in Washington, now added to Marian works in the Mullen Library of the Catholic University of America. Here its usefulness has been enhanced by the presence of a large general theological collection.

At the university, one of the country's leading Mariologists, Eamon R. Carroll, O. Carm., began in 1957 a program in

Scene From Skit on Ave Maria Hour, *conducted by the Society of the Atonement*

Mariology as a regular feature of the summer session. The program provides solidly theological courses on the meaning of the Blessed Virgin within the framework of Catholic theology. Each summer two six-week courses are offered, one a doctrinal survey, the other a more specialized theme, as Our Lady in the Scriptures, etc. Enrollment has been consistently good.

For Catholics the year 1946 would have extra significance as the centennial of our land's dedication to Mary under her title of the Immaculate Conception. In that year a young priest was inspired to enter the publishing field with a little magazine called *Our Lady's Digest.* "Like the Archangel Gabriel, it would announce the praises of the Blessed Virgin."

The magazine is a digest of outstanding Marian articles from Catholic books and magazines, a compendium of Mariology, of Marian history and devotion, especially notable for the relatively high number of theological articles it publishes. Leading Mariologists and Catholic journalists are

on its editorial board. Its founding (and continuing) editor is Father Stanley Matuszewski, whose lifelong devotion to Mary traces to an incident in 1926 when he was saved from drowning while swimming in a branch of the Tioga River near Morris Run, Pennsylvania. It was on "one sunny Sunday summer afternoon, the Feast of the Assumption."

Father Matuszewski joined the Missionaries of Our Lady of La Salette, a society which had been founded in 1852 at La Salette, France, for the purpose of providing priests to care for the Shrine of Our Lady of La Salette. This shrine had been built on the site of Mary's appearances to two children, eleven and fifteen, as they herded their cows on a mountain slope, four miles from the village of La Salette in southeastern France.

On September 19, 1846, on the eve of the feast of the Seven Dolors of Our Lady,

Televising Novena Service at Shrine of the Miraculous Medal, Germantown, Pennsylvania

274

the children saw a brilliant globe of light. The globe seemed to divide and there appeared the form of Mary, seated on a rock on the floor of a dried-up stream. She was weeping bitterly. She beckoned the children to approach her and gave them a message "for her people." They were offending her Son by violating the commandments, swearing and blaspheming the Holy Name, by nonobservance of Sunday and the Lenten fast. She predicted punishment would follow if they remained unrepentant. Afterwards the dry spring of the stream flowed freely and miracles followed. Pope Pius IX declared the apparition a true one, a basilica was built, and the Missionaries of Our Lady of La Salette founded.

Radio, television, the stage — all would join with the press in spreading devotion to Mary. Pioneering in radio was the Society of the Atonement with its *Ave Maria Hour*. The program's originator was Father Anselm, S.A., who was inspired in 1935 to suggest to his superior Father Paul (founder of the society) the idea of broadcasting a religious program.

At first it was decided to present weekly novena devotions in Mary's honor, but a Jewish gentleman encouraged and supported the idea of dramatizing the lives of the saints. The first program brought letters attesting to the good of the program in reference to their personal lives. Many wrote for information about the Church, inquiries resulting in establishing the society's correspondence course in religion.

A young actor, a convert from Anglicanism, had come to the studio in 1938 to meet Father Paul; he eventually joined the order and later became the program's director. The *Ave Maria Hour* has continued uninterrupted and is heard on three hundred stations in this country and Canada and on an equal number in the armed forces. It is but one of the many channels through which the Society of the Atone-

ment is reaching the world to effect its goal of Christian unity.

All media are being utilized by Mary Productions' *Airtime* which originated in 1950. It offers royalty-free scripts for stage, film, radio and tape production. This nonprofit apostolate is conducted by the talented husband-wife team of Mary-Eunice and Joseph Spagnola of Belford, New Jersey.

America's "rocks and rills and templed hills" have many statues of Mary looking down on them in silent contemplation. Some have special American titles, created for a particular observance, for a locality, for love, united through the leaven of the One Mother. Nearly half a continent apart stand Our Lady of the Hudson (New York) and Our Lady of the Rivers (Missouri).

The former, designed by Tom Penning, cradles a towboat in her arm, commemorating the work of hundreds of men who plied the inland waterways from New York City to the Great Lakes in the past century. It is located on the grounds of the Church of the Presentation of the Blessed Virgin at Port Ewen. The port had been established as a depot in 1851, handling the coal coming from Pennsylvania, by way of the Delaware-Hudson Canal, for shipment to northern markets. The statue was commissioned by New York's tow companies, the International Longshoremen's Association, and private individuals.

Near the confluence of the Missouri, Mississippi and Illinois Rivers stands Our Lady of the Rivers, erected in gratitude for Mary's intercession in protecting lives and property at floodtime. Torrential rains in July 1951 had whipped across Kansas, Oklahoma and Missouri. The floods following left forty-one dead and property loss of a billion dollars. Riverbank communities were flooded out and Portage, Missouri, faced destruction.

Father Edward B. Schlattman, pastor of

St. Francis Church, called upon his parish Legion of Mary to direct their prayers to Our Lady of the Rivers for her intercession. Portage people watched as the waters neared their homes, yet the flood finally crested and the city was still high and mostly dry. Father Schlattmann determined that a shrine be erected in gratitude and the idea was given impetus by the deathbed act of a Mississippi boatman. Converted to Catholicism, he asked that friends and relatives make donations of money for a statue of Mary in lieu of sending flowers for his funeral.

Thus the campaign began and the solidly Christian population in the Portage-St. Louis area raised fifty thousand dollars for the memorial. A submerged street was chosen as the site for the twenty-seven-foot, three-thousand-pound statue designed by Mrs. Anthony McClory. The statue was made of plastic, reinforced with glass fibers for resisting dampness, weather changes and discoloration from hot summer suns. In 1957 the statue was mounted on a seventeen-foot concrete pedestal, six hundred feet out from the Portage shore. At night the lighted statue is an official Coast Guard navigational aid.

Two Marian images on the Atlantic coast are as far removed in background as they are in size. The eighteen-foot statue of Our Lady of Good Voyage stands atop a church of that name in Gloucester, Massachusetts. She is the protectress of the Portuguese fishermen whose ancestors came to Gloucester from the Azorean island of Pico, where their forebears were once taken on as crews of American whalers.

When the fishing vessels are homeward bound at night a message is radiotelephoned to shore, asking that the statue be lighted; then the crew watches for Mary's welcoming glow on the horizon. Each June, Gloucester witnesses the blessing of the fleet. After Mass a procession bearing a

replica of Our Lady of Good Voyage moves to the docks where the bishop blesses the vessels and, in memory of those lost at sea, flowers are strewn on the ebbing tide.

The dress of Our Lady of Aquia in Virginia recalls the Indians inhabiting one of Catholicism's most historic localities. At Aquia Creek in 1650 the Brent family established the first English-speaking Catholic colony in Virginia. Close by rose the town of Aquia where a chapel was built and later visited at intervals by Bishop John Carroll, who through his married sister was related to the Brents.

Giles, Margaret and Mary Brent had first come to Maryland from England in 1638. Family and political ties with the Calverts assured Giles of large land grants and official positions. Margaret insisted on recognition, arguing that since she and her sister had brought five men and four servants as colonists, they were entitled to eight hundred acres of land. On securing additional land grants she became the first woman in Maryland to hold land in her own right. When the Assembly refused her "voyce & vote allso" she moved to Virginia and established her home at Aquia Creek. Records list her as "Margaret Brent, Gentleman," but historians use the designation "first American suffragette."

In 1963, members of Catherine Doherty's Madonna House of Combermere, Canada, opened a retreat house in Stafford, Virginia, and named it Our Lady of Aquia. Madonna House is a Pious Union of men, women and priests which trains persons to staff mission centers where positive action is encouraged on the problems of civil rights, housing, labor, interracial justice, school discrimination, juvenile delinquency and migrant work. Another United States house of the Pious Union is La Casa de Nuestra Señora at Winslow, Arizona.

When the French controlled the Missis-

miles around. Not until 1941 was a parish established through the efforts of two zealous women who secured signatures on a petition requesting a resident priest. An abandoned gas station was converted into a "little cathedral," to be succeeded by the present native stone church. Outside its entrance Our Lady of the Ozarks welcomes the area's Catholics and the many vacationers attracted to the mountain's beauty.

The Shrine of Our Lady of the Prairies at Powers Lake, North Dakota, boasts a statue of Mary designed by Father Frederic Nelson, a Scandinavian and a convert. (Catholics are a minority in this northern part of the state, where Scandinavian Protestants first settled.) The sculpture depicts Mary walking barefoot among the wheat.

Our Lady of the Rivers, *Portage, Missouri*

Tom Penning

Our Lady of the Hudson,
Port Ewen, New York

sippi Valley they established Arkansas Post among the Bow Indians. In referring to the post they would say *aux arcs* (at the bows). In time this became Ozarks and two centuries later it would become one more Marian title.

To the Boston Mountain area of the Ozarks Catholics came as early as 1891 to work on the St. Louis and San Francisco railroad beds. A priest came at rare intervals and the event would be reported by a rider on horseback notifying families for

Jack Zehrt

She holds a sheaf of real North Dakota wheat, placed there when crops are blessed at harvesttime.

At Mater Christi Church in North Riverside, Illinois, is the Mother of Mothers statuary: Mary stands on the globe of the earth, her robe enveloping a mother and baby. The figures are deliberately identical in posture and appearance to remind mothers of their closeness to the Mother of God. Mater Christi Church is the first of this name in the United States — an appropriate location for the shrine. When the statuary was erected in 1956, twenty-five hundred mothers participated. Mass is of-

Our Lady of Aquia, Stafford, Virginia

*Our Lady of Good Voyage,
Gloucester, Massachusetts*

fered each day for all mothers giving birth on that day and for the grace of motherhood for all wives. Devotion to Mary under the title of Mother of Mothers is promoted in part through Catholic hospitals in the country, reminding mothers of Mary's powerful spiritual resources.

Many honorary awards are given yearly to persons who by their daily lives exemplify Marian ideals, or whose creative work has contributed to a spread of Marian devotion and the furtherance of brotherhood. The Stella Maris Medal, first given in 1960, is awarded to a woman, regardless of race, color or creed, who has distinguished herself by love and service to her fellowmen in the community in which she lives. Its name, meaning Star of the Sea, is appropriate for the city of Toledo

Mother of Mothers Statuary, North
Riverside, Illinois

Our Lady of the Ozarks, Boston
Mountain, Winslow, Arkansas

Joseph A. Costa, C.P.S.

Mother of Mothers Shrine

Our Lady of the Prairies,
Powers Lake, North Dakota

Rev. Frederic J. Nelson

Stella Maris Medal, Awarded by Mary Manse College, Toledo, Ohio

Shown is the motif of Our Lady of Guadalupe Medal. The medal is awarded by Pi Alpha Sigma (Pan-American Fraternity) of St. John's University, Brooklyn, New York.

Pius XII Marian Award, given by Montfort Fathers, Ozone Park, New York

where Mary Manse College is located. Also in Ohio, the College of Mount St. Joseph gives the Mater et Magistra award to women for social action in the pattern and spirit of the encyclical *Mater et Magistra.*

The Pius XII Marian Award, initiated in 1955, is given for promoting devotion of consecration to the Immaculate Heart of Mary, as called for by Pope Pius XII in his encyclical on Mary's Queenship, *Ad Coeli Reginam.* Its donor, the Montfort Fathers (Missionaries of the Company of Mary), were founded for total consecration to the

Mother of God. The recipient of the medal in 1965 was Frank Duff, founder of the Legion of Mary.

Originated in 1942, Our Lady of Guadalupe Medal is given for promoting understanding among peoples of the Americas. Its 1965 recipient was Felicia Rincón de Gautier, mayoress of Puerto Rico. In 1966 it was awarded to Cardinal Richard Cushing.

Mundelein College, Chicago, awards a Magnificat Medal to Catholic college alumnae for leadership in social action. The University of Dayton, Ohio, bestows

Drawing of Our Lady of the Mist, Dramatizing Mary's Intercession in World War II Incident

a Marianist Award for outstanding contributions to Mariology (until 1966) for outstanding contributions to mankind (from 1967). The Marian Library Medal of the University of Dayton was first given for books in English on the Blessed Virgin. Its 1953 recipient was Fulton Sheen for *The World's First Love* which eventually went to paperback and was translated into five languages; the 1956 medal went to Ruth Cranston, non-Catholic author of the universally acclaimed *The Miracle of Lourdes*, also translated into five languages.

Titus Cranny, S.A., received the medal for *Our Lady and Reunion*. Since 1971 the medal has been awarded every four years to the person who has made the most significant contribution to the advancement of studies anywhere in the world since the last International Mariological Congress.

Many are the incidents that could be told of preservation from death in World War II, but it remained for a U.S. Navy chaplain to make his experience a matter of record and thereby bestow a special title on Mary.

On November 11, 1942, the *U.S.S. Joseph Hewes* was torpedoed during enemy action off the coast of Fedala, in what was then French Morocco. The chaplain, Father Francis J. Ballinger, jumped into the water carrying the Blessed Sacrament in a watertight case about his neck. When rescued by the *U.S.S. Ancon*, Father Ballinger's pyx was missing; it was returned to him several days later by the *Ancon's* coxswain who had recovered it.

During the first week of the Salerno operation the enemy made a particular effort to sink the *Ancon* since she was a prize target, the flagship of Vice Admiral H.K. Hewitt and Lieutenant General Mark Clark. In the brightness of a near-full moon one night, as enemy planes were approaching the ship from two directions and attack seemed imminent, a sudden mist rose from the sea, obscuring the *Ancon*, so that the enemy planes missed her and withdrew.

Father Ballinger had an artist portray these two events in a drawing called "Our Lady of the Mist." In the artist's rendition the flowing robes of Mary signify the mist protecting the *Ancon* which she holds in her hands. Slender cords going down from the ship's bow suspend the pyx which rests in the water below. The prevalence of the symbol "V" is indicative of the prayers offered to God through Mary in petitioning for victory. The words at either side —

"Vide Stellam, Voca Mariam" (Look to the Star, Call upon Mary) — are a prayer known to sailors since time immemorial.

Thousands of our men serving in the Pacific were safely transported on the *U.S.S. St. Mary's*. Official U.S. Navy records give the ship's interesting history. She was built in 1944, exactly a century after the first *U.S.S. St. Mary's* (see section entitled "Virgin Militant"), and like her predecessor was destined to be associated with Japan. The first *St. Mary's* had been part of Commodore Matthew C. Perry's fleet sailing to Gore-Hama, when our government was seeking to engage Japan in commerce, "to open by massive persuasion the gates hitherto hermetically sealed."

Now a century later the second *U.S.S. St. Mary's* would slide down the ways of a Los Angeles shipyard, but her date with Japan would be a bloody one. On November 15, 1944, she carried troops to Leyte Gulf in the Philippines, surviving her first air raid. After bringing troops to Kerama Retto in the Ryukyus Campaign, and re-ceiving the casualties from this operation (March 1945), she again put to sea. When Japanese kamikazes attacked she survived, though four ships around her were hit. She sailed for Okinawa where she again survived kamikaze attacks on April 16. Three days later she took part in a diversionary landing off southern Okinawa, discharging all troops and cargo, never out of sight of burning villages and flashing flame-throwers along the ridges, never out of range of the guns of land and sea attack.

When Japan sued for peace, the *St. Mary's* was changed to a troop transport. Men of the First Cavalry Division were taken aboard and the ship sailed for Tokyo Bay. On September 2, 1945, she had a "ringside seat" when surrender terms with Japan were signed aboard the battleship *Missouri*. On October 11 she became a part of the "Magic Carpet," bringing home over eighteen hundred U.S. Navy and Marine Corps personnel; on the distant shore a huge sign read: WELCOME HOME. WELL DONE.

Attack Transport "U.S.S. St. Mary's,"
Serving in the Pacific Campaign, World War II

From the Motion Picture, "The Song of Bernadette"
Based on the Franz Werfel book of the same title, in this scene the half-blind Bouriette bathes his eyes in the water at Lourdes and is healed.

From the horrors of war emerged a Marian tribute in the form of a book written by a Jew. Franz Werfel — poet, novelist, dramatist — had been expelled from the Prussian Academy of Art for his opposition to the Nazis. When the Germans entered Austria in 1938, he and his wife moved to Paris; when France fell in 1940, the Werfels joined a chaotic migration of Belgians, Dutch, Poles, Czechs and exiled Germans seeking refuge. They were told that Lourdes was the one place where "if luck were kind" one might find a roof.

At Lourdes they found lodgings and then for the first time Werfel became acquainted with the history of Mary's appearances to Bernadette Soubirous and "the wondrous facts concerning the healings." Yet each day was tense with the danger of capture. Werfel wrote: "One day in my great distress I made a vow that if I escaped from this desperate situation and reached the saving shores of America,

I would put off all other tasks and sing, as best I could, the song of Bernadette."

He reached the United States late in 1940 and the following year wrote *The Song of Bernadette*. Describing the eighteen appearances of Mary to the peasant girl in Lourdes between February 11 and July 16, 1858, Werfel stated: "All the memorable happenings which constitute the substance of this book took place in the world of reality. Since their beginning dates back no longer than eighty years, there beats upon them the bright light of modern history and their truth has been confirmed by friend and foe and by cool observers through faithful testimonies. My story makes no changes in this body of truth."

The book won wide acclaim as a best seller here and abroad and was translated into seven languages. The *Saturday Review of Literature* described its "matchless prose . . . that enchants us with the magic

283

The family that prays together stays together

Family Rosary Crusade Billboard, Times Square, New York,
"Crossroads of the World"

of children's voices raised in medieval hymn." Hollywood purchased the film rights and began production in 1943. The movie became a box office attraction and won several awards for its "superb integration of emotional drama and spiritual exaltation."

Werfel died the following year, secure in the knowledge that his work had fulfilled his vow "to magnify the divine mystery and the holiness of man — careless of a period which has turned away with scorn and rage and indifference from these ultimate values of our mortal lot."

Early 1942 found America involved in the war with the months ahead witnessing bitter fighting and many Allied defeats.

War news naturally would overshadow other happenings. Only in retrospect can one appreciate the significance of two anniversaries being celebrated in that year. The Communists were observing the twenty-fifth anniversary of their revolution, the Catholic Church the twenty-fifth anniversary of Mary's appearances at Fatima, Portugal.

To fully understand this seeming coincidence, one must review certain months of 1917 when pressures of World War I obscured the relationship between two important events. Lenin and Trotsky had met on April 16 to plan the revolution which came on November 7. In that same seven-month period Mary appeared six times to three little children at Fatima. She urged daily recital of the rosary, reception of Holy Communion on the First Saturdays in reparation to her Immaculate Heart, and the consecration of Russia to her care that communism would not envelop the world.

In 1942, on the anniversary of those appearances, Pope Pius XII consecrated the world to the Immaculate Heart of Mary and by this act intensified devotion to Our Lady of Fatima and the recitation of the rosary for world peace. At this very time, a prayer program was being initiated in the United States, inspired by Father Patrick Peyton. He had come from Ireland in 1928 to enroll at the Holy Cross Seminary at Notre Dame and ten years later was strick-

en with tuberculosis. He promised Mary that if she would intercede in asking God to restore him to health, he would spend his life in repayment. His condition improved, he continued his studies and was ordained. To express his gratitude a highway shrine was his first consideration. Then he recalled his parents, eight brothers and sisters kneeling each day to recite the rosary. From that recollection the idea of the Family Rosary Crusade was born.

The crusade was launched in late fall of 1942 in Albany, New York; its enthusiastic reception led first to a local, then national, radio rosary program. On May 13, 1945, with millions listening in, the rosary was recited by Bing Crosby and the Sulli-

Rosary Rally, State Capital, St. Paul, Minnesota, 1958

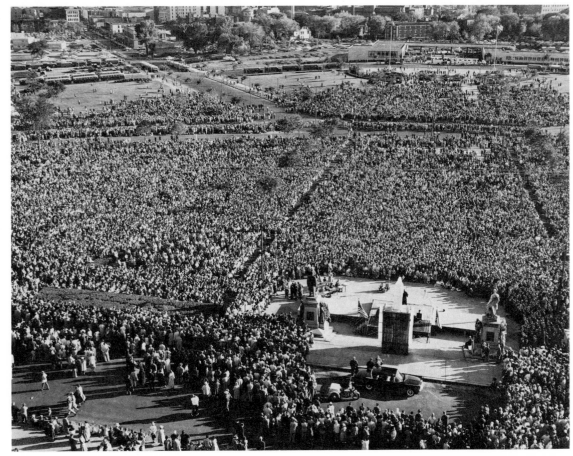

Symbol of Block Rosary Lay Apostolate,
Begun in Detroit, Michigan, 1946

vans (the latter's five sons had died in a single World War II naval engagement). Letters of appreciation prompted country-wide advertising with billboards picturing a family praying and the slogan "The Family that Prays Together Stays Together."

Radio shows between 1948-1970 played to an estimated weekly audience of over five and a half million people around the world. Some one hundred forty stations in this country, forty-one in foreign countries, and over two hundred of the Armed Forces Radio Services carried the programs.

When the Vatican Council suggested that popular public devotions be drawn up in the spirit of liturgical seasons, Father Peyton recognized that a sensitivity to liturgical models could help revitalize the rosary and accordingly changed the name

from Family Rosary Crusade to Campaign for Family Prayer. Top talent through the years — in radio, movies, television and advertising — have carried the program across the land. The aim is to reach Catholics and non-Catholics with the message of family daily prayer. Protestants and Jews have also participated in public prayer endeavors, promoting love and brotherhood.

Films on the fifteen mysteries of the rosary in English, Spanish, Portuguese and French, are shown in countries too numerous to list. On Mother's Day, 1973, a new television series was launched, *A Matter of Faith*, carried on one hundred seventy stations. Father Peyton's guest on that day was Archbishop Fulton Sheen whose message was, he stated, not on woman's liberation, but on woman's consecration through Mary.

286

Today in Hollywood the Family Theater occupies a modern building with editing rooms, sound studios, projection room and film vault. The earlier property and building had been donated in 1948; the present structure was built through the help of the Raskob Foundation and the friends of Father Peyton. There is an oratory for daily Marian devotions.

When world prayers for peace were being requested, a priest in Detroit — Father Solanus Casey, O.F.M. Cap. — suggested to his good friend Nicholas J. Schorn how Fatima might be brought to the United States. Schorn, a sixty-year-old retired businessman, crippled since 1937, began an initial mailing of one hundred thousand reprints of a Fatima article from the *Michigan Catholic.* Soon his work branched out to lecturing on Fatima and through these contacts he met Father Peyton.

Father Peyton told Schorn of a Detroit housewife's claim that Mary had appeared to her while the battle of Iwo Jima was at its height in 1945. She related that she had been praying for the safety of her six brothers in the service; a seventh had al-

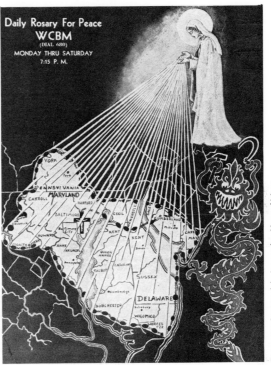

First Poster Issued Announcing "Daily Rosary for Peace" Radio Broadcast, Baltimore, Maryland

Reparation Society of the Immaculate Heart of Mary

Fatima Findings *is the monthly bulletin of the Reparation Society of the Immaculate Heart of Mary. Its subtitle is "The Smallest Newspaper on Earth for the Greatest Cause in Heaven."*

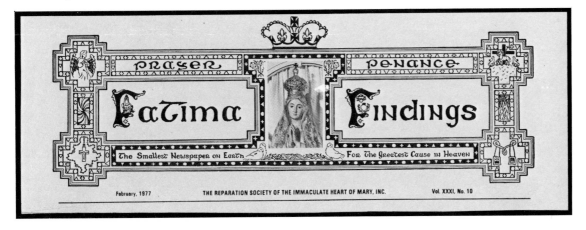

ready been killed and another was then in the division engaged in the Iwo Jima assault. She related that Mary, dressed in black, appeared and told her to bring groups of women together to recite the rosary at each other's homes, house by house, block by block. The woman's parish priest gave permission for these gatherings and soon similar area groups formed.

When Mr. Schorn learned of the success of the gatherings, he founded his rosary apostolate. The vicar general of Detroit,

Original Leaflet Introducing the Blue Army in 1947

BLUE ARMY

PROGRAM REQUESTED BY
OUR LADY OF FATIMA

1. Frequent recitation of the Rosary. Daily, if possible. Family Rosary. This means sacrifice but Our Lady asks for *sacrifice.*

2. Reception of Holy Communion as an act of reparation on the first Saturdays of five successive months. This means the sacrifice of getting up earlier in the morning to go to Mass and Communion, but Our Lady has asked for *sacrifice.*

3. Saying the Rosary on five successive Saturdays. This requires the sacrifice of time and effort but Our Lady asks *sacrifice.*

4. Meditating on the mysteries of the Rosary for fifteen minutes some time during the day of the successive first Saturdays. This requires the sacrifice of thought and concentration, also time and effort, but Our Lady asks for *sacrifice.*

5. To add at the end of each decade of the beads this prayer: "Oh my Jesus, forgive us our sins, deliver us from the fire of Hell, and lead all souls to Heaven, especially those that most need Thy mercy." This requires sacrifice of memorizing the prayer, but Our Lady asks *sacrifice.*

NOTE: Wear a blue ribbon or a blue string by which you will be recognized as a member of the Blue Army, fighting by prayer and penance the Red Army of Communism.

Additional copies of this leaflet may be obtained by sending a three-cent stamped envelope to St. Mary's Church, Plainfield, New Jersey.

Our Lady of Fatima Shrine, St. Mary's Church, Plainfield, New Jersey

Joseph A. De Caro

International Youth and Children's Day

Beaming Faces

A First Communion class poses in the courtyard of St. Cecilia's Church, Dallas, Texas, before the Fatima shrine built with money collected by schoolchildren of the parish.

Bishop Stephen S. Woznicki, gave the movement its name, explaining, "The Block Rosary is an extension of Fatima and has two extra values: It creates spiritual unity among neighbors, now sadly missing, and is Our Lady's answer to the Block System of the Communists." Up into the late 1960s Nicholas Schorn had sent out thirty million pieces of literature on the Block Rosary and corresponded with leaders in sixty countries on all six continents. The Block Rosary continues today, without fanfare or publicity, in many areas.

The broadcasting of the rosary in this country owes its inception to Al Cummings of New Orleans who refused to take "no" for an answer. His suggestions for rosary program broadcasting were being met by one comment: "It can't be done." Cummings persisted and finally got Radio Station WJBW to introduce the program. Its success was immediate. It has been continued each year over the air for the past twenty-eight years and may be heard each night at eight o'clock over Radio Station WSMB which has sponsored the program since April of 1962. In addition, the Rosary Guild, sponsored by the Archdiocesan Union of Holy Name Societies, New Orleans, pledges its members to the daily family rosary.

In Baltimore in 1946 Father John Ryan, S.J., was inspired to found the Reparation Society of the Immaculate Heart of Mary.

289

Vatican Note on New Dogma Proclaimed by Pope

ROME, Nov. 1 (P)—Following is the text of a note in English, issued by the Vatican press office, explaining the Papal Bull "Munificentissimus Deus" ("Most Munificent God") on the dogma of the Assumption. Phrases in quotation marks are direct translations from the Bull, which is in Latin:

The Bull is prefaced by the reflection that the omnipotent providence of God "intersperses and tempers the sorrows of nations and individuals with joy according to His hidden designs so that in many different ways all things may work together unto good for those who love Him."

It then proceeds to examine the historical background of the truth to be defined.

It observes how the privilege of Our Lady's Assumption received new splendor from the definition by Pius IX of the dogma of the Immaculate Conception. These two privileges are intimately related because of the connection between the original sin and death. After that dogma had been defined, the number of petitions from every class of society requesting the definition of the Assumption has steadily grown.

On this account the present Pontiff had a commission appointed to study the question thoroughly, and wrote to the Bishops of the whole world to ask their opinion about the definability of the truth of the Assumption of Our Lady as a dogma and whether they together with their flocks desired its definition.

Bishops Reply Affirmatively

The reply [of] the Bishops to both questions was almost unanimously in the affirmative.

The Bull goes on to say:, "This remarkable unanimity of the Catholic Episcopacy and faithful

POPE PIUS PROCLAIMS DOGMA OF ASSUMPTION

Kneeling before the huge assemblage at St. Peter's in Rome as he declares that Mary, Mother of Jesus, went to heaven in body as well as soul.

Associated Press Radiophoto

And it is the cry of the centuries, your cry of today which breaks in the vastness of this venerable place, already sacred to Christian glories, the spiritual harbor of all people, and now the altar of your overwhelming piety.

As moved by the palpitations of your hearts and the emotion of your lips, the very stones of this patriarchal basilica vibrate and it seems that together with them exult with mysterious quiverings the unnumberable and ancient temples erected everywhere in honor of the Assumption, monuments of a single faith and earthly foundations of the heavenly throne of glory of the queen of the universe.

In this day of joy, under this expanse of sky, together with the wave of angelic exultation, in harmony with that of all the militant church, there cannot but descend upon souls a torrent of grace and teachings, fertile animators of renewed holiness.

Therefore, we raise our eyes with confidence to this lofty creature from this earth, in this, our time, and in this, our generation, shouting to all: 'Lift up your hearts.'

Comfort for Uneasy Souls

To many anxious and uneasy souls—sad result of an uprooted and turbulent era—souls oppressed but not resigned and that no longer believe in life's goodness and, being almost compelled, accept only the momentary, the humble and unknown girl of Nazareth, now glorious in heaven, will open higher visions and will comfort them when contemplating the destiny which befell her, who, elected by God to be the mother of the incarnate word, meekly accepted the word of the Lord.

And you—especially near to our heart, the tormented anxiety of our days and our nights, the

Pope Pius XII Proclaims Assumption a Dogma of Faith, 1950

This society had grown out of a nocturnal adoration society which had as its objectives prayer, reparation, the daily rosary and acts of self-denial. The society became the first in the country to purchase radio time for its "Daily Rosary for Peace Program."

Posters were distributed in the state and interest mounted weekly. The program is now in its twenty-first year and the society has expended nearly a quarter of a million dollars in bringing the rosary to its thousands of listeners. All-male broadcasts, over WBMD, are made at the Fatima Shrine in the Chapel of Grace of St. Igna-

tius Church, for it was here that the society had been founded.

A monthly bulletin, *Fatima Findings*, is published with the subtitle, "The Smallest Newspaper on Earth for the Greatest Cause in Heaven." It is sent to members in all fifty states as well as those in thirty foreign countries. The bulletin carries a monthly rosary meditation for the First Saturdays, Fatima items of world interest, and promotes pilgrimages to area shrines. On these occasions the penitential element advocated at Fatima is stressed.

A simple piece of blue paper, measuring four and three quarters by three inches, was the motivating force enrolling an army of over six million, and the man responsible for that paper was Father Harold V. Colgan, pastor of St. Mary's, Plainfield, New Jersey. His heart attack is part of the story. One day in November 1946, he was rushed to a hospital where five doctors predicted he could not recover. But Father Colgan clung to life. Still alive on December 8, he decided that Mary's feast day would be devoted entirely in prayer to her. He had her statue brought to his room and during the day's meditations promised that if he lived, the balance of his life would be spent in her praise. A week later, though still not fully recovered, Father Colgan returned to his rectory.

For months he could find no appropriate way of fulfilling his promise. Then in October of 1947, while he was rereading of Mary's appearances at Fatima and her plea for prayer, sacrifice and consecration in daily living for the defeat of communism, Father Colgan was suddenly struck by this message: He believed that if a number of people in his large parish would follow Mary's directives "we would have a small army, not with tanks or guns or bullets or instruments of war, but armed with the spiritual implements of prayer and penance ... fighting the errors sweeping the world, and particularly the errors of communism. We would call it the Blue Army in contradistinction to the Red Army of communism." And so Mary's army was conceived.

For ten consecutive weeks Father Colgan presented his idea at church devotions and his parishioners responded. They organized in printing the blue leaflet and distributing it personally and by mail. Soon requests for leaflets came from all over the country; in a year and a half three hundred thousand were mailed. The *Plainfield Courier-News* headlined the progress, PRIEST'S WAR ON COMMUNISM GAINS WORLDWIDE FOLLOWING.

To keep its members informed of the Blue Army's campaign, a publication entitled *Soul* was begun. Father Colgan also began lecturing in 1947 and never stopped until the year before his death in 1972. The priest who almost died in 1946 averaged three hundred speaking engagements a year. The work is now carried on in the hands of an outstanding Catholic author and lecturer — John J. Haffert, only living American layman to have interviewed Lucia, one of the three children to whom Mary appeared at Fatima in 1917. The Blue Army has taken root in fifty-seven nations and more than twenty million people have signed the Blue Army pledge.

Since Mary had chosen to appear to children at Fatima, it seemed obvious to many that children were to be apostles in making her message of prayer and sacrifice known. This thought inspired Catholic mothers in Dallas, Texas, to ask permission of the bishop of the Dallas-Fort Worth Diocese to approve their plan of educating children in Mary's message. One day was to be set apart for this purpose. They reasoned that the children of the United States would be its citizens of tomorrow, the ones most affected by war and unrest, and the decision-makers for America's future.

With the bishop's permission, the Children's Day movement was established. The first Saturday of each October would have children in a special role honoring Mary and asking her intercession for world peace. The first parish observance was that of St. Cecilia's, Dallas; its pastor, Monsignor William Robinson, became the first spiritual director of the movement. The schoolchildren collected money among themselves for erecting in the church courtyard a Fatima shrine before which parish observances could be held.

The Children's Day movement spread rapidly throughout the country, yet remains today under the ecclesiastical jurisdiction of the bishop of Dallas. The governor of Texas issues a proclamation each year, as does the mayor of Dallas. Children's Day has now become International Youth and Children's Day. Observances are held in Canada, Australia, Puerto Rico, the Virgin Islands and Portugal.

Every twenty-five years the Church celebrates a Holy Year, a year of special grace and prayer, which begins and ends with the opening and closing of the holy doors in the major basilicas of Rome on consecutive Christmas eves. The celebration has a historical precedent in the year of jubilee prescribed for the Jews by God.

In the Holy Year of 1950, Pope Pius XII proclaimed as a dogma of faith the Assumption of the Blessed Virgin in body and soul into heaven. The Vatican release (with full coverage in *The New York Times*) observed how this privilege had received new splendor from the definition by Pope Pius IX of the dogma of the Immaculate Conception. In his speech Pius XII reminded the faithful that "nothing must ever prevail over the fact and knowledge that we are all sons of the same Mother, Mary who lives in heaven, a bond of union with the mystical body of Christ, as a new Eve and new Mother of the living, who wishes to lead all men to truth and to the grace of her divine Son."

It is of interest that suggestions for a definition of this dogma had first been made exactly a century earlier. Pope Pius IX in 1849 consulted the bishops of the world on the opportuneness of defining the Immaculate Conception as a dogma of the Catholic Church. Two bishops answered that it would please them if His Holiness would declare not only the Immaculate Conception but also Mary's glorious Assumption as a doctrine of divine faith. Nothing, however, came of these suggestions.

In 1863 an Italian Franciscan, Remigius Buselli, presented the Pope with a theological study on the definability of the Assumption. Some months later Queen Isabella II of Spain entrusted to the apostolic nuncio at Madrid a signature-laden petition asking that the Holy See take steps towards the solemn definition of this Marian privilege. The queen had been inspired to this move by St. Anthony Mary Claret, founder of the Congregation of the Missionary Sons of the Immaculate Heart of Mary (popularly called Claretians). With these two petitions the Assumptionist Movement was on the march.

A Benedictine, Aloys Vaccari, worked from 1868 until 1880 to further the movement, but a decree of the Holy Office judged the movement inopportune at this time. In spite of official frowns, the Assumptionist Movement gained ground. By 1941 the Holy See had received sixty volumes of petitions signed by cardinals, patriarchs, archbishops, bishops, priests, religious and the faithful. In 1942 Pope Pius XII appointed two Jesuits to inventory the growing dossier of petitions, now over eight million in number.

Four years later the Pope asked the bishops of the world what the people and their pastors believed in this matter, not demanding texts, arguments or explanations, but soliciting their personal opinions of the possibility and opportuneness of a dogmatic definition. A deluge of formal requests for the dogma's definition was received. In view of the resulting proclamation, it follows that the actual belief of the universal Church manifest in the preaching of the pastors and in the judgment of the faithful is a safe criterion of the revelation of a truth, and consequently of its definability by the solemn magisterium.

The subject of the Assumption has been considered at many of the international Marian congresses held beginning in 1900, but to the Franciscans goes first place for their series of Assumptionist congresses conducted in various countries. The

292

Operation Deepfreeze Marian Medal. This medal was especially struck for the U.S. International Geophysical Year, 1957-1958.

order's minister general in 1946 had requested each province, university and house of theological studies to petition the Pope for the dogma's definition. Now national Franciscan Marian commissions were established in various parts of the world, with committees appointed in the individual provinces. National Marian congresses were organized every five years, the first in Rome in 1947, followed by those in Lisbon, Madrid, Montreal, Buenos Aires and Puy-en-Velay.

The First Franciscan National Marian Congress in this country was held in San Francisco, logical setting in view of the hallowed associations of its pioneer missionaries in New Spain. The congress met on October 8-11, 1950, in anticipation of the proclamation of the dogma on the first of November.

Continuing in the Franciscan tradition of signal devotion to Mary, Father Juniper B. Carol in 1949 founded the Mariological Society of America, "to promote an ex-

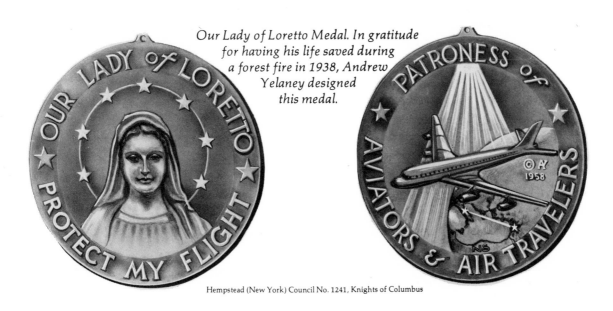

Our Lady of Loretto Medal. In gratitude for having his life saved during a forest fire in 1938, Andrew Yelaney designed this medal.

Hempstead (New York) Council No. 1241, Knights of Columbus

change of views on Marian doctrines and to further research in Mariology." He established his international reputation as Marian theologian with *De Corredemptione Beatae Virginis Mariae* which expresses his life's dedication to the cause of Mary's co-redemption.

In 1954 he began editing the three-volume *Mariology*, embracing every phase of Marian theology and devotion, for theologian, student, priest or religious, yet general enough for lay persons. His editorship of *Marian Studies*, begun in 1950, has continued to the present. Now in preparation is a book entitled *The Controversy over the Debitum Peccati in Our Lady*.

Only a few years intervened between the proclamation of the dogma of the Assumption and the great celebration of the Marian Year, 1954. Exactly a century earlier, Pope Pius IX had formulated, with absolute precision and for all time, the doctrine of the Immaculate Conception when on December 8, 1854, he issued the bull entitled *Ineffabilis Deus*. Its essential word of the definition of the doctrine stated:

"The most blessed Virgin Mary, in the first instant of her conception, was by the singular grace and privilege of almighty God, in view of the merits of Jesus Christ, Savior of the human race, preserved immune from all stain of original sin. This doctrine is revealed by God and therefore must be firmly and constantly believed by all the faithful."

One hundred years later the Church named 1954 as the Marian Year. Since under the title of her Immaculate Conception Mary was the patroness of the United States, it was but natural that American Catholics would express their joy in many ways: Pontifical Masses, pageants, plays, concerts, pilgrimages, exhibits, even a pyrotechnic display over Monterey Bay, California.

In Chicago, Soldier Field was turned

into an outdoor cathedral when two hundred thousand persons assembled for the Marian Year tribute on the feast of the Nativity. A heroic-sized statue — the work of the Dominican priest-sculptor, Thomas McGlynn — was assembled in portions at the north end of the field. Cardinal Samuel Stritch, archbishop of Chicago, celebrated Mass at a specially built altar placed before a gigantic crucifix. Nationality-costumed groups of Croatians, Chinese, Slovaks, Germans, Hungarians, Slovenians, Ruthenians, Filipinos, Irish, Polish, Italians, Ukrainians, Mexicans, Lithuanians, Bohemians — Americans all — took part in the celebration.

When the doctrine had first been formulated in 1854, an American newspaper expressed concern that the dogma had been defined in our "enlightened age"; but a century later the papers of the country gave full publicity to each and all celebrations. Millions of persons were thus brought closer to the knowledge of the true personality and dignity of the Mother of God. The total effect on non-Catholics may never be known, but for one Episcopalian minister attending the Pontifical Mass at Soldier Field, only one course was open — to enter the Catholic Church, because for him "Mary opened the door."

Operation Deepfreeze of the 1957-1958 U.S. International Geophysical Year received a "heavenly" assist when the Catholic officers and men of the U.S. Naval Mobile Construction Battalion Special, Detachment Bravo, placed themselves under the care of Our Lady of the Snows, wearing the medal designed by their chaplain, Father Leon S. Darkowski. The event took place at Mass on October 14, 1956, at the Naval Air Station Chapel, North Kingston, Rhode Island, where the men were being readied for eighteen months' Antarctic duty.

The medal's face shows Mary surrounded by Antarctic activity; she stands be-

Joseph F. Siwak

Entrance to Cathedral of Mary Our Queen,
Baltimore, Maryland

*Dedicated in 1959, this is the first church in
the United States to bear this Marian title.*

neath the aurora australis (southern light) over which an airplane flies; to her right an icebreaker is at work; a snow tractor is beneath her feet, and at her sides are a U.S. Navy explorer in Eskimo clothing and a penguin.

Andrew Yelaney, a commercial airline navigator, in 1959 designed Our Lady of Loretto medal in gratitude for a debt owed Mary since 1938 when he and six Civilian Conservation Corps men were fighting a forest fire in Emporium, Pennsylvania. Trapped by a sheet of flame and unfamiliar with the mountain terrain, they could see no way of escape. Something impelled Yelaney to call his companions to run to one side of a little clearing; before them was a ravine down which they scrambled before flames engulfed the area around them. Six men in another party perished.

Yelaney was convinced Mary had interceded with God in preserving him and his companions from death. His gratitude found expression when later, as chairman of the International Airline Navigators Council, he was asked to draw up a presentation plaque for awarding those promoting air safety. He designed the medal of "Our Lady of Loretto, Patroness of Aviators and Air Travelers" — Loreto, Italy, marking the location of Mary's home miraculously transported from Nazareth in 1294.

The medal's reverse shows Mary's mantle in the form of heavenly light bathing a jet above the Mediterranean. Nazareth and Loreto are the tiny stars. The medal's promotion is handled by the Knights of Columbus, Hempstead, New York, with proceeds going to the training of young men for the priesthood.

As a crowning act of the Marian Year of 1954, Pope Pius XII designated May 31 as the feast of the Queenship of Mary. In Baltimore, in observance of this honor, ground was broken for the Cathedral of Mary Our Queen, first edifice in the

296

country bearing this title. It was consecrated in 1959, coinciding with the delayed observance of the Sesquicentennial Anniversary of the erection of Baltimore as the nation's first diocese. (See section entitled "Mother of Good Counsel.") With its opening the old Basilica of the Assumption did not cease to be a cathedral church, Pope John XXIII having decreed it to be a co-cathedral.

At the cathedral's entrance stands an eight-foot statue of Mary Our Queen; the orb and flowering scepter accent her regal title. She crushes a serpent with her feet, recalling the prophecy in Genesis 3:15 that through a woman would be crushed the head of man's ancient foe. Four designs are repeated in the ornaments outlining the entrance: the black-eyed Susan, official flower of Maryland, bearing the Calvert colors of yellow and black; the rose, symbolic of Mary's love of God; the lily, symbolic of her purity; the pomegranate, emblematic of the divine power of her Son.

When Alaska became the forty-ninth state in 1958 she brought into the Marian family the heroic traditions of her early missionaries who had worked and died in service in the icy wastelands. Outstanding among these valiant men was the saintly Bishop Charles John Seghers whose diocese included no less an area than the entire territory of Alaska. This he traveled from one end to the other, enduring cold, hunger and danger in establishing remote mission stations.

In 1886 Bishop Seghers left Victoria, British Columbia, for Nulato, Alaska, to establish a center there from which Jesuit priests would serve. Accompanying him were the Jesuits, Pascal Tosi and Aloysius Robaut, and a helper, Francis Fuller. Their arduous route led up the gorge of the Dyea, a glacial torrent now famous as the Chilkoot Pass. After crossing the divide, they descended to Crater Lake, one of the sources of the Yukon, arriving at Lake Lin-

Map of Alaska Showing Mary's Mission on the Yukon River

Our Lady of the Snows, Nulato — First Permanent Catholic Mission in Alaska

derman where they constructed a raft to float them, by connecting streams, to Lake Bennett.

They spent a month there, constructing a clumsy scow in which to continue their perilous voyage. After many exciting incidents and narrow escapes, they reached the famous Miles Canyon and successfully negotiated the dreaded White Horse Rapids. They traversed over five hundred miles of what was then an absolute wilderness to reach the first trading post on the Yukon at the mouth of the Stewart River.

Bishop Seghers was impatient to proceed to Nulato before the Yukon would be closed by ice, and he and Fuller continued on, leaving the Jesuits at the Stewart River camp. Along the way Fuller began acting irrationally; suddenly he went berserk and killed Bishop Seghers. When travel permitted, the Jesuits followed only to learn of

Natives at Prayer in Chapel of St. Mary's Mission, St. Marys, Alaska

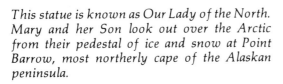

Pictured (top) is St. Mary's Mission, St. Marys, before the 1963 fire. Arrow indicates the building where a statue of Mary was placed when fire threatened. Lower photograph, taken after the fire, shows a distinct break in the conflagration's path of destruction.

This statue is known as Our Lady of the North. Mary and her Son look out over the Arctic from their pedestal of ice and snow at Point Barrow, most northerly cape of the Alaskan peninsula.

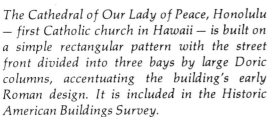

The Cathedral of Our Lady of Peace, Honolulu — first Catholic church in Hawaii — is built on a simple rectangular pattern with the street front divided into three bays by large Doric columns, accentuating the building's early Roman design. It is included in the Historic American Buildings Survey.

Our Lady of Peace in Courtyard of Cathedral, Honolulu

This rare photograph shows the catafalque set up in the Cathedral of Our Lady of Peace, Honolulu, for the Solemn Requiem Mass offered for the repose of the soul of Don Alfonso XII, king of Spain, who died in 1885. (It was customary in Hawaii to honor monarchs of other countries with special ceremonies.) The Mass was attended by the king and queen of Hawaii and their court, attesting by their presence to the cordial relations existing between the monarchy and the Church.

This plaque, honoring Father Damien, can be seen at the Cathedral of Our Lady of Peace, Honolulu, where Father Damien de Veuster was ordained and said his first Mass.

the bishop's death. Father Tosi returned to San Francisco to obtain help, and not until 1899 was he able to go on to Nulato to establish the mission of Our Lady of the Snows, first permanent Catholic mission in the desolate Yukon area.

South and west from Nulato is St. Marys, where in the snowy hills on the banks of the Andreafski River stands St. Mary's Mission, a hundred miles from the Yukon's mouth — as the crow flies. It was built in 1951 by Eskimos working under the direction of James C. Spils, S.J. Its chapel is a place of beauty where natives come from distant villages to pay homage to Mary.

The mission in 1963 suffered serious loss. That all its buildings were not destroyed is miraculous. Fire in five hours wiped out a gymnasium, the priest's and boys' quarters and a priceless library. Fanned by the wind, fire began bridging the narrow corridor leading to the Sisters' quarters, classrooms and chapel. A statue of Mary was placed in the fire's path and over a hundred girls began reciting the rosary. The wind suddenly changed and the fire fanned out. The aerial view taken after the fire shows the clean break in the fire's

300

progress, believed by many to have been halted by Mary.

Interest in Alaska was stimulated and knowledge of the land enriched by the explorations, writings and lectures of Bernard Hubbard, S.J., the "Glacier Priest." His work is represented in Jesuit archives by three hundred thousand negatives and a million and a half feet of film, about ninety percent taken of his "wrestlings" with the Arctic country.

In all his hazardous travels he never suffered serious accident; fervent Hail Marys of thanksgiving appear in his records. On the ice and snow at Point Barrow he placed her statue as the most northerly shrine on the continent in 1931. Six years later he erected a bronze statue of Christ the King on rocky King Island in the Bering Sea. Its

The Church of Our Lady of Sorrows, located at Kaluaaha, Molokai Island, Hawaii, was the first of six chapels built by Father Damien.

National Shrine of the Immaculate Conception, Washington, D.C. — Seventh Largest Church in the World

Pictured is the entrance to the National Shrine of the Immaculate Conception. The statue of Mary flanked by two angels is the work of Ivan Městrović, famed Yugoslav sculptor.

Eskimo inhabitants, entirely Catholic, live in houses built on stilts and lashed to cliffs. On the feast of Christ the King they solemnly proclaimed that their island should be given that name.

The vast northern portion of Alaska is served by over one hundred thirty priests, Sisters, Brothers and devoted volunteers in what Pope Pius XI called "the most difficult mission in the world."

Close on the heels of Alaska's statehood came that of Hawaii. The islands' Catholicity is rich in Marian devotion, the first church having been dedicated to Our Lady of Peace. Three lay Brothers of the French Congregation of the Sacred Hearts of Jesus and Mary (Picpus Fathers) came here in

1827 and erected three grass huts on a small plot of ground, one hut serving as a chapel. On that site, sixteen years later, the Cathedral of Our Lady of Peace was built.

The cathedral is of native coral blocks and stands on a busy street in downtown Honolulu. In its courtyard is Mary's statue, painted in gold leaf, a copy of an ancient one venerated in France. On the four sides of its base are inscriptions in English, Hawaiian, French and Portuguese which read: "In memory of the First Roman Catholic Church, Our Lady of Peace, 1827-1893." (The year 1893 is the date of the statue's erection.) At the cathedral's entrance is a plaque honoring the memory of Father Damien, beloved the world over

301

Mary Altar — Gift of the Marys of America
It is located in the Crypt Church of the National Shrine in Washington, D.C.

for his heroic service to the Molokai lepers.

Father Damien de Veuster's work with the lepers of Molokai is a saga of love, courage and compassion. Soon after joining the Congregation of the Sacred Hearts of Jesus and Mary in his native Belgium, he was sent to the Hawaiian Islands and ordained in the Cathedral of Our Lady of Peace, and there offered his first Mass. In 1873, at his own request, he was made chaplain of the leper colony on Molokai.

He found his charges in tumbledown dirty huts on a shelf of a great dark rock wall rising up out of the Pacific. He inspired the sick to clean their huts and started them on a building campaign which resulted in erecting their own church, decorated with crude bright colors.

A man of many talents, he was especially skilled in carpentry. For the first ten years after arriving at Molokai he built a church or chapel every year. His service to

302

the living was matched by his concern for the dead. For them he made their own coffins and dug their graves. He also treated, spiritually, the non-lepers living in the area.

The first of six chapels built for them he named Our Lady of Sorrows. It is at Kaluaaha, on Molokai Island, topside of the cliffs separating the leper settlement. About five years before his death he recognized the incipient stages of leprosy in his own body and from then, until his passing in 1889, he identified himself with his brother lepers.

In 1969 the State of Hawaii, in recognition of his great contributions, chose his statue to be placed in Statuary Hall in the nation's Capitol.

The tragic year of 1914, which threw the world into turmoil, found an American bishop happily conceiving the idea of a monumental Marian church in the nation's

Capitol. Thomas Shahan, rector of the Catholic University of America, with the warm approval of Pope Pius X, began interesting the Catholic hierarchy of the country in erecting, with national support, a shrine honoring Mary's role as heavenly patroness of the United States.

Five years were spent in considering designs and the architectural form finally chosen was in the Byzantine-Romanesque spirit. The cornerstone was laid in 1920 and the Crypt Church completed six years later, its focal point being the Mary Altar, gift of the Marys of America. The altar was presented on November 19, 1927, by the International Federation of Catholic Alumnae. The mensa, or table, is a five-thousand-pound block of semitransparent golden onyx from Algiers; its base is Roman Travertine marble. Cut into the altar's sides are the figures of Christ, His apostles and St. Paul. At this altar more

than three thousand young men have been ordained to the priesthood and many more to minor orders.

After 1932, lack of funds prevented further construction and for nearly twenty-five years the shrine remained an exquisite church obscured by its truncated exterior shape. To mark the Marian Year of 1954 the bishops of the nation pledged funds to complete the exterior of the upper church. Work was completed late in 1959 and the shrine's dedication occurred on November 20. Its Bell Tower, a Washington landmark, was made possible by the pledge of a million dollars by the Knights of Columbus on June 8, 1957.

The shrine takes its place among the great churches of the world, telling Mary's story in stone. That story begins at the main entrance where on a balcony stands Ivan Městrović's statue of Mary Immaculate and below it the words first sung to

A Portion of the Marian Center and Library, San Francisco, California

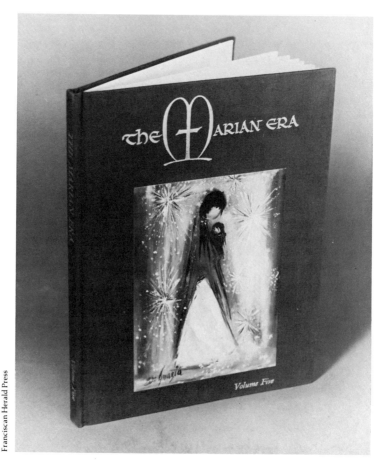

"The Marian Era"

This publication was edited by Marion A. Habig, O.F.M., from 1960-1974. The Navajo Madonna on the cover of this particular volume is the work of Ted De Grazia of Arizona, noted artist of the desert land of the Southwest.

Judith, "Thou art the Glory of Jerusalem, the joy of Israel, the honour of Our People" (Judith 15:10). The center door is surmounted by the scene of the Annunciation, flanked by eight carved panels showing women who prefigured Mary or who are mentioned in the Gospels. Sculpture, mosaics, paintings and memorials, erected by individual orders, complete the paean of praise.

From the Marian Year of 1954, and particularly its observance in the Franciscan National Marian Congress in San Francisco, interest in general information, studies and publications about Mary had slowly been increasing. Contacts were being made with ecclesiastics, religious, and men and women in secular life, which could be developed in the cause of Mary. From this evident interest emerged the establishment of a permanent Marian center in San Francisco, under the direction of Father Alfred Boeddeker, O.F.M.

A further step was the establishment of

*Michelangelo's "Pietà," Loaned by the Vatican
to the 1964-1965 New York World's Fair*

a Marian library. This owed its inspiration to "Our Lady's Week," August 7-15, 1960, under the direction of Eamon R. Carroll, O. Carm., who conducted a forum on Catholic doctrine of Mary. The library was opened and blessed in the Serra Center, San Francisco. Its initial aims were to provide sources of information and their distribution on a knowledge of Mary: doctrine, devotions, plays, radio and TV programs, the collecting, classifying and circulating of books on her from all parts of the world and in all languages. Projected aims included a collection of current Marian periodicals, foreign and domestic, a newspaper-magazine clipping file (indexed by subject), and a catalog of Marian books in other libraries.

Prior to the library's inception, Madonna festivals had been held in San Francisco since 1959, where paintings, sculpture and objects of art showed the universality of Marian devotion. In these exhibits Orthodox and Protestants cooperated in lending their Marian images. The success of this exposure encouraged planning for future displays.

In 1968 the center published a brochure

Altar of Our Lady of the Airways Chapel,
Logan International Airport, Boston, Massachusetts

entitled "What You Can Do for Priests," which offered a "Prayer for Priests" explaining "Why We Invoke Mary." Promoters in every part of the country distributed hundreds of thousands of the brochures to churches, chapels, convents, private homes, hotel rooms, hospitals and institutions. In 1971 the center planned and promoted a National Marian Lecture Tour by Eamon R. Carroll, O. Carm., which lasted three months, given in fifty-seven dioceses in twenty-eight states. Two TV interviews on the east and west coasts reached approximately one hundred thousand viewers.

Extensive publicity by letters and a speaker's bureau promoted the bishops' pastoral on Mary. The following year the center publicized 1973 as "The Year of Faith with Mary the Model of Faith." In this same year the Madonna and Child

306

Committee, cooperating with Pro-Life Movement groups, prepared material, prayer petitions and prayer cards in battling the killing of the innocent. The services of the center at 135 Golden Gate Avenue, San Francisco, are available to all. A dedicated staff sends free on request folios of one to twenty pages on dozens of subjects on solid doctrine and devotion to Mary.

Pope John XXIII, in 1959, addressing the Second World Congress of Sodalities of Our Lady, South Orange, New Jersey, stressed: "Unquestionably signs seem to point to the fact that ours is a Marian Age; and it likewise becomes clearer day by day that the way for men to return to God is assured by Mary, that Mary is the basis of our confidence, the guarantee of our security, the foundation of our hope."

The Pope's designation, "Marian Age,"

Interior of Our Lady of the Skies Chapel, Kennedy International Airport, New York

Situated before the altar of Our Lady of the Skies Chapel, Kennedy International Airport, this processional cross first hung in Pope Paul's airplane cabin on his 1965 peace mission to the United Nations.

inspired Father Marion Habig, O.F.M., to begin editing in 1960 a publication called *The Marian Era.* It was approximately magazine size, though with permanently bound covers, on the cover appearing an artistic representation of Mary by Virginia Broderick, who is identified with high-quality work of religious artistic expression.

Father Habig's introduction stated that "the publication is not a strictly learned journal, nor is it a popular magazine. . . . It holds a middle place. . . . Both in contents and in form it is designed to be of lasting

value and worthy to be placed on the shelves of any library."

The magazine contained scholarly articles on Marian devotion by specialists in each field, and many reproductions of time-honored images of Mary found in cathedrals, art galleries, as well as the work of contemporary artists.

Father Habig was well qualified to undertake the publication from his wide experience as author of many books and articles in professional journals and encyclopedias, as well as historical research in Franciscan and Marian fields. *The Marian*

307

Era continued from 1960 to 1974, each of the eleven volumes fulfilling Father Habig's prediction of "lasting value."

Few peacetime events have commanded the publicity attendant on the Vatican's loan of Michelangelo's "Pietà" to the New York World's Fair of 1964-1965. Communication media of the entire world gave it full coverage, much praise and some criticism for exposing the masterpiece to possible damage in transit. Vatican officials, however, decided that sharing the "Pietà" with millions justified any risk involved.

The sculpture had never been away from Rome since its completion in 1499 and the decision to send it to New York was made in 1962 by Pope John XXIII, at the request of Cardinal Francis Spellman of New York. After many months' planning, the three-thousand-pound sculpture was fitted in three packing cases nesting one inside the other. The cases were shockproof, fireproof and designed to float. The vessel chosen to transport the precious cargo was, appropriately, the *Cristoforo Colombo*. It deposited the "Pietà" safely in New York, almost to the day of the four-hundredth anniversary of the sculptor's death.

Visitors to the fair's Vatican Pavilion saw the "Pietà" to better advantage than they could have in Rome. It was displayed, as Michelangelo intended, mounted on a low pedestal on an inclined plane. For maximum protection the display was placed behind a wall of bulletproof glass. A slow-moving platform carried viewers past the sculpture at about a distance of sixteen feet. A special area was provided for those who wished to stand and view the work at leisure.

Michelangelo began the "Pietà" when he was twenty-three, and in it he expressed his faith and his humanity more tenderly than in many of his later works. He represented Mary as she existed in his own mind and when critics complained that she

appeared too young he replied, "So chaste and undefiled a being would never age."

The sculpture was first installed in Old St. Peter's Basilica and survived the sacking by the armies of Charles V and the later razing of St. Peter's, suffering no more damage than the loss of four fingers on Mary's inert left hand; these were restored in 1736. It is by this very left hand and the attitude of her body that Mary so poignantly expresses the two emotions of love and grief in the death of her Son.

On May 21, 1973, Laszlo Toth, deranged thirty-three-year-old Hungarian-born Australian, battered the statuary with a hammer, breaking off the left hand and forearm and damaging the nose and left eye. Many months of expert work have effected complete restoration.

Air travelers approaching Boston's Logan International Airport can easily identify the tower of the Old North Church, famous in history as the tower where two lanterns were hung one night centuries ago to guide Paul Revere for the start of his famous ride.

Inside the airport is Our Lady of the Airways Chapel, welcoming arriving and departing travelers. Part of the chapel's altar is a wing-like pillar on which is inscribed the prayer beloved of millions: "We fly to thy patronage, O Holy Mother of God; despise not our petitions in our necessity but deliver us always from all dangers, O Glorious and Blessed Virgin."

At the foot of the bronze statue of the Assumption are three airliners encircling the earth. The chapel was the inspiration of Cardinal Richard Cushing who dedicated it in 1952. It is used for Mass and devotional visits every day of the week.

Millions of persons enter and leave our country via New York's Kennedy International Airport and at some time in their journey view the Tri-Faith Chapels Plaza opposite the arrivals building. At this plaza, completed in 1966, Jew, Protestant

Praying for Peace in the World
Pupils of Our Lady Queen of Peace School, Maywood, New Jer-
sey, recite the rosary at the school shrine in observance of Pope
Paul's "World Day of Prayer for Peace," October 4, 1966.

and Catholic worship side by side in graphic proof of America's religious freedom.

Along a six-hundred-fifty-five-foot central lagoon are three structures: a concrete hexagon adorned with forty-foot-high twin tables of the Ten Commandments and a stylized menorah, an A-frame whose roof slants toward a giant cross, and a corrugated glass and concrete oval, the latter Our Lady of the Skies Chapel. The building suggests in form the wing of a plane or the body of a fish and on its facade is the figure of Mary poised on a propeller.

The chapel succeeds an earlier one built

in October 1955, from which building a fourteen-foot gold anodized aluminum Virgin and propeller were removed to be placed in the reredos of the new structure. The building accommodates five hundred persons, is one hundred twenty-five feet long and forty-two feet high; its forty-two-foot floor-to-ceiling recessed lancet windows heighten the light and airy effect. Eventually the windows will be of stained glass, in earth-sea-sky motifs with figures of birds, fish and plant life. The white marble altar faces the congregation and back of it is a marble screen with a carving of the Last Supper. Before the altar is the

309

cross which, unmounted, hung in Pope Paul's airplane cabin on his peace mission to the United Nations in 1965. Also at the chapel is the chalice which he used at the Mass in Yankee Stadium.

A Marian distinction was the 1966 Christmas postage stamp, the first to use a sacred painting for its design. Reproduced was the central section of Hans Memling's fifteenth-century "Madonna and Child with Angels," an excellent example of the detail with which the German-born artist executed his works. The painting hangs in the National Gallery of Art and is thus a part of our national art heritage.

Carter Brown, then the gallery's assistant director, had recommended the painting to the Citizens Stamp Advisory Committee, experts in the fields of art, painting, history and philately. The stamp's religious theme evoked protests from the American Civil Liberties Union, the Amer-

In 1961 the Scriptural Rosary *(cover and two random pages shown) introduced a modern version of the medieval way in which the rosary was once prayed.*

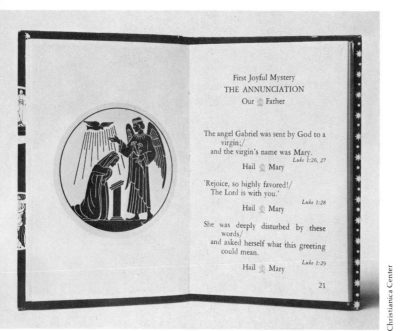

ican Jewish Congress, Protestants and Other Americans United for Separation of Church and State (P.O.A.U.), and Americans United. Their clamor helped to promote sales. When the stamp was first issued at Christmas, Michigan, sales totaled 793,632 of which 537,650 were first-day cover cancellations. The initial printing of 1.2 billion was a sellout.

The stamp was reissued in 1967, again over protest, and its popularity equaled that of the previous year. P.O.A.U. sought an injunction against the postmaster general but Federal District Judge Alexander Holtzoff denied it, stating that "while the Constitution provided for 'a separation of church and state' it did not require a separation of religion and state."

In 1966 the world faced a year of continuing unrest. Mindful of burdens of the human family, Pope Paul VI issued an encyclical, *Christi Matri Rosarii* ("Rosaries to the Mother of Christ"), urging that prayers be offered during the month of October so that through Mary's intercession peace would be established. He noted:

"We can see nothing more appropriate or efficacious than for the whole Christian family to raise its voice amid its many stresses and difficulties to pray the Mother of God, whom we also address as Queen of Peace, to be generous, as a good mother, with her gifts. During the Second Vatican Council we gave our confirmation to a point of traditional doctrine when we gave her the title of Mother of the Church, a title acclaimed by the council Fathers and the Catholic world."

He urged that during the entire month the rosary be recited, stressing that "this prayer is well suited to God's people, acceptable to the Mother of God and powerful in obtaining gifts from heaven."

In this country all faiths joined in the Pope's request. Typical of Catholic schoolchildren's participation was that of pupils of Our Lady Queen of Peace School, Maywood, New Jersey, reciting the rosary at the school's outdoor shrine.

On October 4, the anniversary of Pope Paul's peace mission to the United States, he celebrated an evening Mass in St. Peter's Square. It was carried to millions through a European television linkup and worldwide radio coverage, so that "the one voice of the Church will resound on all the continents of the Earth and reach the very gates of Heaven."

Emphasis on the rosary in the 1960s found a new and individual recitation emerging. The scriptural rosary appeared in 1961, described as a modern version of the old medieval way in which the rosary

Rosary Rally, With Estimated 20,000 Persons Attending
The rally was held on October 5, 1969, at Roosevelt Raceway, Westbury, New York. His Excellency, Bishop Walter P. Kellenberg, is shown standing at the altar.

The Long Island Catholic

U.S. Air Force Academy Chapel, Colorado

The chapel's spectacular setting in Colorado's Rocky Mountains dominates the entire area, symbolic of the leading role that religion plays in our national life. The chapel has separate facilities for each of the three major religious denominations.

Our Lady of the Skies Chapel in the Air Force Academy Chapel

had once been prayed. In a book entitled *Scriptural Rosary* the publisher recalled that about 1425-1525 A.D., people prayed the rosary by reciting a different little thought or meditation, with each Hail Mary. These little thoughts described some teaching or incident in the lives of Jesus and Mary; their purpose was to tell the story of each rosary mystery and at the same time help to avoid the distraction of repetition as the Hail Marys were said.

The small, easy-to-carry book, had eighty pages printed on mellow, antique paper. Its strong case-bound cover had a blue and white dust jacket, making the book durable enough for daily use for many years. It was issued by the Scriptural Rosary Center of Chicago (now Christianica Center). The cost was nominal, with price reductions for large orders. The scriptural quotations could be recited privately, or in a group; for the latter the leader read the versicle and the rest of the group answered with the response, enabling a group to pray in the same familiar way of praying the Angelus.

From the book's first appearance interest continued, inspiring the making of a two-record set for fuller appreciation. The Speech and Drama Department of the Catholic University of America recorded the scriptural rosary under the direction of Father Gilbert V. Hartke, O.P. A cast of twelve talented actors spoke the words of Jesus, Mary, Elizabeth, Gabriel, Simeon, Pilate, Peter and others. The beautiful and powerful words of scripture appealed to the imagination and inspired an awareness of the joys, sorrows and glories of Mary. Included in the recording were nine Marian hymns and motets sung by the A Capella Choir of the Music Department of the university.

Again, in 1969, Pope Paul reminded the

313

Our Lady of Kansas Mosaic, Mount Carmel Academy, Wichita, Kansas

faithful of the month of October's dedication to the rosary. He issued an apostolic exhortation proposing that the seriousness

Sister Fleurette is pictured at work arranging tesserae in place before pasting. Visible are the symbols of Kansas: oil wells, meadowlarks, sunflowers and a steer head.

and urgency of restoring peace among men be recognized by offering prayers toward that goal:

"Despite some progress and some legitimate hopes, murderous conflicts are continuing, new points of tension are appearing. Within the Church itself, misunderstandings arise between brothers who mutually accuse and condemn each other. Hence it is more urgent than ever to work and pray for peace. . . . How can we do otherwise than lovingly to depend upon the incomparable intercession of Mary?"

Following his directive, rosary rallies were held in all parts of the country. One particularly impressive gathering was that of the Diocese of Rockville Centre, New York. Long Island Legion of Mary groups had worked two months in promoting and making arrangements for the October 5 rally at Roosevelt Raceway, Westbury, New York. The public had been invited and an estimated twenty thousand persons attended.

Bishop Walter P. Kellenberg presided and was principal celebrant of the Mass. The program included the recitation of the full rosary; a group of children led the Joyful Mysteries, five handicapped persons

Indoor Marian Garden

*Our Lady of the Cape (Canada) is surrounded by Marian plants;
among them are: angel-wing begonia, palm, Our Lady's Mantle,
Heart of Mary begonia, rosary plant, Lady Mary geranium, Our
Lady's Hair, prayer plant and Christ in Cradle. The unique Marian
garden is owned by Mrs. Bonnie Roberson of Hagerman, Idaho.*

Mrs. Bonnie Roberson

the Sorrowful, and teenagers the Glorious.

It is inspiring that all branches of our country's armed forces provide facilities and opportunities for the exercise of religious observance. Young men and women, "watchmen on the walls of world freedom," cannot help but meditate on the full meaning of preparedness, militarily and spiritually.

The Catholic chapel of the U.S. Air Force Academy Chapel in Colorado is designed to represent a grotto. The reredos behind the altar is composed of varying shades of blue, turquoise, rose and gray tesserae to form an abstract portrayal of the firmament. Superimposed on the mural are two ten-foot marble figures: Our Lady of the Skies to the left, Guardian Angel to the right. Above a sculptured silver crucifix is a marble dove symbolizing the Holy Spirit.

In the sacristy is a six by four-foot painting of Our Lady of the Air by Peter Bianchi of Kenosha, Wisconsin, a staff art-

315

mary songs

by bill peffley

Bill Peffley

Shown is the album cover of Mary Songs. Words and music are by Bill Peffley of Norristown, Pennsylvania.

GO TELL THE WORLD ABOUT MARY

Go tell the world about Mary,
Go tell the world about her joy,
God the creator was her little boy
And she'd lull him to sleep
With a song for him deep in her heart.

Go tell the world about Mary,
Go tell the world about her pain,
God the redeemer was her young
    son slain
And his love she would keep
And would ponder it deep in her heart.

Go tell the world about Mary
Go tell the world about her place,
Mother of Christ in the whole human
    race,
And his life she will keep
And will care for it deep in each heart.

Bill Peffley

One of the Mary Songs *Describing Peffley's Apostolate*

ist of the National Geographic Society. Every Monday evening the perpetual novena to Our Lady of the Air is held. Mary is honored as special patroness and protectress of those who travel, not only through the air but also in outer space.

316

Furnishings, liturgical fittings and adornments were gifts from private individuals and donations from Easter offerings made at air force bases. The classical pipe organ was bought by the U.S. Air Force Command Welfare Fund. Both the Stations of the Cross and the reredos were designed and completed by Lumen Martin Winter who created "The Conversion of St. Paul" for the facade of the Church of St. Paul the Apostle, New York City.

The U.S. Air Force Academy's religious program includes intense discussion of contemporary religious problems, adult theology courses and a rich and creative liturgy, to deepen the cadet's theological sense for the moral and religious challenges of the future.

Mary acquired a new title when the love, art and limitless patience of one woman created the mosaic of Our Lady of Kansas. Sister Mary Fleurette Blameuser, a Sister of Charity of the Blessed Virgin Mary, viewed the forty-six-foot foyer in Mount Carmel Academy, Wichita, where she taught art and knew immediately that Mary would be the starting point for a mosaic beautifying that curved wall.

Whatever spare time she had in the next four years went into the work. The mosaic, to cover an area of two hundred square feet, had to first be designed on Kraft wrapping paper. A working surface had been provided her on a special workbench of adjustable aluminum sheets supported by sawhorses. Next, the design had to be transferred to special tile paper on which the mosaic pieces (tesserae) would be pasted. Predetermined sections, two hundred ten of them, had to be planned for eventual incorporation into the whole; everything had to be so accurate that the finished mosaic would fit the prescribed wall space.

The mosaic involved nearly one hundred forty thousand pieces of tesserae (small bits of stone, glass or tile), one hundred forty-five variations in color, thirty-seven in blue tones alone. Dominating the panel is Mary encompassed in a mandorla of light, twelve stars in her halo, the moon at her feet. Her billowing veils symbolize the south wind, for Kansas means South Wind People. The Christ Child's open arms welcome those entering the foyer. Since Kansas is noted for its colorful sunsets and clear starry nights, the two ideas were combined in the background of astral bodies.

At Mary's feet are stalks of wheat, candelabra-like, a guard of honor in attendance. To her left, the state motto, symbols of industry, grain elevators; to the right sunflowers, a steer head and oil wells. The airplanes in the sky are characteristic of Wichita. The State of Kansas motto, "Ad Astra Per Aspera" (To the Stars Through Difficulties) is the testimonial of the work of Sister Fleurette.

Robert Herrick, seventeenth-century English poet, used a rose to explain Mary:

> *To work a wonder God would have her shown*
> *At once a Bud and yet a Rose full-blown.*

A woman of today, Mrs. Bonnie Roberson, uses Marian flowers and plants to arouse and enrich devotion. Her apostolate rightly could be called "Say It With Flowers." Mary Gardens are her life. Their historical background places the earliest Mary Garden at Norwich Priory, England, in 1531.

Researching old dictionaries and early gardening books Mrs. Roberson found three hundred plant names relating to such a garden. Through the years that list has grown to twelve hundred: plants, flowers, healing herbs, all with Marian origin. She realized how this knowledge could become a constructive and rewarding means of combining love of Mary with love of planting — giving dignity and joy to the gardening done by men and women everywhere.

Persons can become Mary Garden missionaries, local and national, whose gardens can attract those of other faiths, where Mary can be discussed in Christian friendship and sociability, the sharing of seeds, plants and gardening information. Literature is available listing annuals, perennials and biennials. Marian indoor gardens can provide beauty and inspiration, a comfort to shut-ins or those in hospitals. A recent endeavor is planning gardens for the blind, using plants especially fragrant or of strong texture.

Bill Peffley of Norristown, Pennsylvania, member of the Legion of Mary since 1956, became concerned that Mary's part in the fullness of the Church's life, especially in the liturgy, was being deemphasized. Though not a musician or trained composer, he recorded ten inspirational tributes in an album, *Mary Songs*, soon to be followed by *More Mary Songs* — sim-

This statue of Our Lady of Fatima can be seen at the House of Mary Shrine, Yankton, South Dakota. Its inscription conveys the shrine's dedication of honoring God and His Blessed Mother.

Shown is one of the thirteen Stations of the Cross at the House of Mary Shrine in Yankton, South Dakota. Beyond is Lewis and Clark Lake and the Nebraska shore.

ple, humble, haunting melodies written with poetic care and melodic loveliness.

Both albums have been acclaimed by critics, educators and clergy of many denominations throughout the world. A Lutheran educator commented, "It is a privilege to share in the production of one of the better religious albums." Peffley claims that he is an "emphasizer" only, saying: "I believe the songs came *through* me and not *from* me." The treatment of the songs avoids the sentimental approach; it fea-

Honoring the Sacred Heart of Jesus
and the Immaculate Heart of Mary
*This heart-shaped pond, forming a rosary made of beads
of rock, was erected to give veneration to Jesus and Mary.*

tures the role of Mary in her relationship to Christ, and includes several works on St. Joseph.

Bill's wife, Mary, also a member of the Legion of Mary, is the author of the book *Woman of Faith*, a biography of Edel Quinn, Catholic lay missionary, who brought the legion to Africa in 1936. The Peffleys own and operate three Catholic bookstores in Norristown, West Reading and Willow Grove, Pennsylvania, and have established Balance House Publications to promote the *Mary Songs* records

and music books. Their three children — Edel, Francis and Natia — are also Legionaries, working to make Mary better known and loved.

In the historic Lewis and Clark country of South Dakota is a very new Marian shrine, built entirely by dedicated men, on ten acres of woodland. Called the House of Mary Shrine, it was begun in 1971; it will not be completed until these men are satisfied they have considered every possible means of honoring God and His Mother.

First object of veneration to be installed

319

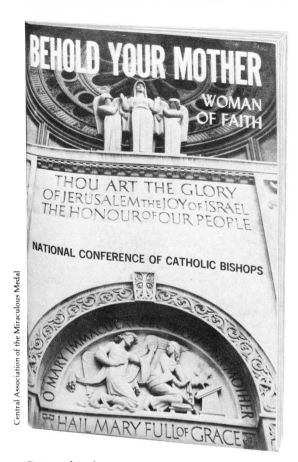

*Pictured is the cover
of a manual for teachers of
religious education. The manual was made
available at a workshop of the Philadelphia
Archdiocese sponsored by the Central Association of the Miraculous Medal.*

white for the Our Fathers, red for the Hail
Marys, nature itself providing the agency
of veneration. The "rosary way" consists
of all one hundred fifty-three Hail Mary
and sixteen Our Father beads, of four by
four-inch redwood beads, strung on a
heavy chain elevated about two feet from
the ground, weaving among the woods.

A natural sheltered area provides for the
celebration of Mass. This is the meditation
area. A sculptured six-foot statue of Moses
is here, the focal point for eventual surrounding by the Ten Commandments of
concrete. St. Michael the Archangel, protector against the devil, is not forgotten.
To be developed are small shrines of St.
Therese of the Child Jesus, St. Joseph, St.
Benedict, St. Isidore and the Infant Jesus

*In observance of the bishops' pastoral letter,
"Behold Your Mother, Woman of Faith," this
book cover, featuring a contemporary painting
entitled "The Annunciation," was distributed
to schoolchildren by the Knights of Columbus.*

were the Stations of the Cross, each of simple construction and each donated by different people. The Thirteenth Station, the
Crucifixion, is of three large wooden
crosses fifty feet high, and can be reached
ascending the hill of Mount Carmel. The
crosses are illumined at night making them
visible from the distant Nebraska shore.

Honoring the Sacred Heart of Jesus and
the Immaculate Heart of Mary is a heart-
shaped pond which forms a rosary, with
beads of rock. Here every Sunday at four
o'clock in the afternoon the rosary is recited; the public is always invited. Those
coming on Sunday evenings are cautioned
to bring flashlights for there are other rosary areas. One is made up of rosebushes,

"Pentecost"

This is from the Don Bosco filmstrip on the pastoral letter, "Behold Your Mother, Woman of Faith." In writing of the bond between Mary and the Holy Spirit the bishops (in the section, "Mary — Mother of the Church," paragraph 112) point out: "Christ sent His Spirit as the new Advocate, as the Intercessor who comes to help us in our weakness. Any correct understanding of Mary's role must be seen in connection with the predominant role of the Holy Spirit. The Bible provides us with a starting point: St. Luke presents Mary as the humble woman overshadowed by the Holy Spirit in order that Christ be formed. 'God sent his Son born of a woman . . . that we might receive the adoption of sons' (Gal. 4:4)."

of Prague, all to bear testimony of the desire and need of persons for the traditional type of Catholic devotions.

The entire shrine surroundings are of much historic interest. Lewis and Clark, on their exploring trip up the Missouri, made camp on the Nebraska side and there met the friendly Yankton Sioux. For the Indians the river valley was a highway and a home, providing shelter, wild game and planting areas. Scattered campsites and burial grounds today attract historians,

and particularly those in archaeology.

Between Yankton and the Nebraska shoreline is the Lewis and Clark Lake and Reservoir, part of a development of water resources embracing the Missouri River and Basin. The dam and reservoir were built by the U.S. Army Corps of Engineers who estimate that visitors to the area will grow to five million annually by 1980. The shrine then will be of interest to non-Catholics as well. Many people are cooperating in the shrine's development: Legion

321

Our Lady of the Island, Eastport, New York
The eighteen-foot, twenty-ton granite statue overlooks Moriches Bay
and the Atlantic Ocean. Bishop John R. McGann of the Rockville
Centre Diocese is shown officiating at its dedication on October 2, 1976.

of Mary, South Dakota Third Order Carmelites and Rosary Makers. Already the shrine has been the site of the South Dakota Marian Conferences of 1973, 1974 and 1976.

In 1973 the United States Conference of Catholic Bishops issued a pastoral letter, "Behold Your Mother, Woman of Faith." The fifty-five-page document had been two years in preparation and was largely based on the ecumenical dialog of Vatican Council II. The letter was published on

November 21, the ninth anniversary of the major council document on Mary, *Lumen gentium.* The responsible episcopal committee had as chairman Cardinal John Carberry of St. Louis. Other members were Cardinal Timothy Manning (Los Angeles), Cardinal Humberto Medeiros (Boston), Archbishop William W. Baum (Washington, D.C.), Bishop David M. Maloney (Wichita) and Auxiliary Bishop John J. Dougherty of Newark. Consultants on the board were Eamon R. Carroll, O. Carm.,

322

In the aftermath of the Vietnam War, the Vietnamese Congregation of the Mother Co-Redemptrix was forced to flee its homeland. Its members have found refuge in the United States at Our Lady of the Ozarks, Carthage, Missouri.

Bishop Bernard F. Law is shown with twelve newly ordained deacons of the Vietnamese Congregation of the Mother Co-Redemptrix, Carthage, Missouri. Their ordination took place on April 30, 1976.

Frederick Jelly, O.P., Bernard Theall, O.S.B., and Monsignor Thomas Falls.

The letter was an extended reflection on current teaching of the Church about Mary, both doctrinal and devotional. It considered the historical development of Catholic teaching on her and related the cult of Mary to various vocations. The introduction stressed the bishops' faith in the truths concerning Mary and their filial love for her, the need for everyone to recognize Mary's special place in God's plan for the salvation of mankind, ecumenical difficulties and hopes.

The pastoral letter received enthusiastic response in pulpit and press. A full Spanish-language translation was published, the full text appeared in *The Marian Era* and other religious publications. Three particularly impressive acknowledgments of the importance of the letter were of an audio-visual nature. Don Bosco Filmstrips prepared four filmstrips with matching cassettes in two editions — children's and adult tracks; the Confraternity of Christian Doctrine and Religious Education Office of the Archdiocese of Philadelphia also prepared a filmstrip and cassette, and the Diocese of Rockville Centre, New York, prepared a series of ten television color programs (each lasting twenty minutes) for grades four through six.

In the letter's appendix, "Mary's Place in American Catholic History," the bishops stated: "It is evident that a loyal and loving devotion to our Lady has been, from the very beginning, an important part of American Catholicism. It is up to the American Catholics of today to cherish

Shown is Cardinal John Carberry of St. Louis, Missouri, who celebrated the special Marian Mass at the Forty-first Eucharistic Congress in Philadelphia.

tact was made with the noted Franciscan architect, Cajetan Baumann, who drew up the initial plans. The property for the shrine, sixty-plus acres, was the gift of Crescenzo Vigliotta, Sr., one of whose fifteen children is a Montfort Father. He gave the land because, as he put it, "God has been good to me."

The statue of Our Lady of the Island was designed by Raphael DeSota and interpreted in Vermont granite by sculptor Frank Marchini. Eventually the shrine grounds will include Stations of the Cross, rosary walk, various chapels, monastery convent and offices, guest house, pilgrim hall, library and picnic areas — all easily accessible from Sunrise Highway and the well-known Long Island Expressway.

An entire Vietnamese Marian congregation, scattered by the tragedy of the war, would find sanctuary in a former Marian seminary in the hills of Missouri. Cooper-

This is the cover of a booklet for a special liturgy of the Mass honoring Mary, entitled Mary, Tabernacle of the Lord. *It was celebrated by Cardinal John Carberry at the Forty-first International Eucharistic Congress in Philadelphia on August 7, 1976.*

and to pass on to succeeding generations of Catholics this rich heritage of devotion to Mary, the Mother of God and Mother of the Church."

In the Bicentennial Year, Mary acquired one more American title — Our Lady of the Island (Long Island). The idea for the title originated with the Montfort Missionaries, publishers of *Queen of All Hearts*, whose headquarters on the island are at Bay Shore.

In 1953 the Fathers, Brothers and lay helpers decided to build a small outdoor shrine to Mary Queen of All Hearts. Through a series of events, "some of which bordered on the miraculous," con-

MARY,
TABERNACLE
OF THE LORD

324

NC News Service

ating in this happy ending were many people, including the U.S. Army and Navy.

In 1975, two hundred members of the Vietnamese Congregation of the Mother Co-Redemptrix were attempting to escape in fishing boats from the Vietnam coastline. Turbulent waves threatened their small boats to being forced back to shore, with possible reprisals by the Viet Cong who had some months previously driven them out of North Vietnam. The priests and Brothers had had to leave their schools and retreat house and now, under the leadership of Father Ignatius Dai, were trying to reach safety. Others of their congregation had remained in the homeland to carry on the work.

U.S. Navy boats saw their plight and assisted them in reaching land. In the deployment of the refugees some were transported to Guam by ship; others were

Legion of Mary Display, Eucharistic Congress, Philadelphia, 1976

Legion of Mary

flown to Camp Pendleton, California, Indiantown Gap, Pennsylvania, and Fort Chaffee, Arkansas. It was at the Arkansas fort that the army chaplain, Father Thomas F. McAndrew, was then enjoying a visit from Bishop Bernard F. Law of the Diocese of Springfield-Cape Girardeau, Missouri. Hearing of the congregation's need of locating, he thought of a vacant seminary at Carthage in his diocese.

The Oblates of Mary Immaculate some four years before had moved their minor seminary, Our Lady of the Ozarks, and the

325

St. John Neumann Shrine

Twenty-seven windows record the life of St. John Neumann. This one commemorates a decisive turning point in his priesthood. He is shown wearing the Redemptorist fifteen-decade rosary.

buildings and chapel were vacant. The order's provincial, Father William Woestman, as well as Father John Weissler, O.M.I., pastor of St. Ann's in Carthage, were contacted and readily agreed to lend the facilities of the former seminary to the Vietnamese. In due time the scattered groups were reunited in Carthage.

On April 30, 1976, twelve of the members were ordained to the diaconate in

326

preparation for ordination to the priesthood. On that occasion Bishop Law reminded them: "Of all the things you are, and of all the things you are to become, you are to always be a sign of hope." When final arrangements have been made the Vietnamese would like to move to a rural setting where they can engage in farming to support themselves. In the meantime their simple faith, gentle culture and a devotion to family life are leaving a deep impression on their American friends.

Philadelphians will long remember the million persons coming into their city in August 1976 — young and old, handicapped, priests and religious, military per-

One of the Many Artifacts in the St. John Neumann Shrine, Philadelphia

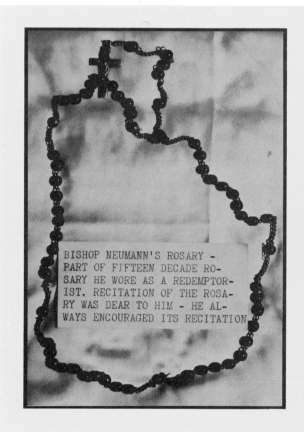

BISHOP NEUMANN'S ROSARY – PART OF FIFTEEN DECADE ROSARY HE WORE AS A REDEMPTORIST. RECITATION OF THE ROSARY WAS DEAR TO HIM – HE ALWAYS ENCOURAGED ITS RECITATION

Peter Gentile

This window best exemplifies the saint's deep devotion to Mary — Mother of God and Mother of Mankind.

sonnel, organizations, ethnic groups — attending the Forty-first International Eucharistic Congress. From morning to night, special events stressed world hunger, family life, freedom and justice and many other themes. All the events were fully reported by the news media and televised newscasts on Philadelphia stations.

In Mary's honor a Mass, *Mary, Tabernacle of the Lord,* was celebrated by Cardinal John Carberry of St. Louis, with the homily given by Archbishop Fulton J. Sheen. The Blue Army of Our Lady of Fatima conducted a Marian vigil from 11:00 p.m., August 6, to 6:00 a.m., August 7. Master of ceremonies was the Blue Army's national president, Monsignor Anthony J. Connell. A eucharistic procession with flags of all nations was led in five divisions by cardinals of Europe, Latin America, Asia, Africa and the United States. Each cardinal led a decade of the world rosary, the fifth decade by Cardinal Carberry.

Father Patrick Peyton spoke on the rosary's power for peace in individual families and the "family of the world." Monsignor Connell likened the heart of Jesus to a fulcrum, the center of our lives, and Mary's intercession as the great lever which could pry the world from hopelessness and immorality. John Haffert, editor of *Soul* (organ of the Blue Army), spoke on the queenship of Mary. His talk was followed by the coronation of the International Pilgrim Virgin Statue of Our Lady of Fatima by Cardinal Ribeiro, patriarch of Portugal. Under the auspices of the Blue Army this statue has been venerated since 1947 in this country and abroad. For the congress it had been flown in from Rio de Janeiro on the first of August and reserved in St. Paul's Church in Princeton, New Jersey, where more than a thousand congress

participants had been housed in nearby Princeton University.

Mother Teresa of Calcutta was most acclaimed of the twenty persons speaking on the general theme "Woman and the Eucharist." She began by saying: "I think our Mother Church has raised womanhood to something beautiful for God by making Our Lady Mother of the Church. God loved the world so much that He gave

327

His Son, and I think that was the First Eucharist, the giving of the Son to Our Lady, and Our Lady was the first altar."

Citing the Visitation and Cana as exemplary of Mary's compassion, she called Mary "the most beautiful of all women, the greatest, most humble, most pure, most holy, through whom God was able to show His love and compassion for the world."

She challenged her audience: "Do we have the eyes of Mary to see the need of others? ... Are we like Mary to others in the community, to recognize their failings, their sufferings? ... Mary's understanding love of others? ... Our Lady is so great because she had this understanding love. And you and I, being women, have that tremendous thing in us, that understanding love."

She described the fearlessness which members of her order ventured into all kinds of places in accomplishing their care of the poor: "They walk down the street with rosary in hand because Our Lady is our Mother, but she is also our strength and our protection. ... [In five years' work in New York City] the Sisters have never heard a rude word, an ugly remark, never a touch to hurt, but always great respect, great dignity, shown. Our Lady is always with us because she is the cause of our joy and we try to be the cause of her joy. Together, learning from her, keeping close to her, we are able to go through the most terrible places, fearlessly, because Jesus in us will never deceive us, Jesus in us is our love, our strength, our joy and our compassion. And that is why God has created a woman, maybe not to do big things, ... but small things with great love."

More than three thousand Legionaries from thirty-four states and six foreign countries "hit the streets" of Philadelphia during the congress, sharing their faith and comforting the afflicted. They visited one hundred twenty nursing homes and

hospitals and made more than twenty-one thousand contacts with persons on the street whom they approached about the Catholic faith. They talked to seven hundred lapsed Catholics and met one hundred sixty-nine prospective converts. Another fifty-four persons gave their names and addresses for further information about Catholicism.

More than five thousand Miraculous Medals were sold and twenty-five thousand leaflets (designed for non-Catholics) were distributed. On display stands were such pamphlets as "Face the Facts — One Holy Catholic Apostolic Church," "The Rosary Made Easy for Non-Catholics" and "The Mother of Mankind."

Many heroic men and women have been considered in this book. Now, veritably, the last shall be first — John Neumann — first male American saint, canonized on June 19, 1977. "Give to me holiness," he prayed at his first Mass. That and more is now his, "in good measure ... and running over." A Redemptorist, Michael J. Curley, has written Neumann's biography, dedicated "To the Memory of the Bishops of the United States who like Bishop Neumann struggled valiantly to save the faith of countless immigrants." Today's emphasis on ethnicity makes the reading of the life of this modest, self-effacing man, of special interest. What he thought, what he believed, the obstacles — physical and spiritual — which he mastered in meriting sainthood, serve as a guide for all in this nearly ended twentieth century.

From early boyhood in Bohemia, Neumann was devoted to Mary. Serious by nature, he would turn aside from the games of his companions and ask them to join him in saying the rosary. At twenty he entered the diocesan seminary in Budweis, following this by study at the archdiocesan seminary at Prague. While there he resolved to be a missionary in the United States.

On passing his examinations he found that an abundance of priests would delay his ordination. Unordained and troubled, he left for America. Bishop John Dubois of New York greeted him with enthusiasm; priests were desperately needed for serving the German immigrants whose faith might weaken while adjusting to American life. The bishop did not bother to wait for Neumann's canonical endorsement from Europe but ordained him a deacon on June 19, 1836. On *that* day Neumann vowed to say the rosary every day of his life in gratitude to Mary for bringing him this far.

For four years he ministered to German and Irish immigrants in a nine-hundred-square-mile area west of Rochester, New York — mostly woods and farmlands, log or dirt roads. A chance meeting with Father Joseph Prost, a Redemptorist, had gradually attracted him to this order; with the decision made, he was received in September of 1840. Now would begin a novitiate which would test him spiritually and physically.

Master of eight languages, he needed them all as he served eight assignments in one year, traveling three thousand miles through New York, Pennsylvania and Maryland, on horseback, bumpy stage-coaches, single-track railroads or small steamers and canal boats. "The temptations of the soul," he wrote, "are doubtless as numerous as the disorders of the body, but to remain steadfast and to persevere in all this turmoil of spirit, there is no better remedy than prayer to the Blessed Virgin for the grace of perseverance."

Persevere he did, and pronounced his religious vows in 1842, the first Redemptorist profession in America. Writing of the trials he experienced, the diary is charitable of others, sparkling with confidence in God and the patronage of Mary. His daily schedule included rising at 4:30 a.m., with little relaxation or rest in the next eighteen hours. On retiring at 10:30 p.m.,

he recited the Litany of the Blessed Virgin. When any parish groups came with petty grievances, he asked that they first pray with him. "Let us say the stations of the cross or the rosary and then we shall talk over the matter." Few had the ready will to pray and those who did, seldom troubled him further.

In the short span of five years Neumann was named vicegerent, highest on-the-scene superior of the Redemptorists. Four years later he became rector of St. Alphonsus Church, Baltimore, where Archbishop Francis Kenrick realized his great strength of character and asked that he be his confessor. Kenrick hinted that he might soon have to get himself a miter. In 1852, against his will, Neumann was named fourth bishop of Philadelphia. When first visiting his Redemptorist brothers, as they admired his episcopal attire he smilingly said, "The Church treats her bishops like a mother treats a child. When she wants to place a burden on him, she gives him new clothes."

In one of the three synods he called for his clergy, he recommended the Litany of Our Lady of Loretto be sung on all Sundays and holy days before the principal Mass, with the added invocation, "Queen conceived without sin, pray for us." If no choir was available, the litany was to be recited with five decades of the rosary added. Both in the pulpit and the confessional he loved to talk of Mary's greatness and goodness, recommending sinners to seek her intercession.

For over two years he worked strenuously in establishing churches and schools, encouraging religious orders to come to his diocese, and faithfully visiting the one hundred thirteen parishes in the thirty-five thousand square miles then included in the Diocese of Philadelphia. A respite came when he was invited to Rome for the solemn ceremony of the definition of the dogma of Mary's Immaculate Conception. Before leaving he composed a pastoral letter which concluded: "Let all experience thy protection, Virgin and Mother, through whom the nations are brought to penitence, the demons brought to flight, and they that sit in darkness and in the shadow of death be filled with the knowledge and love of Thy Son."

The great festivities at Rome intensified his devotion; on his return his second pastoral urged all pastors to celebrate the event by a triduum.

In attending the Eighth Provincial Council in Baltimore in 1855, he proposed that December 8 (the anniversary of the promulgation of the dogma of the Immaculate Conception) be set aside as a holy day of obligation, a suggestion which was not then followed.

In the less than eight years as bishop he established eighty churches, instituted Forty Hours Devotion, brought seven religious orders to his diocese, and put in operation a central board of education which was the genesis of the present diocesan system of parochial schools in the United States. He died suddenly on January 5, 1860, at age forty-nine. Complying with his often stated request, he was buried in a chapel in the basement of the Redemptorist Church of St. Peter's on Vine Street, Philadelphia, where thousands come weekly to pray at his tomb and view the artifacts of his saintly life.

Epilogue

There can be no end to a book on Mary, the timeless woman. The historian may limit himself to a premise of time and area only to be confronted with infinity — ". . . all ages to come shall call me blessed" (Luke 1:48).

In the shaping of today's "instant" history, we are caught up in the unrest attendant on world problems, with an accelerating emphasis on science, the occult and paranormal phenomena. One's purity of vision may become obscured. Wordsworth put it this way:

The world is too much with us; late and soon,
Getting and spending, we lay waste our powers:
Little we see in Nature that is ours.

Mary *is* ours, given to us by Christ from the cross when He said, "This is your mother" (John 19:27). It is a tradition of our nature to honor the mother of an illustrious son. Because Mary bore Christ, she has a right to our veneration.

In his magnificent prose-poem, Father John W. Lynch called Mary "a woman wrapped in silence." It is a silence which thunders if we will only listen.

Bibliography

Abel, Anna Heloise. "Indian Reservations in Kansas." *Transactions Kansas State Historical Society*, VIII (1903-1904), 82-83.

Adams, Eleanor B. "The Chapel and Cofradia of Our Lady of Light in Santa Fe." *New Mexico Historical Review*, XXII (1947), 327-341.

Allen, William. *The History of Norridgewock*. Norridgewock, Me.: Edward J. Peet, 1849.

Alsberg, Henry G. *The American Guide: a Source Book and Complete Travel Guide for the United States*. New York: Hastings House, 1949.

America's Historylands. National Geographic Society. Washington, 1962.

Anderson, Floyd. *Father Baker*. Milwaukee: Bruce, 1960.

Anthony, Sister Mary, O.L.M. *Teen-Age Foundress: Teresa Barry, Foundress of the Sisters of Charity of Our Lady of Mercy*. Charleston, n.d.

Antony, C.M. "Lulworth Castle, its History and Memories." *Catholic Historical Review*, I (1915), 243-257.

Aradi, Zsolt. *Shrines to Our Lady Around the World*. New York: Farrar, Straus and Young, 1954.

An Army of Peace: The Story of the Sisters of Loretto at the Foot of the Cross. Loretto, Ky., 1957.

Art in the United States Capitol. Architect of the Capitol, compiler. Washington: U.S. Government Printing Office, 1976.

Auerbach, Herbert S. "Father Escalante's Journal with Related Documents and Maps." *Utah Historical Quarterly*, XI (1943), 1-10.

Auger, Leonard A. "St. Francis Through 200 Years." *Vermont History*, XXVII (1959), 287-304.

Bacchiani, Alessandro. "Giovanni da Verrazano and His Discoveries of North America, 1524." *American Scenic and Historical Preservation Society*, XV (1910), 135-226.

Badin, Stephen T. *Origine et Progrès de la Mission du Kentucky*. Paris, 1821.

Baldwin, Ava S. *The History of Florence, Arizona, 1866-1940*. Thesis, Graduate College, University of Arizona, Tempe, 1941.

Bancroft, Hubert Howe. *History of the Pacific States of North America*. 34 vols. San Francisco, 1875-1890.

Barnum, Francis, S.J. "Catholic Missions in Alaska: A Compendium of their History from the Foundation until 1900." *United States Catholic Historical Society Historical Records and Studies*, XIII (1919), 87-100.

Barrington, Daines. *Miscellanies*. London, 1781.

Barry, Colman J., O.S.B. *Catholic Minnesota: Historic Places and Tours*. St. Paul, 1958.

Barry, J. Neilson. "The First Explorers of the Columbia and Snake Rivers." *Geographical Review*, July 1932, 443-456.

Baudier, Roger. "The First Sodality of the Blessed Virgin, New Orleans, 1730." *United States Catholic Historical Society Historical Records and Studies*, XXX (1939), 47-53.

————. *Through Portals of the Past; the Story of the Old Ursuline Convent of New Orleans*. New Orleans, 1955.

Bayley, James Roosevelt, Bishop of Newark. *Frontier Bishop: The Life of Bishop Simon Bruté*. Nevins, Albert J., M.M., editor. Huntington: Our Sunday Visitor, Inc., 1971.

Bayliss, Joseph E., and Estelle L. *River of Destiny, The Saint Marys*. Detroit: Wayne University Press, 1955.

Beauchamp, William Martin. *Past and Present of Syracuse and Onondaga County, New York*. New York: S.J. Clarke Publishing Co., 1908.

Bennett, William Harper. *Catholic Footsteps in Old New York — a Chronicle of Catholicity in the City of New York from 1524 to 1808.* New York: Schwartz, Kirwin and Fauss, 1909.

Bentley, William. *The Diary of William Bentley, D.D.* 4 vols. Salem: Essex Institute, 1905-1914.

Biever, Albert H., S.J. *The Jesuits in New Orleans and the Mississippi Valley.* New Orleans: Hauser, 1924.

Blake, William J. *The History of Putnam County, New York.* New York: Baker & Scribner, 1849.

Bodega y Quadra, Juan Francisco. "Viajes de exploracion (en la costa occidental de América)." *Dirección de hidrografia,* Madrid, Anuario, Año 3 (1865), 279-336.

Boisthibault, Doublet de. *Les Voeux des Hurons et des Abnaquis a Notre Dame de Chartres.* Chartres, 1857.

Bolton, Herbert E. *Anza's California Expeditions.* 5 vols. Berkeley: University of California Press, 1930.

———. *Cross, Sword and Gold Pan.* Los Angeles: The Primavera Press, 1936.

———. *Pageant in the Wilderness.* Salt Lake City: Utah State Historical Society, 1950.

———. *Rim of Christendom; a Biography of Eusebio Francisco Kino, Pacific Coast Pioneer.* New York: Macmillan, 1936.

——— and Ross, Mary. *The Debatable Land: A Sketch of the Anglo-Spanish Contest for the Georgia Country.* Berkeley: University of California Press, 1925.

Bonano, Salvatore, O.F.M. "Our Lady's Influence in the Discovery of America and During the Colonial Period of the United States." *Ephemerides Mariologicae,* V (March 1955), 47-86.

Bowen, Charles F. *Lost Virgin.* Boston: Bruce Humphries, 1959.

Brown, John Marshall. "The Mission of the Assumption on the River Kennebec, 1646-1652." *Maine Historical Collections,* second series, I (1890), 87-99.

Brown, Mark H. *The Plainsmen of the Yellowstone.* New York: Putnam, 1961.

Burke, Eugene M., C.S.P. "Nuestra Señora." *American Ecclesiastical Review,* CXXXI (1954), 27-33.

Burns, James A., C.S.C., and Kohlbrenner, John B. *History of Catholic Education in the United States.* New York: Benziger, 1937.

Burton, Katherine. *Children's Shepherd* (Father John Drumgoole). New York: Kenedy, 1954.

Butler, James Davis. "Father Samuel Mazzuchelli." *Wisconsin State Historical Society Collections,* XIV (1898), 155-161.

Byrne, John F., C.SS.R. *The Glories of Mary in Boston: Church of Our Lady of Perpetual Help.* Boston: Mission Church Press, 1921.

———. *The Redemptorist Centenaries, 1732-1932.* Philadelphia: The Dolphin Press, 1932.

Campbell, Thomas, S.J. *Pioneer Priests of America.* 3 vols. New York: America Press, 1911-1914.

Carol, Juniper B., O.F.M., ed. *Mariology.* 3 vols. Milwaukee: Bruce, 1954-1961.

Cartas Esféricas y Planos de los Puertos Situados Sobre las Costas Septentrionales de las Californias, 1799. Collection of maps in the Library of Congress.

Castelnau, Francis, Comte de. *Vues et Souvenirs de l'Amerique du Nord.* Paris, 1842.

Cather, Willa. *Death Comes for the Archbishop.* New York: Knopf, 1927.

Catholic Builders of the Nation. Thomas F. Meehan, ed. 5 vols. Boston: Continental Press, 1923.

Charland, Thomas M., O.P. *Histoire de Saint-François-du-Lac.* Ottawa: Dominican College, 1942.

Charlevoix, Pierre François. *Histoire et description generale de la Nouvelle France.* 6 vols. Paris, 1744.

Chase, John. *Frenchmen, Desire, Good Children, and Other Streets of New Orleans.* New Orleans: Robert L. Crager & Co., 1949.

Chavez, Angelico, O.F.M. *La Conquistadora: Autobiography of an Ancient Statue.* Paterson, N.J.: St. Anthony Guild Press, 1954.

Chittenden, Hiram M., and Richardson, Alfred T. *Life, Letters and Travels of Father Pierre Jean DeSmet, S.J.* 4 vols. New York: Francis P. Harper, 1905.

Christensen, Erwin O. *The Index of American Design.* New York: Macmillan, 1950.

Cicognani, Amleto Giovanni. *Sanctity in America.* Paterson, N.J.: St. Anthony Guild Press, 1941.

Clairborne, John F. H. *Mississippi, as a Province, Territory and State.* Jackson: Power & Barksdale, 1880.

Clapesattle, Helen B. *The Doctors Mayo.* Minneapolis: University of Minneapolis Press, 1941.

Coffee Run, 1772-1960; the Story of the Beginnings of the Catholic Faith in Delaware. Hockessin, Del., 1960.

"The Colony of Saint Mary in Pennsylvania, North America, with a Notice of the Voyage and a Map." *American Catholic Historical Researches,* new series, I (1905), 97-115.

Cortes, José. *Memorias Sobre las Provincias del Norte de Nueva España,* 1799. Manuscript in Library of Congress, Washington.

Cottrell, Alden T. *The Trenton Battle Monument and Washington's Campaign, December 26, 1776 to January 3, 1777.* Department of Conservation, State of New Jersey, Trenton, 1947.

Coues, Elliott. *On the Trail of a Spanish Pioneer; diary and itinerary of Francisco Garcés in his travels through Sonora, Arizona and California.* 2 vols. New York: Francis P. Harper, 1900.

Coulter, E. Merton. *A Short History of Georgia.* Chapel Hill: University of North Carolina Press, n.d.

Covington, Harry F. "The Discovery of Maryland or Verrazano's Visit to the Eastern Shore." *Maryland Historical Magazine,* X (1915), 199-217.

Cranny, Titus, S.A. "A New Title for Mary." *Unity Studies,* 12 (1954).

———. *Our Lady and Reunion.* Garrison, N.Y.: Chair of Unity Apostolate, 1962.

Crespi, Juan. *Fray Juan Crespi, Missionary Explorer on the Pacific Coast, 1769-1774.* Herbert Eugene Bolton, ed. Berkeley: University of California Press, 1927.

Cronin, Kay. *Cross in the Wilderness* (Oblates of Mary Immaculate). Vancouver: Mitchell Press, 1959.

Cuba and the Wrecked Maine. Chicago: Belford, Middlebrook & Co., 1898. Cummings, E.C. "Father Biard's Relation of 1616 and Saint Saveur." *Maine Historical Collections,* series 2, V (1894), 81-99.

Curley, Michael J., C.SS.R. *Bishop John Neumann, C.SS.R.,* Philadelphia: Bishop Neumann Center, 1952.

Dablon, Claude, S.J. *Relation de ce qui s'est passé de plus Remarquable aux Missions des Peres de la Compagnie de Jesus en la Nouvelle France, les Années 1670 & 1671.* Paris, 1672.

Dahlinger, Charles W. "A Place of Great Historic Interest: Pittsburgh's First Burying Ground." *Western Pennsylvania Historical Magazine,* II (1919), 204-211.

Davis, George Lynn-Lachlan. *Day-Star of American Freedom or the Birth and Early Growth of Toleration in the Province of Maryland.* New York: Scribner, 1855.

Davis, Royden, S.J. "The Plentiful Harvest (Conewago, Pennsylvania)." *The Jesuit Maryland Province,* August 1959, 3-30.

Day, Gordon M. "Dartmouth and Saint Francis." *Dartmouth Alumni Magazine,* November 1959, 28-30.

De Costa, Benjamin F. *Cabo de Arenas; or the Place of Sandy Hook in the Old Cartology, as indicated in the map of Alonzo Chaves.* New York: D. Clapp & Son, 1885.

———. "The Globe of Pope Marcellus II and its Relation to the Voyage of Verrazano, with notes on the Discovery of the Hudson." *United States Catholic Historical Society Records and Studies,* III (1903), 24-37.

———. "The Verrazano Map." *Magazine of American History,* II (1878), 449-469.

———. *Verrazano the Explorer.* New York: Barnes, 1880.

Dedication of the National Shrine of the Immaculate Conception, 1959. *Marian Library Studies,* No. 76, Dayton, Ohio.

De Goesbriand, Louis. *Catholic Memoirs of Vermont and New Hampshire.* Burlington, Vt., 1886.

Delanglez, Jean, S.J. *El Río del Espíritu Santo.* New York: United States Catholic Historical Society Monograph Series XXI, 1945.

De Smet, Peter J., S.J. *Oregon Missions and Travels over the Rocky Mountains in 1845-46.* New York: Edward Dunigan, 1847.

Discalced Carmelite Fathers. *History of Holy*

Hill: *Shrine of Mary, Help of Christians.*
Hubertus, Wisc., 1958.

Domínguez, Francisco Atanasio. *The Missions of New Mexico, 1776; a Description by Francisco Atanasio Domínguez, with other Contemporary Documents.* Translated and annotated by Eleanor B. Adams and Angelico Chavez, O.F.M. Albuquerque: University of New Mexico Press, 1956.

Donnelly, Joseph P., S.J. "A Silver Crown for the Statue of the Virgin." *Missouri Historical Society Bulletin,* V (1949), 207-210.

Donnelly, W. Patrick. "Father Pierre-Jean DeSmet: U.S. Ambassador to the Indians." *United States Catholic Historical Society Historical Records and Studies,* XXIV (1934), 7-142.

Doyon, Bernard, O.M.I. *The Cavalry of Christ on the Rio Grande, 1849-1883.* Milwaukee: Bruce, 1956.

Dragon, Antonio, S.J. *Enseveli Dans Les Neiges.* Montreal: Les Editions Bellarmin, 1951.

Du Creux, François, S.J. *Historiae Canadensis seu Novae-Franciae.* Paris, 1664.

Duffy, Consuela Marie, S.B.S. *Katharine Drexel: A Biography.* Cornwells Heights, Pa., 1972.

Duggan, Thomas S. *The Catholic Church in Connecticut.* New York: State History Co., 1930.

Dunn, Jacob Piatt. "Father Gibault: the Patriot Priest of the Northwest." *Transactions of the Illinois State Historical Society,* X (1906), 15-34.

Duratschek, Sister M. Claudia, O.S.B. *The Beginnings of Catholicism in South Dakota.* Washington: Catholic University of America Press, 1943.

Dworaczyk, Edward Joseph. *The First Polish Colonies of America in Texas.* San Antonio: The Naylor Co., 1936.

Earle, Alice Morse. *Colonial Days in Old New York.* New York: Scribner, 1896.

The Early Jesuit Missions in North America; compiled and translated from the letters of the French Jesuits. William Ingraham Kip, ed. New York: Wiley and Putnam, 1846.

Early Western Travels, 1748-1846. Reuben Gold Thwaites, ed. 32 vols. Cleveland: The A. H. Clark Co., 1904-1907.

Ellis, John Tracy. *American Catholicism.* (The Chicago History of American Civilization.) Chicago: University of Chicago Press, 1956.

———. "Catholics in Colonial America." *American Ecclesiastical Review,* CXXXVI (1957), 11-27, 100-119, 184-196, 265-276, 304-307.

———. *Documents of American Catholic History.* Milwaukee: Bruce, 1956.

———. *A Select Bibliography of the History of the Catholic Church in the United States.* New York: The Declan X. McMullen Co., 1947.

Engelhardt, Zephyrin, O.F.M. "Missionary Labors of the Franciscans among the Indians of the early days." *Franciscan Herald,* I (1913), 110-112, 143-146, 175-177, 213-215, 247-249, 286-291, 319-321, 355-358, 391-393; II (1914) 22-24, 62-64, 104-106, 142-144, 182-184, 222-224, 264-266, 300-301, 342-343.

———. *The Missions and the Missionaries of California.* 4 vols. San Francisco: James H. Barry, 1908-1915.

English, William H. *Conquest of the Country Northwest of the River Ohio, 1778-1783.* 2 vols. Indianapolis: The Bowen-Merrill Co., 1896.

Eskildson, J. F. *Our Lady's Shrine: an Account of Some of the Miraculous Cures performed at the Mission Church, Boston Highlands, 1870-83.* Boston: Cashman, Keating & Co., 1883.

Eustis, Edith Morton. "Eighteenth Century Catholic Stone Carvings in New Mexico." *Liturgical Arts,* Spring 1932, 112-115.

Everett, Edward. *The Life of George Washington.* New York: Sheldon and Co., 1860.

The Far West and the Rockies Historical Series, 1820-1875. Glendale, Calif.: Arthur H. Clark Co., 1954-1961.

"Father De Smet's Sioux Peace Mission of 1868 and the Journal of Charles Galpin." *Mid-America,* XIII, No. 2, new series II (1930), 141-163.

Father Peyton and the Family Rosary. Albany: Family Rosary, Inc., 1960.

Father Skelly Memorial Edition. *The Miraculous Medal,* XXXVI (1963), 1-83.

Fink, Leo Gregory. *Old Jesuit Trails in Penn's*

Forest; the Romance of Catholicism in the Footprints of the Pioneer Missionaries of Eastern Pennsylvania. New York: The Paulist Press, 1936.

Fiske, John. *The Dutch and Quaker Colonies in America.* 2 vols. New York: Houghton Mifflin, 1903.

Flanigen, George J. *Catholicity in Tennessee, 1541-1937.* Nashville: Ambrose Printing Co., 1937.

Flynn, Joseph M. *The Catholic Church in New Jersey.* New York: The Publishers Printing Co., 1904.

Foik, Paul J. *Pioneer Catholic Journalism.* New York: United States Catholic Historical Society Monograph Series XI, 1930.

Forbes, Allan, and Cadman, Paul F. *France and New England.* 3 vols. Boston: State Street Trust Co., 1925, 1927, 1929.

Forman, Henry C. *Jamestown and St. Mary's, Buried Cities of Romance.* Baltimore: Johns Hopkins Press, 1938.

The Founding of a Young Ladies' Academy; Georgetown Visitation Convent Sesquicentennial, 1799-1949. Washington, 1949.

Fowle, Otto. *Sault Ste. Marie and its Great Waterway.* New York: Putnam, 1925.

French, Benjamin F. *Historical Collections of Louisiana.* 5 vols. New York: Wiley and Putnam, 1846-1853.

Gallagher, Joseph. "The See of Baltimore." *The Catholic Market,* July-August 1964, 29-33, 58-60.

Gannon, David, S.A. *Father Paul of Graymoor.* New York: Macmillan, 1959.

Garand, Philias Stanislas. *The History of the City of Ogdensburg.* Ogdensburg, N.Y., 1927.

Garraghan, Gilbert J., S.J. "Catholic First Things in the United States." *Mid-America,* X (1939), 110-186.

———. *The Jesuits of the Middle United States.* 3 vols. New York: America Press, 1938.

———. "Nicholas Point, Jesuit Missionary in Montana of the Forties." In *Conference on the History of the Trans-Mississippi West, University of Colorado, 1929.* James F. Willard and Colin B. Goodykoontz, editors. Boulder: University of Colorado, 1930.

———. "The Trappists of Monks' Mound."

Illinois Catholic Historical Review, VIII (1925), 106-136.

Garrett, Thomas M., S.J. "Devotion to Our Lady in Catholic Men's Colleges." *American Ecclesiastical Review,* CXXXII (1955), 31-37.

Geiger, Maynard J., O.F.M. *The Franciscan Conquest of Florida, 1573-1618.* Washington: Catholic University of America, 1937.

———. "Mormons, Franciscans and the Blessed Virgin." *The Immaculate,* August 1964, 12-14.

———. "Our Lady in Franciscan California." *Franciscan Studies,* XXIII (1942), 99-112.

Gerow, Richard O., Bishop, ed. *Civil War Diary (1862-1865) of Bishop William Henry Elder, Bishop of Natchez.* Jackson, Miss., 1960.

Gibson, John. *Gibson's Guide and Directory of the State of Louisiana and the Cities of New Orleans and Lafayette.* New Orleans: John Gibson, 1838.

Gibson, Sister Laurita. *Some Anglo-American Converts to Catholicism Prior to 1829.* Washington: Catholic University of America, 1943.

Gillett, H. M. *Famous Shrines of Our Lady.* 2 vols. London, 1960-1961.

Gilmary, Elizabeth. "A Vision of Our Lady in the Alleghenies." *The Catholic Home Journal,* January 1957, 3, 19, 30.

Gilman, Richard. "Spain in America." *Jubilee,* June 1955, 18-39.

"Gothic in America (St. Mary's Chapel)." *The Voice,* November 1952, 8-9, 30.

Gould, Charles N. *Oklahoma Place Names.* Norman: University of Oklahoma Press, 1933.

Graham, A.A. "The Military Posts, Forts and Battlefields within the State of Ohio." *Ohio Archaeological and Historical Quarterly,* III (1895), 300-311.

Grassmann, Thomas, O.F.M. Conv. *The Indian Maiden: Catherine Tekakwitha.* Fonda, N.Y., 1956.

Green, Mary Fitzgerald. *History of St. Mary's Parish, Independence, Missouri, 1823-1964.* Independence, 1964.

Griffin, Martin I.J. *Catholics and the American Revolution.* 3 vols. Ridley Park, Pa., 1907-1911.

———. "Did Washington Die a Catholic?" *American Catholic Historical Researches*, XVII (1900), 123-129.

———. "Rev. Robert Harding." *American Catholic Historical Researches*, VII (1890), 82-92.

Griffith, Lucille. *History of Alabama, 1540-1900, as recorded in Diaries, Letters and Papers of the Times.* Northport, Ala.: Colonial Press, c. 1962.

Griswold, Bert Joseph. *The Pictorial History of Fort Wayne, Indiana.* Chicago: Robert O. Law Co., 1917.

Groves, Don. "Please, Come In, Mister" (Convent of Mary Immaculate, Key West, Florida). *Columbia*, July 1964, 8-9, 42-43.

Gudde, Erwin G. *California Place Names.* Berkeley: University of California Press, 1949.

Guide to Historic Markers in Delaware. Dover: Historic Markers Commission, 1933.

Guilday, Peter Keenan. *The Life and Times of John Carroll, Archbishop of Baltimore, 1735-1815.* Westminster, Md.: Newman Press, 1954.

———. *The National Pastorals of the American Hierarchy, 1792-1919.* Westminster, Md.: Newman Press, 1954.

Habig, Marion, O.F.M. "The Cult of the Assumption of Our Lady in the United States." *Studia Mariana*, VII (1952), 83-119.

———. "The First Immaculate Conception Mission." *American Ecclesiastical Review*, CXXXI (1954), 73-80.

———. "The First Marian Shrine in the United States." *American Ecclesiastical Review*, CXXXIV (1957), 81-89.

———. *Heralds of the King: the Franciscans of the St. Louis-Chicago Province, 1858-1958.* Chicago: Franciscan Herald Press, 1958.

———. "Our First Church of Mary Immaculate." *American Ecclesiastical Review*, CXXXI (1954), 313-319.

Hafen, LeRoy R. *Old Spanish Trail.* The Far West and the Rockies Historical Series, 1820-1875. Glendale, Calif.: Arthur H. Clark Co., 1954.

Hamilton, Edward P. *The French and Indian Wars.* Mainstream of America Series. Lewis Gannett, ed. New York: Doubleday, 1962.

Hamilton, Peter J. *Mobile of the Five Flags.* Mobile, Ala.: Gill Printing Co., 1913.

Hamlin, Talbot. *Greek Revival Architecture in America.* New York: Oxford, 1944.

The Handbook of Texas. Walter P. Webb, ed. 2 vols. Austin: Texas State Historical Association, 1952.

Hanson, John Wesley. *History of the Old Towns, Norridgewock and Canaan.* Boston, 1849.

Haran, John P., S.J. *Mary, Mother of God.* Huntington: Our Sunday Visitor, Inc., 1973.

Harldy, Virginia. "A Visit to the Loretto of America." *Records of the American Catholic Historical Society*, XXVI (1915), 166-173.

Harris, George H. *Aboriginal Occupation of the Lower Genesee Country.* Rochester, N.Y., 1884.

Harris, John Brice. *From Old Mobile to Fort Assumption.* Nashville, Tenn.: Parthenon Press, 1959.

Heming, Harry H. *The Catholic Church in Wisconsin.* Milwaukee: Catholic History Publishing Co., 1895-1898.

Hewett, Edgar L. *Handbooks of Archaeological History.* Albuquerque: University of New Mexico Press, 1943.

——— and Fisher, Reginald G. *Mission Monuments of New Mexico.* Albuquerque: University of New Mexico Press, 1943.

——— and Mauzy, Wayne L. *Landmarks of New Mexico.* Albuquerque: University of New Mexico Press, c. 1940.

Hill, Charles F. "Roman Catholic Indian Relics in the Possession of the Wyoming [Pa.] Historical and Geological Society." *Wyoming Historical and Geological Society Proceedings*, IX (1905), 171-174.

Historic American Buildings Survey. Library of Congress, January 1, 1938. John P. O'Neill, National Park Service, ed. Washington: Government Printing Office, 1938; supplement, 1959.

Historical Churches of the South. Collection of articles in *Holland's* (magazine of the South). Atlanta: Tupper & Love, Inc., 1952.

Hoecken, Christian, S.J. *Pewani Ipi Potewatemi Missinoikan, Eyowat Nemodjik Cath-*

oliques Endjik. Baltimore: John Murphy, 1846.

Hoelle, Philip C., S.M. "The Legion of Mary." *Marian Era*, III (1962).

Hoffman, M.M. *Arms and the Monk! The Trappist Saga in Mid-America*. Dubuque, Iowa: Wm. C. Brown Co., 1952.

Hofstadter, Richard; Miller, William; Aaron, Daniel. *The United States: The History of a Republic*. Englewood Cliffs: Prentice-Hall, 1957.

Homan, Helen Walker. *Knights of Christ*. Englewood Cliffs: Prentice-Hall, 1957.

Hope, Arthur J. *Notre Dame, 100 Years*. South Bend: Notre Dame Press, 1943.

Horgan, Paul. "Devil in the Desert." *Saturday Evening Post*, May 6, 1950, 24-25.

Horn, Stanley P. "Nashville During the Civil War." *Tennessee Historical Quarterly*, IV (1945), 3-22.

Hough, Emerson. *The Passing of the Frontier*. Vol. 26 of The Chronicles of America Series. Allen Johnson, ed. New Haven: Yale University Press, 1920.

Hughes, Thomas A., S.J. *History of the Society of Jesus in North America, Colonial and Federal*. 4 vols. New York: Longmans, Green, 1907-1917.

———. "Properties of the Jesuits in Pennsylvania, 1730-1830." *American Catholic Historical Society of Philadelphia Records*, XI (1900), 177-195, 281-294.

Irving, Washington. *The Life and Voyages of Christopher Columbus and the Voyages and Discoveries of the Companions of Columbus*. 3 vols. New York: Putnam, 1892.

Ives, Joseph Moss. *The Ark and the Dove; the Beginning of Civil and Religious Liberty in America*. New York: Longmans, Green, 1936.

Jackson, Orton P., and Evans, Frank E. *The New Book of American Ships*. New York: Stokes, 1926.

Jesuit Relations and Allied Documents. Reuben Gold Thwaites, ed. 73 vols. Cleveland: Burrows Brothers, 1896-1901.

Johnson, Frances Ann. *Robert Rogers and His Rangers*. Littleton, N.H., 1953.

Jolly, Ellen Ryan. *Nuns of the Battlefield*. Providence, R.I.: Visitor Press, 1927.

Jones, John William. *Christ in the Camp*. Richmond, Va.: B.F. Johnson & Co., 1887.

Jones, William M. *Texas History Carved in Stone*. Houston: Monument Publishing Co., 1958.

Julian, Brother, C.F.X. *Men and Deeds: The Xaverian Brothers in America*. New York: Macmillan, 1930.

Kenny, Michael, S.J. *The Romance of the Floridas*. Milwaukee: Bruce, 1934.

Kenton, Edna, ed. *The Jesuit Relations and Allied Documents; Travels and Explorations of the Jesuit Missionaries in North America (1610-1791)*. New York: Vanguard, 1954.

Ketchum, Richard M., ed. *The American Heritage Book of Great Historic Places*. New York: Simon and Schuster, 1957.

Keyes, Nelson B. *The American Frontier: Our Unique Heritage*. Garden City, N.Y.: Hanover House, 1954.

King, Kenneth M. *Mission to Paradise*. Chicago: Franciscan Herald Press, 1956.

Knight, Lucien Lamar. *Georgia's Landmarks, Memorials and Legends*. 2 vols. Atlanta: Byrd Printing Co., 1913-1914.

Kohl, John G. *A History of the Discovery of Maine*. Portland: Bailey and Noyes, 1869.

Kretschmer, Konrad. *Die Entdeckung Amerika's in Ihrer Bedeutung für die Geschichte des Weltbildes*. Berlin, 1892.

Kull, Irving S., ed. *New Jersey, a History*. 6 vols. New York: American Historical Society, Inc., 1930.

Kurjack, Dennis C. "Historic Philadelphia (St. Joseph's and St. Mary's Churches)." *Transactions American Philosophical Society*, new series XLIII (1953), 199-209.

Lambing, Andrew A. *Mary's First Shrine in the Wilderness*. Pittsburgh: Myers, Shinkle & Co., 1882.

Lanning, John Tate. *The Spanish Missions of Georgia*. Chapel Hill, N.C.: University of North Carolina Press, c. 1935.

"The Last Years of Kaskaskia." *Illinois State Historical Society Journal*, XXXVII (1944), 229-241.

Laveille, E. *The Life of Father de Smet, S.J.* New York: Kenedy, 1916.

Leeson, Michael A. *History of the Counties of McKean, Elk and Forest, Pennsylvania*. Chicago: J.H. Beers & Co., 1890.

Leger, Sister Mary Celeste. *The Catholic Indian Missions in Maine, 1611-1820.* Catholic University of America Studies in American Church History. Washington, 1929.

Lenz, Paul A. *A Pilgrimage to Loretto.* Loretto, Pa., 1955.

Lewis, Clifford M., S.J., and Loomie, Albert J., S.J. *The Spanish Jesuit Mission in Virginia.* Chapel Hill, N.C.: Virginia Historical Society, University of North Carolina Press, 1953.

Lexau, Joan M. *Convent Life: Roman Catholic Religious Orders for Women in North America.* New York: Dial Press, 1964.

Library of Congress. *Manuscripts in Public and Private Collections in the United States.* Washington: Government Printing Office, 1924.

Lipinsky, Lino S. *Giovanni da Verrazano, the Discoverer of New York Bay.* New York, 1958.

Looking Eagle. *We Wore Our Feathers High.* Pine Ridge, S. Dak., 1958.

Lord, Daniel A., S.J. "Our Lady in the United States." *Lumen Vitae,* VIII (1953), 311-314.

———. *Played by Ear.* Chicago: Loyola University Press, 1956.

Lord, Robert H.; Sexton, John E., and Harrington, Edward T. *History of the Archdiocese of Boston in the Various Stages of Its Development, 1604 to 1943.* 3 vols. New York: Sheed & Ward, 1944.

Lovell, Caroline Couper. *The Golden Isles of Georgia.* Boston: Little, Brown, 1939.

Lucey, William Leo, S.J. *The Catholic Church in Maine.* Francestown, N.H.: Marshall Jones Co., 1957.

Lummis, Charles F. *Mesa, Cañon and Pueblo.* New York: The Century Co., 1925.

McCarry, Charles. "The Pietà: Masterpiece at the Fair." *Saturday Evening Post,* March 28, 1964, 25-28.

McDermott, Edwin J., S.J. "The Saga of Father Kino." *Arizona Highways,* XXXVII (1961), 6-29.

Macleod, Xavier Donald. *Devotion to the Blessed Virgin Mary in North America.* New York: Virtue & Yorston, 1866.

McMenamy, Claire. "Our Lady of Guadalupe at Conejos, Colorado." *Colorado Magazine,* XVII (1940), 180-182.

McQueen, Alexander S. *History of Charlton County (Georgia).* Atlanta: Stein Printing Co., 1932.

Maes, Camillus P. *Life of Reverend Charles Nerinckx.* Cincinnati: Robert Clarke & Co., 1880.

Mahan, Bruce E. "New Melleray Abbey." *The Palimpsest,* XLII (1961), 81-145.

Manton, Joseph E., C.SS.R. *Madonna of Mission Hill (Our Lady of Perpetual Help).* Roxbury, Mass., 1960.

Manucy, Albert C. "The Founding of Pensacola — Reasons and Reality." *Florida Historical Quarterly,* XXXVII (1959), 223-241.

Marden, Luis. "Gloucester Blesses Its Portuguese Fleet." *National Geographic,* July 1953, 75-84.

Marion, William L. "St. Mary's Stage Station." *Annals of Wyoming,* XXX (1958), 40-41.

Marriner, Ernest. *Kennebec Yesterdays.* Waterville, Me.: Colby College Press, 1954.

Martin, Sister M. Aquinata, O.P. *The Catholic Church on the Nebraska Frontier, 1854-1885.* Catholic University of America Studies in American Church History. Washington, 1937.

Martin, Richard A., ed. *Florida Times Union Centennial Edition,* Jacksonville, December 27, 1964.

Mason, Edward G. "Kaskaskia and its Parish Records." *Magazine of American History,* VI (1881), 161-182.

Mathews, Stanley, S.M. "Know Your Mother Better: A Marian Bibliography." *Marian Library Studies,* No. 26. Dayton, Ohio.

Maurault, J.A. *Histoire des Abénakis.* Sorel, Canada, 1866.

Maynard, Theodore. *The Story of American Catholicism.* 2 vols. New York: Macmillan, 1941.

Mazzuchelli, Samuel Charles. *Memoirs historical and edifying of a missionary apostolic.* Translated by Sister M.B. Kennedy, O.S.F. Chicago: W.F. Hall Printing Co., 1915.

Merlet, M. Louis. *Histoire des Relations des Hurons et des Abénakis en Canada.* Chartres, 1858.

Merlet, René. *La Cathédrale de Chartres.* Paris, 1918.

Metzger, Charles H. *Catholics and the Ameri-*

can *Revolution*. Chicago: Loyola University Press, 1962.

Miller, David E. "Discovery of Glen Canyon, 1776." *Utah Historical Quarterly*, XXVI (1958), 221-237.

Miss Columbia's Public School; or Will It Blow Over? New York: Francis B. Felt & Co., 1871.

Morison, Samuel Eliot. *Admiral of the Ocean Sea*. 2 vols. Boston: Little, Brown, 1942.

———. *The European Discovery of America: The Northern Voyages, AD 500-1600*. New York: Oxford University Press, 1971.

———. *The European Discovery of America: The Southern Voyages, AD 1492-1616*. New York: Oxford University Press, 1974.

Morton, Julius Sterling. *Illustrated History of Nebraska*. 3 vols. Lincoln: Jacob North & Co., 1907.

Munsell, Joel. *The Annals of Albany*. 10 vols. Albany: J. Munsell, 1850-1859.

Murrett, John C. *The Story of Father Price*. New York: McMullen Books, 1953.

Nardini, Louis R. *No Man's Land; El Camino Real*. New Orleans: Pelican Publishing Co., 1962.

Narratives of Early Maryland, 1633-1684. Clayton Colman Hall, ed. New York: Scribner, 1910.

National Conference of Catholic Bishops. *Catholics in America, 1776-1976*. Robert Trisco, ed. Washington: Committee for the Bicentennial, 1976.

National Park Service. *National Register of Historic Places*. U.S. Department of the Interior. Washington: Government Printing Office, 1976.

National Survey of Historic Sites and Buildings, Vol. V: *Explorers and Settlers*. Washington: Government Printing Office, 1968.

National Survey of Historic Sites and Buildings, Vol. XII: *Soldier and Brave*. Washington: Government Printing Office, 1971.

Nevins, Albert J., M.M. *Our American Catholic Heritage*. Huntington: Our Sunday Visitor, Inc., 1972.

Nieberding, Velma. "St. Mary's of the Quapaws, 1894-1927." *Chronicles of Oklahoma*, XXXI (1953), 2-14.

O'Callaghan, Edmund Bailey, ed. *The Docu-* mentary *History of the State of New York*. 4 vols. Albany, 1849-1851.

O'Connor, Edward S., ed. *The Mystery of the Woman: Essays on the Mother of God*. South Bend: University of Notre Dame Press, 1956.

O'Connor, Sister Mary Paschala, O.P. *Five Decades: A History of the Congregation of the Most Holy Rosary*. Sinsinawa, Wisc.: Sinsinawa Press, 1954.

O'Connor, Paul C., S.J. *Eskimo Parish*. Milwaukee: Bruce, 1947.

O'Connor, Peter B. *History of Queen of Peace Parish, North Arlington, New Jersey, 1922-1947*. North Arlington, 1947.

O'Connor, Richard. *Johnstown: The Day the Dam Broke*. New York: Lippincott, 1957.

O'Daniel, Victor, O.P. *Dominicans in Early Florida*. New York: United States Catholic Historical Society Monograph Series XII, 1930.

O'Gorman, Thomas. *A History of the Roman Catholic Church in the United States*. New York: Christian Literature Co., 1895.

Ohlmann, Ralph, O.F.M. "The Assumptionist Movement and the Franciscan Marian Congresses; a Survey." First Franciscan National Marian Congress in Acclamation of the Dogma of the Assumption, October 8-11, 1950. *Studia Mariana*, VII (1952). Burlington, Wisc.

———. "The Immaculate Conception and the United States." *Marian Library Studies*, No. 21. Dayton, Ohio.

Olmstead, William A. "An Incident of the Civil War." *United States Catholic Historical Society Historical Records and Studies*, V (1909) 510-512.

Olson, Sigurd F. "Relics from the Rapids." *National Geographic*, September 1963, 412-435.

One Hundred Years of Progress; a Graphic, Historical and Pictorial Account of the Catholic Church of New England. James S. Sullivan, ed. Boston, 1895.

Orsini, Mathieu. *The Life of the Blessed Virgin Mary*. New York: Peter F. Collier, 1861.

Ortelius, Abraham, *Theatrum Orbis Terrarum*. Antwerp, 1595.

"Our Lady of the Rivers." *Monsanto Magazine*, March-April 1957, 21-22.

Ousley, Clarence. *Galveston in Nineteen Hundred*. Atlanta, Ga.: Wm. C. Chase, 1900.

Palladino, Lawrence B., S.J. *Indian and White in the Northwest: A History of Catholicity in Montana, 1831-1891*. Lancaster, Pa.: Wickersham Printing Co., 1922.

Palm, Sister Mary Borgias, S.N.D. *The Jesuit Missions of the Illinois Country, 1673-1763*. Dissertation, St. Louis University Graduate School. Cleveland, 1933.

Palou, Francisco, O.F.M. *Noticias de la Nueva California*. 4 vols. San Francisco: California Historical Society Publication, 1874.

"A Papal Crown for La Conquistadora." *St. Anthony Messenger*, LXVIII (1961), 30-35.

Pareja, Francisco. *Catecismo en Lengua Castellana y Timuquana*. Mexico, 1612.

Parkman, Francis. *Jesuits in North America in the Seventeenth Century*. Boston: Little, Brown, 1888.

Parsons, Wilfrid, S.J. *Early Catholic Americana, a List of Books and Other Works by Catholic Authors in the United States, 1729-1830*. New York: Macmillan, 1939.

––––––. "Marian Devotion in the early United States." *Marian Studies*, III (1952), 236-250.

Pena, Juan Antonio de la. *Derrotero de la Expedición en la Provincia de los Texas, Nuevo Reyno de Filipinas*. Mexico, 1722.

Peterson, Edward. *History of Rhode Island*. New York: John S. Taylor, 1853.

Phillips, P. Lee. *Alaska and Northwest Part of North America, 1588-1898*. Maps in Library of Congress, Washington, 1898.

Pictorial Americana: a select list of photographic negatives in the Prints and Photographs Division of the Library of Congress. Washington, 1955.

Pierce, Arthur D. *Iron in the Pines; the story of New Jersey's Ghost Towns and Bog Iron*. New Brunswick: Rutgers University Press, 1957.

Pike, Robert E. "The Lost Treasure of St. Francis." *American Heritage*, Winter 1953-1954, 14-19.

Pittman, Philip. *The Present State of the European Settlements on the Mississippi*. London, 1770.

Plowden, Charles. *A Short account of the establishment of the New See of Baltimore in Maryland and of Consecrating the Right Rev. Dr. John Carroll, First Bishop Thereof*. Dublin, 1790.

Podmore, Harry J. *Trenton, Old and New*. Trenton: The Kenneth W. Moore Co., 1927.

Pouchot, M. *Memoir upon the Late War in North America between the French and English, 1755-60*. 2 vols. Roxbury, Mass.: W. Elliot Woodward, 1866.

Pourade, Richard F. *The Explorers*. San Diego: Union-Tribune Publishing Co., 1960.

Priestley, Herbert Ingram. *The Luna Papers. Documents Relating to the Expedition of Don Tristan de Luna y Arellano for the Conquest of La Florida in 1559-1561*. Deland, Fla.: Florida State Historical Society Publications, 1928.

––––––. *Tristan de Luna; Conquistador of the Old South. A Study of Spanish Imperial Strategy*. Glendale, Calif.: Arthur H. Clark Co., 1936.

Putnam County History: The Last 100 Years. Third Work Shop, Putnam Valley Historical Society, Cold Spring, N.Y., 1957.

Raabe, Evelyn M. "El Carmelo." *Mary*, July-August 1963, 16-23.

Reed, Henry Hope, Jr. "The City Still Waits for its Artist." *New York Herald Tribune Sunday Magazine*, September 1, 1963, 3-4, 13.

Reed, Merrill A. *Historical Statues and Monuments in California*. San Francisco, 1956.

Reily, John T. *Conewago — a Collection of Catholic Local History*. Martinsburg, W. Va.: Herald Print, 1885.

A Relation of Maryland. London, 1635.

"Remarks on a Latin Inscription lately found at Castine, in the State of Maine." *American Antiquarian Society Proceedings*, XL (1864), 59-66.

Riggs, Arthur S. "The Twentieth Century Reproduction of Columbus's Flagship at the Seville Exposition." *Art and Archaeology*, July-August, 1929, 27-34.

Riley, Arthur Joseph. *Catholicism in New England to 1788*. Catholic University of America Studies in American Church History. Washington: 1936.

Rines, Edward F. *Old Historic Churches of America*. New York: Macmillan, 1936.

Riobo, John, O.F.M. "An Account of the Voyage Made by the Frigates 'Princesa' and 'Favorita' in the year 1799 from San Blas to Northern Alaska." *United States Catholic Historical Society Historical Records and Studies*, XII (1918), 76-89.

Riordan, Michael J. *Cathedral Records from the Beginning of Catholicity in Baltimore to the Present Time*. Baltimore: The Catholic Mirror Publishing Co., 1906.

Riordan, Robert. *Medicine for a Wildcat*. Milwaukee: Bruce, 1956.

Robinson, James Troy. "Fort Assumption: the First Recorded History of White Man's Activity on the Present Site of Memphis." *West Tennessee Historical Society Papers*, V (1951), 62-78.

Roemer, Theodore, O.F.M. Cap. *The Catholic Church in the United States*. St. Louis: Herder, 1950.

——. *The Leopoldine Foundation and the Church in the United States, 1829-1839*. New York: United States Catholic Historical Society Monograph Series XIII, 1933.

Rooney, James A. "Early Times in the Diocese of Hartford, Connecticut, 1829-1874." *Catholic Historical Review*, I (1915), 148-163.

Ross, Ishbel. *Angel of the Battlefield*. New York: Harper, 1956.

Ross, Mary. "The Restoration of the Spanish Missions in Georgia, 1598-1606." *Georgia Historical Quarterly*, X (1926), 171-199.

Rusk, William Sener. "Godefroy and Saint Mary's Chapel, Baltimore." *Liturgical Arts*, Third quarter, 1933, 141-145.

Ryan, Abram J. *A Crown for Our Queen*. Philadelphia: H. L. Kilner & Co., 1882.

Ryan, John, S.J. "Fifteenth Anniversary of Radio Rosary." *Fatima Findings*, XIX (1965), 1, 7.

——. "Queen of the Ether Waves." *Fatima Findings*, V (1951), 1-2.

Ryan, Joseph P., O.F.M. "Travel Literature as Source Material for American Catholic History." *Illinois Catholic Historical Review*, X (1928), 179-238, 301-363.

St. Augustine's Historical Heritage: 400th Anniversary. St. Augustine Historical Society, Florida, 1965.

St. Mary's Seminary and University Memorial Volume, 1791-1891. Baltimore: J. Murphy & Co., 1891.

Samuel, Ray, et al. *Tales of the Mississippi*. New York: Hastings House, 1955.

Sargent, Daniel. *Our Land and Our Lady*. New York: Longmans, 1939.

Scharf, John Thomas. *History of the Confederate States Navy, from its Organization to the Surrender of Its Last Vessel*. New York: Rogers & Sherwood, 1887.

Schlarmann, John J. *From Quebec to New Orleans: the Story of the French in America*. Belleville, Ill.: Buechler Publishing Co., 1929.

Schoenberg, Wilfred P., S.J. *A Chronicle of Catholic History of the Pacific Northwest, 1743-1960*. Portland, Ore.: Catholic Sentinel Printery, 1962.

——. *Jesuits in Montana, 1840-1960*. Portland, Ore., 1960.

——. *Jesuits in Oregon, 1844-1959*. Portland, Ore., 1959.

Schrott, Lambert, O.S.B. *Pioneer German Catholics in the American Colonies, 1734-1784*. New York: United States Catholic Historical Society Monograph Series XIII, 1933.

Semple, Henry C., S.J. *The Ursulines in New Orleans and Our Lady of Prompt Succor; Record of two centuries, 1729-1925*. New York: Kenedy, 1925.

"Seventy-five Years' Growth of Holy Name Sisters." *Catholic Sentinel*, October 25, 1934.

Shambaugh, Benjamin F. *The Old Stone Capitol Remembers*. Iowa City: State Historical Society, 1939.

Shanahan, Emmett A. *Minnesota's Forgotten Martyr, Jean Pierre Aulneau, S.J.* Crookston, Minn., 1949.

Sharkey, Donald C. "This is Your Mother." *Ave Maria*, April 30, 1955; August 20, 1955; March 2, 1957.

——. *The Woman Shall Conquer*. Milwaukee: Bruce, 1952.

Shea, John Gilmary. *The Catholic Church in Colonial Days, 1521-1763*. New York: the author, 1886.

———— *Discovery and Exploration of the Mississippi Valley.* New York: Redfield, 1852.

———— *History of the Catholic Church in the United States.* 4 vols. New York: the author, 1886-1892.

———— "Log Chapel on the Rappahannock." *Catholic World,* XX (1875), 847-856.

Sheedy, Morgan M. "Historical Address on the 169th Anniversary of the Organization and the 57th Anniversary of the Consecration of St. Mary's Church, Lancaster, Pennsylvania." *Records of the American Catholic Historical Society,* XXVI (1915), 346-360.

"A Short Account of the Establishment of the New See of Baltimore." *American Catholic Historical Researches,* VII (1890), 161-175.

Shrine of the Blessed Virgin Mary, Mother of God, Whitemarsh, Maryland. Whitemarsh: Osma Caravan No. 110, Order of the Alhambra, 1960.

Sigsbee, Charles D. *The "Maine," an Account of her Destruction in Havana Harbor.* New York: Century Co., 1899.

Simmons, Agatha Aimar. *Brief History of St. Mary's Roman Catholic Church, Charleston, South Carolina.* Charleston, 1961.

Slater, John M. *El Morro, Inscription Rock, New Mexico.* Los Angeles: The Plantin Press, 1961.

Slocum, Charles E. *History of the Maumee River Basin.* Indianapolis: Toledo, Bowen & Slocum, 1905.

Solis de Meras, Gonzalo. *Pedro Menéndez de Avilés . . .* Deland, Fla.: The Florida State Historical Society, 1923.

Spalding, Martin J. *Sketches of the Early Catholic Missions of Kentucky from their Commencement in 1787 to the Jubilee of 1826-27.* Louisville: B.J. Webb & Brother, 1844.

Steck, Francis Borgia, O.F.M. *A Tentative Guide to Historical Materials on the Spanish Borderlands.* Philadelphia: American Catholic Historical Society, 1943.

Stokes, Isaac Newton Phelps. *The Iconography of Manhattan Island, 1498-1909.* 6 vols. New York: R.H. Dodd, 1915-1928.

Stotz, Charles Morse. *Defense in the Wilderness.* Pittsburgh: Historical Society of Western Pennsylvania, 1958.

Sweeney, Elizabeth Ann. "The Catholic Church at Central City." *Colorado Magazine,* XVIII (1941), 181-186.

Tanner, Mathias, S.J. *Societas Jesu usque ad sanguines et vitae profusionem militans.* Prague, 1675.

Taylor, Coley. "Our Lady of Guadalupe." *Marian Library Studies,* No. 85. Dayton, Ohio.

Thomas, Alfred Barnaby. *After Coronado — Spanish Explorations Northeast of New Mexico, 1696-1727.* Norman: University of Oklahoma Press, 1935.

Thompson, Zadock. *History of Vermont, Natural, Civil, and Statistical.* Burlington: Chauncey Goodrich, 1842.

Thorman, Donald J. "Ave Maria." *Catholic Press Annual,* 1961, 45-48.

Thornton, Francis B. *Catholic Shrines of the United States and Canada.* New York: Funk & Wagnalls, 1954.

Titterington, P.F. *The Cahokia Mound Group and its Village Site Material.* St. Louis, 1938.

Torquemada, Juan de. *The Voyage of Sebastian Vizcaino to the Coast of California, 1602.* San Francisco: The Book Club of California, 1933.

Treacy, William P. *Old Catholic Maryland and its Early Jesuit Missions.* Swedesboro, N.J., 1889.

U.S. Army, Engineer Department. *Report of Explorations Across the Great Basin of the Territory of Utah . . . in 1859 by Captain James H. Simpson.* Washington: Government Printing Office, 1876.

U.S. Works Progress Administration. Federal Writers' Project. *American Guide Series;* various publishers.

Vancouver, George. *A Voyage of Discovery to North Pacific Ocean and around the World, 1792-94.* 6 vols. London, 1801.

Vetromile, Eugene, S.J. *The Abenakis and their History.* New York: James B. Kirker, 1866.

———— *Indian Good Book for the Benefit of the Penobscot, Passamaquoddy, St. John's, Micmac, and other Tribes of the Abenaki Indians.* New York: Edward Dunigan & Brother, 1856.

Vogt, Berard A., O.F.M. *The Cradle of the Catholic Church in Northern New Jersey.* Butler, N.J., 1930.

Vollmar, Edward R., S.J. *The Catholic Church in America: an historical bibliography.* 2d ed. New York: Scarecrow Press, Inc., 1963.

Wagner, Henry R. *Cartography of the Northwest Coast of America to the Year 1800.* 2 vols. Berkeley: University of California Press, 1937.

————. "Saints' names in California." *Historical Society of Southern California Quarterly,* XXIX (1947), 49-58.

Waite, Otis F.R. *History of the Town of Claremont, New Hampshire, 1764 to 1894.* Manchester, 1895.

Walker, Fintan Glenn. *The Catholic Church in the Meeting of Two Frontiers: The Southern Illinois Country, 1763-1793.* Washington: Catholic University of America Press, 1935.

Walsh, Henry L., S.J. *Hallowed Were the Gold Dust Trails.* Santa Clara: University of Santa Clara Press, 1946.

Walsh, Louis S. *Origin of the Catholic Church in Salem.* Boston: Cashman, Keating & Co., 1890.

Walsh, William J. *The Apparitions and Shrines of Heaven's Bright Queen — in Legend, Poetry and History from the Earliest Ages to the Present Time.* 4 vols. New York: T.J. Carey Co., 1904.

Walsh, William S. *Curiosities of Popular Customs.* Philadelphia: Lippincott, 1925.

Walton, M. Maury. *Old Saint Joseph's, Philadelphia, 1733-1933.* Philadelphia: The Dolphin Press, 1933.

Waterman, George S. "Afield-Afloat; Notable Events of the Civil War." *Confederate Veteran,* VI (1893), 170-171.

Waugh, Julia Nott. "Saint Mary's Quest." *Commonweal,* XXV, January 29, 1937, 382-383.

Wellman, Paul I. *Glory, God and Gold.* New York: Doubleday, 1954.

Welsh, William D. *A Brief History of Port Angeles, Washington.* Port Angeles, 1961.

Werfel, Franz. *The Song of Bernadette.* New York: Viking, 1942.

"West Point Foundry." *Report of New York State Historical Association,* XV (1916), 190-203.

West Virginia State Road Commission. *Historic and Scenic Markers.* Charleston, W. Va., n.d.

Western Guidebook to Historic Places in Western Pennsylvania. Pittsburgh: University of Pittsburgh Press, 1938.

Wheeler, George A. *Castine, Past and Present.* Boston: Rockwell and Churchill Press, 1896.

Wightman, Orrin Sage, and Cate, Margaret D. *Early Days of Coastal Georgia.* St. Simons Island, Ga.: Ft. Frederica Association, 1955.

Willis, Nathaniel P. *American Scenery; or Land, Lake and River, Illustrations of Transatlantic Nature.* 2 vols. New York: James S. Virtue, 1840.

Winthrop, Alice W. "The Work of the Sisters in the War with Spain." *Ave Maria,* IL (1899), 385-388, 426-430.

Wirmel, Sister Mary Magdalen, O.S.F. "Sisterhoods in the Spanish American War." *United States Catholic Historical Society Historical Records and Studies,* XXXII (1941), 7-69.

Wolle, Muriel Sibell. *The Bonanza Trail.* Bloomington: Indiana University Press, 1953.

Wood, Henrietta D. *Early Days of Norridgewock.* Skowhegan, Me.: The Skowhegan Press, 1941.

Wright, John J. "Mary Immaculate, Patroness of the United States." *Thomist,* XVII (1954).

Wright, William. *The Big Bonanza.* Hartford, Conn.: American Publishing Co., 1876.

Wynne, John J., S.J. *The Jesuit Martyrs of North America.* New York: Universal Knowledge Foundation, 1925.

Yzermans, Vincent A. "Churches of Mary in the United States." *American Ecclesiastical Review,* CXXXII (1955), 169-180.

Zornow, William Frank. *Kansas: a History of the Jayhawk State.* Norman: University of Oklahoma Press, 1957.

Zwierlein, Frederick J. "The Catholic Contribution to Liberty in the United States." *United States Catholic Historical Society Historical Records and Studies,* XV (1921), 112-136.

Index

344

346